VMware ESX
Essentials in the
Virtual Data Center

VMware ESX
Essentials in the
Virtual Data Center

David Marshall

Stephen S. Beaver

Jason W. McCarty

CRC Press
Taylor & Francis Group
Boca Raton London New York

CRC Press is an imprint of the
Taylor & Francis Group, an **informa** business

Auerbach Publications
Taylor & Francis Group
6000 Broken Sound Parkway NW, Suite 300
Boca Raton, FL 33487-2742

© 2009 by Taylor & Francis Group, LLC
Auerbach is an imprint of Taylor & Francis Group, an Informa business

Library of Congress Cataloging-in-Publication Data

Marshall, David (David W.)
   VMware ESX essentials in the virtual data center / David Marshall, Stephen S. Beaver, and Jase McCarty.
      p. cm.
   Includes bibliographical references and index.
   ISBN 978-1-4200-7027-9 (alk. paper)
   1. VMware. 2. Operating systems (Computers) 3. Virtual computer systems. I. Beaver, Stephen S. II. McCarty, Jase. III. McCarty, Jase. IV. Title.

QA76.76.O63M3647 2008
005.4'3--dc22   2008030526

Visit the Taylor & Francis Web site at
http://www.taylorandfrancis.com

and the Auerbach Web site at
http://www.auerbach-publications.com

Contents

Acknowledgments xi

About the Authors xiii

1   Introduction to Server Virtualization 1
Sorting out the Terminology...2
History of Virtualization 3
Overview of Server Virtualization Technology 7
    Server Virtualization Technology 10
        Discovering the Benefits 11
    Summary...14

2   VMware's Hypervisor Platform...15
VMware ESX Product Background 15
ESX Platform Specifics 17
    VMkernel...17
    Console Operating System (COS)..17
    Virtual Machine File System (VMFS)...18
    VMware VirtualCenter 18
    Core Features 20
        Large-scale management..20
        Centralized licensing model...20
        Deployment Wizard 20
        Editable virtual machine templates...20
        Cloning of virtual machines 20
        Live Migration (VMotion)..21
        Distributed Resource Scheduler (DRS)...21
        Distributed Power Management (DPM)...21
        High Availability (HA)..21
    Features Available from Plug-ins 22
        Integrated Physical to Virtual machine conversion or P2V with
        VMware Converter Plug-in..22

Consolidation Plug-in..22
Update Manager Plug-in...22
Ability to Create Custom Plug-ins 22
VirtualCenter—Physical or Virtual.............................23
VirtualCenter Location 24
VirtualCenter Authentication.....................................24
VMware ESXi..25
Summary...28

3   VMware ESX Architecture 31
Physical Host Server 32
CPU Resources 33
Memory Resources..33
Storage Resources... 34
Network Resources 35
The Service Console 36
The VMkernel..38
Summary... 40

4   Installing VMware ESX Server 41
Planning for Deployment 42
Hardware 42
Host Server Usage..43
Software Licenses..43
Supported Versus Unsupported Guest Operating Systems 45
Support from Software Vendors....................................... 46
Unexpected Server Growth.. 46
Virtual Machine Density... 46
Data and System Backup Considerations 48
Monitoring Considerations 49
Network Considerations..49
Performance Considerations...50
Security Considerations..50
Use Case...51
Use Case Document Outline...52
Requirements 54
Deployment Plan 55
Planning Complete—Ready to Begin 55
VMware ESX 3.5 Hardware System Requirements..........55
VMware ESX 3.5 Installation......................................57
Automating Installations 68
Summary...93

5   **Virtual Machines**..**95**
Virtual Machine Concepts..95
Virtual Machines...96
   Guest Operating Systems 98
      Power State Options 99
      Snapshots and Virtual Disk Modes....................100
      VMware Tools 101
Creating a Virtual Machine 102
   Installing a Guest Operating System 105
   Installing VMware Tools..105
Summary..107

6   **Interacting with VMware ESX** **109**
VI Client 110
   Inventory..113
      Scheduled Tasks 114
      Events 114
      Administration 114
      Maps..115
      Additional Buttons 115
   Web Client...116
   VMware Remote Console (VMRC)........................117
   Service Console (COS)...118
   VI SDK..120
   CIM 121
Summary..121

7   **Console Operating System Explained** **123**
What is the Console Operating System? 123
   How to Access the COS...125
   Commands 128
      Service Console Configuration and Troubleshooting Commands ..128
      Networking and Storage Commands....................130
      VMware Consolidated Backup Commands............131
   Summary...132

8   **Networking** **133**
Networking Architecture..133
   Virtual Network Interface Cards..............................133
      vswif..134
      vmknic 134
      vlance 134

vmxnet 135
e1000 135
Virtual Switches 135
Physical Network Adapter Teaming and Link Aggregation (IEEE 802.3ad) 137
Load Balancing 138
Fault Tolerance 139
VLAN Tagging (IEEE 802.1Q) 139
External Switch Tagging 140
Virtual Guest Tagging 141
Virtual Switch Tagging 141
Summary 142

9   Storage **145**
Virtual Machine File System 145
Direct Attached Storage 146
Network Attached Storage 146
Fibre Channel SAN 147
Internet Small Computer System Interface 148
Summary 150

10   Advanced Features **151**
VMotion 151
Distributed Resource Scheduler 152
VMware High Availability 154
Virtual Machine Failure Monitoring 156
Storage VMotion 157
VMware Consolidated Backup 158
Virtual Desktop Infrastructure 162
Summary 163

11   Resource Management **165**
Processor 165
VMware Virtual SMP 166
Memory 166
Disks 169
Network 169
Summary 169

12   Performance Optimization **171**
Configuration of the Host Server 172
Upgrade your Version of VMware ESX 172
Host Server Processor Performance 174
Host Server Memory Performance 175

Host Server Storage Performance 176
Host Server Network Performance 178
Configuration of the Virtual Machine 179
Remove Unneeded Virtual Hardware 179
Power off Idle Virtual Machines.. 179
Virtual Machine Processors.. 180
Virtual Machine Memory 181
Virtual Machine Networking... 182
Configuration of the Guest Operating System............... 182
Updating VMware Tools 183
Microsoft Windows˚ Guest Operating System Performance 184
Linux Guest Operating Systems Performance................ 185
Backups and Anti-Virus Configuration 186
Summary 187

13 Automating and Extensibility **189**
Software Development Kits and Toolkits............................. 190
VI SDK.. 190
VI PERL Toolkit... 191
VMware VI Toolkit (for Windows)..................................... 192
VMware CIM APIs... 193
VMware VDDK 193
VMware Guest SDK 194
VI Client Extensions 194
Storage VMotion Plug-in 195
Add Port Groups Plug-in.. 196
Juxtaposition RDP Plug-in... 197
Console Plug-in.. 198
Invoke Plug-in... 198
Summary 199

14 Additional Useful Resources **201**
Product Vendor Resources 201
VMware Web Site 201
VMware User Group... 203
VMware Appliance Marketplace 203
VMTN Blogs 204
VMworld Conference... 204
Third-Party Vendor Resources.. 204
Blue Lane Technologies 205
Catbird 205
Gear6 206
PlateSpin.. 206

rPath 207
Surgient 208
Veeam 208
Vizioncore 209
VKernel 210
VMLogix 211
Information Resources and Web Links 211
VMBlog.com 211
InfoWorld Virtualization Report 212
Virtual Strategy Magazine 213
RTFM Education 213
Virtualization.Info 214
TechTarget 215
Virtualization Events 216
Summary 216
Index **231**

Acknowledgments

We realize that this book would not be possible without the work and support of many different people. It would be impossible to thank everyone by name, but we hope they each know just how much they meant to us during the process of creating this book. We appreciate all of the hard work, dedication, and energy that people contributed along the way.

All three of the authors of this book have the highest respect for what VMware has accomplished and created over the years. Virtualization is a technology that we eat, sleep and breathe, and we are excited to see more and more people join the virtualization community. The three of us are active virtualization community members, and we sincerely hope that this book can help to bring in new members to this wonderful group of virtualization enthusiasts.

Collectively, we'd like to thank everyone at Auerbach Publications, Taylor and Francis Group. Our editor, John Wyzalek, has once again proven himself to be incredibly easy and flexible to work with during the course of this project. At every twist and turn, John was there to help keep things on course and on track.

Virtualization is our passion, but family is the most important thing in our lives. Without the support from our family members, this book would have been impossible to write.

"Trying to put thought to paper can sometimes prove to be an exhausting exercise. As a child going through school, I was always told to write about something you know and love, and everything will flow naturally. I thought to myself, what better topic to write about than virtualization? And the words and ideas did flow. The first book I wrote covered server virtualization from Microsoft and VMware. Lucky for me, VMware has continued to innovate, create and build a better mouse trap. So I thank VMware for continuing to challenge me and for inspiring my own ideas around their product. But the people that deserve my most sincere gratitude and thanks are my family. My wife Donna and my children Megan and Haley deserve more thanks than I can ever give them for their patience, understanding and support during this book writing process. And special thanks to my parents, David and Sandra and my sister Tammy for their constant support of me as well.

Finally, I'd like to thank my co-authors and friends, Stephen and Jason, for stepping in and helping me to create what I believe is a fantastic VMware ESX book."

David Marshall

"First and foremost, I have to give the most thanks to my wife, Tracy, and my two sons, Shane and Brandon. My family is and always has been my greatest supporters throughout my career and I truly believe that they, my family, are the real secret to my success. I would like to give thanks to my friends and co-authors David, for thinking of me for this project and Jase for stepping to up the plate and hitting a home run. I would like to thank my Uncle Doug for being an inspiration to me my whole life. Doug, you showed me a picture of my dad in his plane that he gave to you that said, "Study, work hard and then come soar with me." Well I am soaring on top of the world and the view is great just like you said it is. I would like to thank everyone from the VMware Community Forums. There are just too many of you to mention, but each and every one of you has helped in making a great community and helped to share ideas for all. Finally, I would like to give thanks to my mother and father, may they rest in peace. You may not have gotten to see your son grown and on his own but I pray each and every day that I have made you proud."

Stephen S. Beaver

"I have to start by giving thanks to my wife, Toni, and my children, Emma, Ethan, and Parker. They have been my best source of strength through my professional career and personal life. I would not have been able to achieve the goals, for myself or my family, without their continued support and love. I would also like to thank my parents, Ronny and Ginger for expecting the most from me. Without their love and encouragement, I would have never become the person that I am today. Making them proud has been one of my biggest goals in life. I look forward to every accomplishment as an opportunity to make them proud. I would like to thank my good friends, Stephen Beaver and David Marshall, for making me a part of this project. I would have never had this opportunity without their faith in me. And finally, I would like to thank all of the people that have helped me learn over the years."

Jason W. McCarty

About the Authors

David Marshall is an industry recognized virtualization expert that focuses on product marketing and community development. He has been in the industry for over 15 years and has been a virtualization industry advocate for the past 8 of those years. David is currently employed as the Director of Marketing at Austin-based Hyper9 and was at InovaWave before that. Prior to his marketing career, David was a Senior Architect at Surgient and a Deployment Manager at ProTier where he was responsible for creating and implementing a number of complex virtualization solutions for a number of Fortune 1000 clients. And before joining ProTier, he enjoyed a very successful 7-year career working in and managing a number of departments within BankOne. David is a co-author of the very successful virtualization book, *Advanced Server Virtualization: VMware and Microsoft Platforms in the Virtual Data Center*, was the Technical Editor of *Virtualization for Dummies* and *VMware VI3 for Dummies*, and he also authored numerous articles for a number of well known technical magazines. He founded one of the oldest and more popular virtualization news sites, VMblog.com, authors the InfoWorld Virtualization Report, and can be heard regularly on InfoWorld's Virtualization Report Podcast. He has also appeared on a number of conference panels focused on the subject of virtualization, including a well received session about performance at VMword 2006. He is a Microsoft Certified Professional and holds numerous certifications from CompTIA. David graduated with a bachelor's degree in Finance and an Information Technology Certification from the University of New Orleans. He can be contacted through VMBlog.com.

Stephen S. Beaver is the Co-Author of *"Scripting VMware Power Tools: Automating Virtual Infrastructure Administration"* and *"How to cheat at configuring VMware ESX Server"* as well as the Technical Editor of *"VMware ESX Server: Advanced Technical Design Guide."* Stephen is currently a systems engineer with one of the largest private hospitals in the United States, Florida Hospital in Orlando, Florida. Stephen is the lead architect for all the virtual systems throughout the hospital. As such, his main focus is to develop and touch every aspect off all virtual things throughout the systems complete life cycle from design, testing, integration and deployment to operation management and strategic planning. Stephen's background also includes a position as a Senior Engineer at the law firm Greenberg Traurig in Miami, FL, where he designed and deployed the firm's virtual infrastructure worldwide. Stephen has a solid background of over ten years in the industry and has been focused on virtualization for the last five years. Stephen is one of the most active participants and a moderator on the VMware Community forum. Stephen has been invited to speak at several virtualization seminars and events as well as being a presenter at the last three VMworld events.

Jason W. McCarty is currently a Senior Systems Engineer with an ASP component of Equifax Inc., in Baton Rouge, LA. As the team lead and virtualization architect, Jason is responsible for managing a datacenter that delivers loan origination software to banks, credit unions, and other lending institutions across North America. Through the use of VMware's virtualization technologies, he has created a dynamic and cost effective implementation of production, test, and development environments. Jason's education includes a Master's of Science in Engineering Technology, a Bachelor's of Science in Electronic Engineering Technology, and an Associate's Degree in Computer Information Technology, all of which have contributed to his technical and business success. Jason's background spans approximately 19 years, with technical experience in a wide variety of platforms, and business experience in areas including finance, insurance, academic, and military operations. In addition to technical and business experience, Jason taught technology courses as an adjunct instructor at Tulane University College in New Orleans, LA for 3 years and at the University of Phoenix in New Orleans, LA and Baton Rouge, LA for 5 years. Jason is a very active in the VMware Community Forums, and has obtained the rank of Virtuoso. Jason has presented on various topics through the years, as well as maintaining a technical blog on his web site at jasemccarty.com.

Chapter 1

Introduction to Server Virtualization

Virtualization is one of those IT buzzwords being thrown around the industry more and more lately, and unfortunately, it can have so many different meanings that it needs to be put into better context when discussed by so many different people. It was only about four years ago that the topic of virtualization itself was thought of as some obscure, black art technology that only a handful of people cared about, and yet today, it is thought of as a mainstream "must have" technology for any IT organization.

For those of us in the know because we have been using virtualization technologies for years now, it has become quite commonplace for us to advertise or tout the technology's benefits to as many people that are willing to listen. And beginning about two years ago, members of the press and analyst firms started picking up steam talking about the technology as well, which in turn caused a huge surge in the number of venues and mediums willing to discuss the subject. However, what really brought virtualization into the spotlight weren't its many benefits or anything else technical for that matter. Oddly enough, it was two financial events that helped trigger the explosive growth in server virtualization. In the month of August 2007, VMware's parent company, EMC, took the virtualization company public, earning itself nearly $1 billion dollars and becoming one of the most successful technology IPO offerings since Google. And interestingly, only one day later, Citrix announced that it was going to acquire a VMware competitor, XenSource, for an amount somewhere in the neighborhood of $500 million dollars. These two incredible sets of financial numbers made everyone, technical and non-technical, stand up and take notice of this technology, and it squarely placed virtualization on the front page everywhere for everyone to read.

1

In this chapter, we will provide you with a high-level overview and the background information you need to help explain just "what is this virtualization technology all about?" And to help answer that question, we'll introduce some of the most basic concepts in this chapter as well as create a discussion around some of the differences between the various technologies in order to help you better grasp the overall concept.

Sorting out the Terminology

If you have made it this far by purchasing this book, you probably already have somewhat of a commitment to virtualization in your organization or you are at least starting down the path of exploration. The next step is becoming more familiar with some of the terminology that you are going to be faced with throughout the book or throughout your research and implementation of server virtualization.

- **Host Machine**—A host machine is the physical machine on which the virtualization software is installed. It contains the physical resources such as the processors, memory, hard disks, network adapters and other resources that the virtual machine utilizes.
- **Virtual Machine**—The virtual machine (VM) is the virtualized representation of a physical machine that operates and is maintained by the virtualization software. A virtual machine is typically comprised of either a single file or a group of files that can be read and executed by the virtualization platform. Each virtual machine is a self-contained operating environment that behaves as if it is a separate computer. A virtual machine emulates a complete hardware system, including but not limited to a processor, memory, network adapter, removable drives and peripheral devices. Multiple virtual machines configured with different guest operating systems are capable of operating on the same host machine simultaneously.
- **Virtualization Software**—Virtualization software is a generic term denoting a software technology that provides a layer of abstraction in order to create logical environments for operating systems or application instances to execute in isolation from one another.
- **Virtual Disk**—The term refers to the virtual machine's physical representation on the disk and is composed of a single file or a group of files that are located on the host machine's hard drive or on a remote storage location. It appears to the virtual machine as if it were a physical hard disk. Virtual disks offer a number of benefits over their physical counterparts such as portability and ease of backup.
- **Guest Operating System**—The operating system that is installed and runs inside of a virtual machine environment that would otherwise operate directly on a separate physical machine.

- **Virtual Machine Monitor**—A virtual machine monitor (VMM) is the software that runs in a layer between a hypervisor or host operating system and one or more virtual machines that gives the virtual machine abstraction to the guest operating systems. The VMM virtualizes certain hardware resources such as the CPU, memory and physical disk, and it creates emulated devices for virtual machines running on the host machine. The VMM can export a virtual machine abstraction that is identical to a physical machine so that the standard operating system can run just as if it were on physical hardware.

- **Hypervisor**—A hypervisor is a thin layer of software that provides access to hardware resources and provides virtual partitioning capabilities, and it runs directly on the hardware or on the 'bare-metal' of the machine, but underneath higher-level virtualization services. The hypervisor is directly responsible for hosting and managing virtual machines running on the host, although overall benefits can vary widely from one vendor's hypervisor to another.

- **Hosted Virtualization**—In this virtualization approach, partitioning and virtualization services run on top of a standard operating system on the host machine. With this method, the virtualization software relies on the host operating system to provide the services needed to talk directly to the underlying hardware.

- **Paravirtualization**—A virtualization approach that exports a modified hardware abstraction which requires the guest operating system to be modified and ported before it can be allowed to run in the virtualized environment as a virtual machine. Therefore, its use requires an open source operating system whose source is publicly available and open to modification such as Linux.

- **Hardware-level Virtualization**—In this approach, the virtualization layer sits on top of the hardware exporting the virtual machine abstraction. And since the virtual machine looks like the hardware, all of the software written for it can operate successfully in the virtual machine.

- **Operating-System Virtualization**—Here, the virtualization layer sits between the operating system and the applications that install and run on the operating system. The virtual instances are written for the particular operating system being virtualized.

History of Virtualization

In order to move forward, we need to know where we've been. And so, it's important to see where today's virtualization technology came from. And believe it or not, the history of virtualization technology goes back further than most people might think. In fact, the idea of virtualization was first discussed as far back as the late 1950's. The following information will attempt to chronicle the significant events that have occurred since the early 1960's as well as cover the impact that it had on x86 server virtualization.

In the early 1960's, IBM introduced us to the term "Time Sharing" which was the original driving force behind virtualization. Today, many people associate time sharing with mainframe computers, but arguably x86 could be headed in this direction under the name On-Demand Computing. In 1964, IBM introduced the IBM System/360, which provided limited virtualization capabilities and was architected by the legendary Gene Amdahl. Later in 1964, the CP-40 was released and gave way to the first mentions of Virtual Machines and Virtual Memory. In 1965, the System/360 Model 67 and TSS (Time Sharing System) were developed. This was followed in 1967 by another release of CP-40 and CMS, which put into production a system supporting 14 VMs each having 256K of Virtual Memory.

A new iteration of the CP-40 called CP-67 Version 1 debuted in 1968. This provided a much needed boost in both performance and stability to CP-40. CP-67 Version 2 in 1969 gave way to a new scheduler and PL/I support and in 1970 CP-67 Version 3 had free storage sub pool support which provided additional performance and the addition of SLT instruction. Finally in 1971, Version 3.1 of CP-67 was released with high speed I/O enhancements.

In 1972, the System/370 Advanced Function was released and had new Address Relocation Hardware and now supported four new operating systems (VM/370, DOS/VS, OS/VS1, and OS/VS2). As VM technology became more popular in the IBM community, the MVMUA (Metropolitan VM User Association) was founded in New York in 1973. The introduction of VM/370 Release 2 in 1974 contained the first iteration of VMA (Virtual Machine Assist) Microcode. Also in 1974, Gerald J. Popek and Robert P. Goldberg created a set of formal requirements for architectures titled "Formal Requirements for Virtualizable Third Generation Architectures."

This led to a quiet period in the virtualization space from 1974 to 1987, when the rise of the Internet gave way to the need for TCP/IP support. In 1987, VM TCP/IP also known as FAL made TCP/IP available to VMs. During the 1980s and 1990s, the need for virtualization was effectively abandoned with the introduction of the low-cost mini-computer and the personal desktop. Instead of sharing resources centrally in the mainframe model, organizations began to use these low cost distributed systems. The broad adoption of Windows and Linux as the emerging server operating systems in the 1990s established the x86 server as the new industry standard. However, the high demand and strong growth of the x86 server and desktop environments introduced a whole new set of IT Infrastructure and operational challenges that had to be addressed.

The following events directly lead to the current set of available x86 server virtualization technologies and platforms.

In 1988, a small company called Connectix Corporation was founded and provided solutions for Apple Macintosh (Mac) systems. Connectix became well known for its innovative approach to solving problems that Apple either could not or would not solve. One such example of this was Mode32, a solution to the 24-bit memory addressing problem on the Motorola 68020 and 68030 processors used in early Macs. Another product by Connectix was SpeedDoubler, a product that provided a high-performance emulation bridge from the Motorola 68000 processors to the Power PC-based processors. Following SpeedDoubler was RAM Doubler, which provided a way to double a Mac's memory by compressing and decompressing the contents of RAM on the fly.

Connectix's experience with the Mac and PC world would lead them to create a new product named Connectix Virtual PC 1.0 for the Mac. The Virtual PC 1.0 product was quite a feat of programming in that it incorporated a binary translation engine to translate instructions from a virtual Intel x86 processor to a physical Power PC processor used in the Mac. This example of emulation would lead Connectix into virtualization technologies.

In 1998, a company called VMware was founded by Diane Greene and husband Dr. Mendel Rosenblum along with two students from Stanford University and a colleague from Berkley. On October of 1998, these founders filed for a patent regarding new virtualization techniques based on research conducted at Stanford University. The patent was awarded on May 28, 2002.

On February 8, 1999, VMware introduced "VMware Virtual Platform" to market. This product is considered by many to be the first commercially available x86 virtualization platform, and it would later morph into what we now call the VMware Workstation product.

In late 2000, VMware released their first server virtualization platform, VMware GSX Server 1.0. This product was aimed at workgroup class server implementations and installed on top of either a Linux or Windows operating system. The following year, VMware took x86 server virtualization to the next level with the release of VMware ESX Server 1.0, a mainframe class server virtualization platform. Unlike VMware GSX Server, VMware ESX Server installed on bare-metal and provided a more stable and high performance computing environment due to its native hypervisor—otherwise known as a Virtual Machine Monitor (VMM) and which requires much less overhead. From 2002 to the present, VMware has continued to release updated versions of both GSX Server (ultimately renamed to VMware Server) and ESX Server platforms adding new capabilities and enhancing performance.

Connectix had built a relationship with Microsoft which was based on the bundling of Microsoft operating system packs with the Connectix Virtual PC for Mac product. And later, they provided the PocketPC emulation technology embedded in Microsoft's Visual Studio.NET application. Connectix entered the x86 server virtualization arena with their release candidate version of the Connectix Virtual Server product in early 2003. However, Connectix Virtual Server never actually made it to market as a Connectix branded product because before it could, Microsoft acquired the intellectual property rights of both Virtual PC for Mac and Windows as well as Connectix Virtual Server.

Microsoft's virtualization plan was focused on supporting legacy application re-hosting, server consolidation and automation of software development and test environments. They released their first virtualization product, Microsoft Virtual

PC 2004, on December 2, 2003. Microsoft's planned entry into the x86 server virtualization market with Microsoft Virtual Server 2004 was delayed in order to implement heavy security modifications due to the new Microsoft security initiative. The final product, Microsoft Virtual Server 2005, was released in mid-2004 with two versions being made available—Microsoft Virtual Server 2005 Standard Edition (supporting up to four physical processors) and Microsoft Virtual Server 2005 Enterprise Edition (supporting up to 32 physical processors).

Like Connectix, VMware too was acquired. The company was purchased by EMC Corporation on January 9, 2004. At first glance, this appeared to many as quite a surprise; however the underlying reason for the acquisition was that, like EMC's acquisition of Documentum and Legato, EMC was searching for software applications which consumed very large quantities of storage space to help further their storage sales agenda. Since the acquisition, VMware continues to operate as an independent subsidiary of EMC and is still headed by CEO Diane Greene. In August 2007, EMC took VMware public and sold off around 10 percent of the company—earning it somewhere in the neighborhood just short of $1 billion dollars.

Around the same period of time that people were focused on watching what VMware and Microsoft were doing in the virtualization space, another server virtualization technology was actively being developed called Xen. The Xen project was first described in a paper presented at SOSP in 2003. In October of that same year, the first public release of a 1.0 version of Xen made its appearance. Xen was originally developed by the Systems Research Group at the University of Cambridge Computer Laboratory as part of the XenoServers project, and it was funded by the UK-EPSRC. Since then, Xen has significantly matured into a fully-fledged project that enabled research into better techniques to virtualize resources such as the CPU, memory, disk and network. Ian Pratt, a senior lecturer at Cambridge, lead the project and helped to found XenSource, Inc., a company that supported the development of the open source Xen project and also created and sold a commercial, enterprise version of the software. Project contributors included such notables as AMD, HP, IBM, Intel, Novell, RedHat and XenSource.

In late 2006, XenSource released its first version of XenEnterprise 3.0, a product based on Xen v3.0.3 and created to compete directly with VMware's ESX product. In August 2007, XenSource announced the release of XenEnterprise v4 which was based on Xen 3.1, was more stable and tried to become closer in feature parity to competitor platforms such as VMware ESX. It was also during this same month that Citrix announced that it would follow EMC and Microsoft on the virtualization platform acquisition path by acquiring XenSource for nearly $500 million dollars.

With hypervisor technology like VMware ESX and Xen becoming the dominant platform in server virtualization, Microsoft had to take a stand and shift its focus onto something more competitive rather than resting its laurels on Microsoft Virtual Server. So with the development of Longhorn or Windows Server 2008, the company started to develop its own hypervisor technology, originally called

Viridian and later named Hyper-V. Microsoft anticipates that the virtualization platform will be out in the second half of 2008. However at launch time, its feature set isn't expected to be in parity with competitor products based on Xen nor will it offer the same features that can be found in VMware's virtualization suite, VI3.

Chip manufacturers Intel and AMD continue to introduce new technologies to provide much better support for virtualization at the hardware layer. These technologies include multi-core processors, Intel's Virtualization Technology (originally known as Vanderpool and Silvervale), and AMD-V/SVM (originally known as Pacifica). These hardware virtualization technologies allow virtualization platforms to efficiently handle certain unsafe x86 instructions that a virtual machine may call during normal operation. Intel-VT and AMD-V technology intercepts these instructions and pass control to the hypervisor to avoid the need for a complex and performance hindering layer of software. The added virtualization instructions in the AMD and Intel processors have helped spawn a number of new virtualization platforms since the additional technology has removed one of the barriers of entry into the virtualization market.

Overview of Server Virtualization Technology

Wikipedia describes virtualization in the broadest sense stating that the technology "refers to the abstraction of computing resources." For a 20,000 foot view of the technology, that's really not a bad place to start. As stated earlier though, when talking about virtualization, context becomes extremely important. However, since we are focusing on VMware's ESX technology, we will primarily be discussing hypervisor server virtualization; but for completeness, we will also touch on other forms of virtualization so that you have a better understanding of the technology.

Server virtualization technology is a way of making a physical computer function as if it were two or more computers where each non-physical or "virtualized" computer is provided with the same basic architecture as that of a generic physical computer. There are several ways to do this, and each has its own set of pros and cons.

In order to make a physical computer function as more than one computer, its physical hardware characteristics must be recreated through the use of software. This is accomplished by a software layer called abstraction. Abstraction software is used in many software systems, including inside the Windows operating system families. The Windows Hardware Abstraction Layer (HAL) is an excellent example of abstraction. The Windows HAL provides a common way for all drivers and software to talk to the hardware in a common/unified format. This makes the job of writing software and drivers easier because developers no longer have to write custom software for each brand or type of computer that they want their code to run on. Abstraction, as it relates to virtualization, is the representation of a set of common hardware devices that are entirely software driven. This is basically software that looks and acts like hardware. Virtualization technology therefore allows the installation of an operating system on hardware that doesn't really exist.

Virtualization is a concept that allows a computer's resources to be divided or shared by multiple environments simultaneously. These environments can interoperate or they can be totally unaware of one another. A single environment may or may not even be aware that it is running in a virtual environment. These environments are most commonly known as "virtual machines" or VMs. VMs will almost always house an installation of an operating system (e.g., Linux, Windows, etc.). These operating system installations are commonly referred to as "guest operating systems". The guest operating system running in the virtual machine sees a consistent, normalized set of hardware regardless of what the actual physical hardware components are in the host server.

Instructions for a VM are usually passed directly to the physical hardware, doing so allows the environment to operate faster and more efficiently than emulation, although more complex instructions must be trapped and interpreted in order to ensure proper compatibility and abstraction with the physical hardware.

In order to better understand a virtualized computer environment, it is beneficial to compare the basic computer organization of a typical physical computer to that of a computer running a virtualization platform and virtualized environments. The arrangement of a typical computer has a set of hardware devices onto which is installed an operating system (e.g., Linux or Windows) and one or more applications that get installed into the operating system. Figure 1.1 shows this arrangement.

Inside a computer hosting a virtualization platform, the arrangement may be slightly different because the computer itself has a set of hardware onto which the operating system (e.g., Linux or Windows) is installed. The operating system has a virtualization platform installed into which one or more virtual machines are created where each can act as its own set of separate hardware and are capable of having an operating system and applications installed as shown in Figure 1.2.

And finally, another common arrangement of a virtualized computing system is one in which the virtualization platform is installed directly onto the computer's hardware or installed on "bare-metal"—such as VMware ESX. This form of virtualization provides a platform on which one or more virtual machines can be created

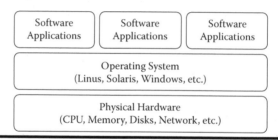

Figure 1.1   The Arrangement of a Typical Computer.

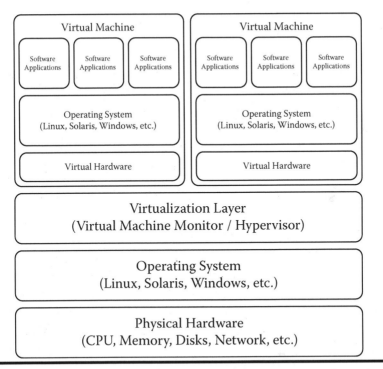

Figure 1.2   The Arrangement of a Hosted Architecture.

with each capable of having a unique guest operating system and its own set of applications installed. This layout is shown in Figure 1.3.

Common implementations of server virtualization include:

- **VMware ESX**—This is the fastest performing and most mature x86 server virtualization platform to date. VMware ESX installs and operates directly on the bare-metal of the physical hardware in order to maximize efficiency. Its hypervisor technology is proprietary.

- **Citrix XenServer**—The foundation for the Citrix family of product is the open-source Xen hypervisor. The server virtualization platform installs and runs directly on the physical hardware and is enhanced by Intel and AMD hardware virtualization assist capabilities. Citrix acquired the technology with the acquisition of XenSource. The company offers both a free and pay version of its solution.

- **Virtual Iron**—Virtual Iron provides enterprise class software for server virtualization and virtual infrastructure management. Their solution runs directly on the physical hardware and leverages the hardware-assisted virtualization capabilities provided by Intel and AMD processors. Its virtualization platform is based on the open-source Xen technology. Virtual Iron offers both a free and pay version of its software.

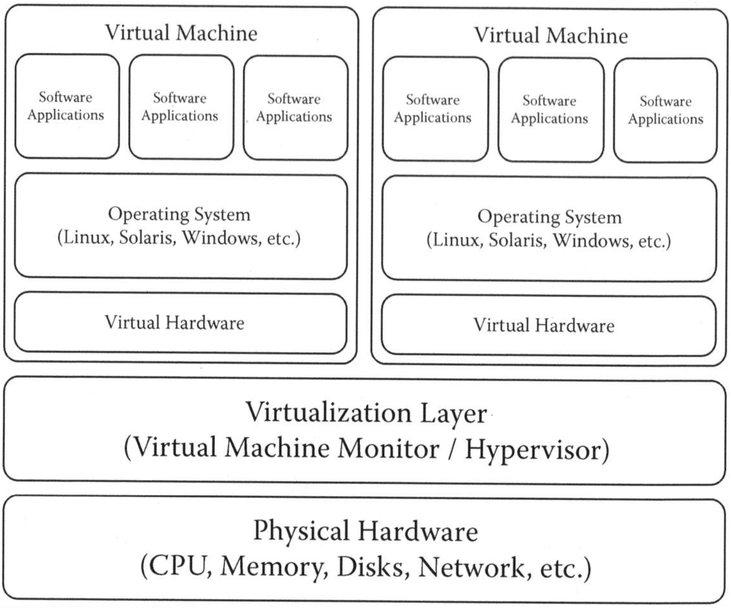

Figure 1.3   The Arrangement of a Hypervisor (Bare-Metal) Architecture.

■ **VMware Server**—VMware Server is a free lightweight hosted server virtualization platform that was originally based on VMware's Workstation product. VMware Server must be installed on either a Linux or Windows host operating system.

■ **Microsoft Virtual Server**—Microsoft Virtual Server is a free hosted server virtualization platform that is based on technology acquired from Connectix Corporation. Virtual Server 2005 R2 must be installed on a Windows Server 2003 Edition or Windows XP Professional operating system (although Microsoft does not officially support Virtual Server on Windows XP Professional for production use).

■ **Microsoft Hyper-V**—Microsoft's Hyper-V, code-named 'Viridian', is Microsoft's latest virtualization hypervisor technology and replaces Microsoft Virtual Server as the company's focused virtualization platform. Unlike Microsoft Virtual Server, Hyper-V technology is included in Microsoft's operating system, specifically the x64 versions of Microsoft Windows Server 2008. The Hyper-V hypervisor is also available as a stand-alone offering, without the Windows Server functionality, for bare-metal installations.

Server Virtualization Technology

Reducing hardware and software needs, reducing down time, increasing scalability and improving performance are all key factors in creating success within today's

IT environments. And server virtualization can help provide the necessary means for your organization to achieve these goals.

The following is a brief overview of some of the benefits you can expect to achieve with the implementation of server virtualization in your environment as well as an overview of when and when not to use the technology.

Discovering the Benefits

- **Portability**—Virtualization gives the ability to have a consistent hardware platform, even if the real underlying hardware comes from different manufacturers. Hardware independence makes it easy to move a virtual machine from one physical server to another.
- **Manageability**—Virtual environments can be easily managed. Virtualization offers flexibility in creating and managing complex initiatives.
- **Efficiency**—When properly implemented, server virtualization allows the physical hardware to be used more efficiently, allowing higher utilization of the hardware's resources. It can also help reduce power, space and cooling issues through consolidation.

When to use server virtualization:

- **Server Consolidation**—Server consolidation allows many physical servers to be virtualized and hosted on as little as a single physical server leveraging virtualization. Most servers today are far underutilized, running between 8 and 12 percent utilization. Consolidating multiple virtual servers onto one physical server can bring efficiency to the hardware and raise its utilization safely beyond 70 percent.
- **Legacy Application Support**—Server virtualization provides an upgrade path for migrating legacy applications and operating systems from older failed, failing or unsupported hardware platforms onto newer hardware without incurring problems or facing issues because of incompatibilities between the application or the operating system and the newer hardware platforms (for example, because of the lack of drivers or general vendor support).
- **Multiple Operating System Support**—Having the ability to host live, multiple operating systems on a single piece of equipment becomes extremely beneficial within an organization such as software development or testing. Being able to run multiple operating systems reduces the amount of downtime that is associated with constantly having to rebuild servers in order to swap out the operating system.
- **Software Demonstration**—By using server virtualization, software demonstrations and beta software can be run in a consistent manner. Users are more apt to install a demo or beta software inside of a virtual machine as opposed

to installing it within a physical production server that is already hosting another application. Virtualization can also help a salesperson demonstrate multiple software instances to a customer from a single physical machine.

■ **Software Development, Testing, and Debugging**—Because of the strong isolation between the environment and the virtualization platform, it becomes easy to perform software development, testing and debugging. A complex development and testing matrix can more easily and readily be produced.

■ **Technical Training and E-Learning**—In order to teach many of today's advanced courses, more than one computer is required for each student. By using server virtualization, training companies can not only reduce the number of computers that are required to teach a single classroom, but they can also greatly decrease the amount of time it takes them to setup or rebuild the computer environment for each class.

■ **Business Continuity**—Virtualization can help a business more easily achieve the "five nines" of uptime by helping to eliminate planned downtime, deliver high availability and disaster recovery solutions, and assist with backing up data.

■ **Security Honey Pot**—Virtual machines can easily help with setting up a honey pot in your network environment in order to view the threats and attacks that your network or applications may be susceptible to from unscrupulous forces.

When server virtualization should not be used:

■ **Virtualization of x86 Virtualization**—Installing and operating server virtualization inside of another instance of virtualization is probably not an ideal situation. Attempting to do so can cause double time slicing and quite frankly, in many cases, would probably prove to be unusable. Many people have reported that it is possible to install VMware ESX inside of a VMware Workstation 6 virtual machine; and while this may prove to be successful, it should probably only be used to learn the technology and not used as any sort of production environment architecture to be sure. This limitation only applies to x86 virtualization as IBM's original virtualization technology was engineered to support this very type of usage.

■ **Graphic Intensive Applications**—The performance requirements are simply too great to successfully test and/or play high end games in virtual environments. As virtualization platforms continue to progress, this will become less of an issue. As an example, some desktop virtualization platforms have recently started to support the capability of operating some 3-D games.

■ **Specialized hardware and peripherals**—There is no way today to leverage custom hardware peripherals/cards in a virtualization platform. This is because there is no emulation or representation of these devices in the virtual environment. As virtualization continues to catch on and spread throughout the IT industry, this will change.

- **Performance testing**—The overhead caused by virtualization will usually give an inaccurate view of the performance metrics being measured inside the virtual machine. As the technology continues to advance, this problem becomes less of an issue.
- **Hardware driver debugging**—Because all virtual machines in each version of virtualization are the same and the hardware is fixed and emulated, there is no way to test or debug hardware drivers on this platform.

So what about Emulation and Simulation? Where do they fit in?

Emulation is a concept that allows one environment to act or behave as if it were another environment. This could also be described as sophisticated impersonation. An environment is an execution platform, operating system, or hardware architecture. Instructions are interpreted from the executing environment into instructions that the real, underlying environment understands. Emulation is used for running legacy environments, operating system development, and software testing. Emulated environments incur a high performance penalty when compared to virtualized systems due to the overhead of the interpreter.

Common implementations of emulation include:

- Bochs—Bochs is an open source x86 emulator which emulates the x86 processor, devices, and BIOS.
- MAME—The Multiple Arcade Machine Emulator allows arcade ROM soft-ware to run on Windows. It emulates the arcade hardware for which the games were originally programmed.
- Virtual PC for Mac—Virtual PC for Mac emulates the x86 hardware environment which allows Microsoft Windows operating systems to be installed and run.
- WINE—WINE enables Windows applications to run on Linux, FreeBSD, and Solaris. It emulates portions of the Windows operating system, but the code executes natively on the x86 processor. Ironically, the name WINE is a recursive acronym which stands for "WINE Is Not an Emulator."

Simulation is a concept in which an environment imitates another environment. This imitation simply accepts pre-defined inputs and provides pre-defined responses. This is arguably the easiest or least complex concept to implement. An environment is an execution platform, operating system, or hardware architecture. Simulators are used differently than both emulation and virtualization. They are primarily used in hard-ware and microchip design and prototyping. By doing this, testing can be done on hardware and microchips yet to be built! This reduces the costs and risks associated with mistakes being made on hardware and chips before they are fabricated.

Common implementations of simulation include:

- **Cadence and Synopsis**—These companies provide chip design software along with simulators to test viability, performance and other metrics. These are great examples of the capability that simulators provide.
- **Simics**—The Simics evolved from gsim in 1991. Simics is able to run unmodified operating systems using its simulated processors and devices.
- **SimOS**—The SimOS project was developed at Stanford University in 1992. It simulated the SPRITE system on SPARC hardware. Other implementations of SimOS supported MIPS-based SGI systems, Digital Alpha Processors and the Power PC.

Summary

The use of emulators and simulators have their places, however virtualization is the only technology that enables revolutionary capabilities in the datacenter. Virtualization provides the benefits necessary to give IT organizations the ability to save costs on hardware and increase the efficiency of server deployments, provisioning, and management. Virtualization also enables physical hardware independence, which gives IT the flexibility and freedom of not being locked in to a single vendor's hardware solution.

The history of virtualization goes back much further than most people realize. Several significant developments occurred in the early 1960s, in the late 1980s, and the early 1990s. These developments lead to the founding of the two pioneering companies in the x86 server virtualization space, VMware and Connectix. Together these two companies have defined x86 server virtualization and helped pave the way for server consolidation efforts. Both companies have since been acquired (VMware by EMC and Connectix by Microsoft) but their technology continues to lead to innovations in the computer industry.

While virtualization can solve many of today's IT problems, it is not a universal solution capable of solving all problems. Even with all of the advancements that have been made, there are still times in which virtualization is not yet mature enough of a technology to be applied, such as with certain applications requiring high, intensive I/O access or when the need for high-end graphics display is needed (such as doing 3D design work in a CAD/CAM application like Unigraphics). These challenges are being met head-on, so hopefully these issues will be solved in the not so distant future.

Chapter 2

VMware's Hypervisor Platform

VMware ESX is undoubtedly the most widely deployed and most stable server virtualization platform on the market today. The platform was built and architected to be a production ready, enterprise-class server virtualization product that is feature rich and designed to have the smallest possible overhead thanks to its hypervisor design. In this chapter, we will take a look at the platform's background and then cover some of the specific features found in VMware ESX and the VMware Infrastructure 3 suite. And finally, we'll take a look at what VMware is doing with their hardware embedded version of the hypervisor, VMware ESXi.

VMware ESX Product Background

For those of you just starting out with VMware, believe it or not, VMware ESX was first released back in March of 2001. The release followed VMware GSX Server and VMware Workstation. VMware GSX Server (now called VMware Server) was developed to be a workgroup class solution providing simple administration on a familiar host platform, while VMware Workstation was designed as a desktop virtualization product. Both products, however, suffered performance loss due to the high overhead that came along with installing the virtualization technologies on top of a host operating system. During early pre-release versions of VMware ESX, it was necessary to install a copy of Red Hat Linux first, then after completing the install, the kernel would have to be replaced with a custom kernel written by VMware. Indeed, a tedious task to say the least.

VMware ESX is a hypervisor-based virtualization platform. A hypervisor provides the most efficient use of resources in a virtualization platform because it does not rely upon a host operating system and can minimize the resource overhead. VMware's decision to build an incredibly lightweight bare-metal operating system was a simple one. The company wanted to create an enterprise class virtualization platform and realized early on that to be successful, performance and granularity of resource control would be critical components. In May of 2002, VMware released ESX Server 1.5 providing support for uniprocessor virtual machines, tight SAN integration, and advanced resource controls. In July of 2003 VMware announced ESX Server 2.0 which provided support for up to two processors with the VMware Virtual SMP add-on product. Virtual SMP is supported only by ESX Server 2.x and above. At the end of 2004, VMware released VMware ESX Server 2.5 and with it the ability to directly boot from SAN and automatically script the hypervisor's installation, as well as adding improved support for clustered virtual machines.

In October of 2005, VMware unveiled the next generation of VMware ESX Server, 3.0. And then in June of 2006, the company officially launched the third generation of the industry leading virtualization software and wrapped a number of applications and features around it to make a new virtualization suite called VMware Infrastructure 3 (VI3). Automation capabilities were added and enhanced, including VMware High Availability, Distributed Resource Scheduling, VMware VMotion and VMware Consolidated Backup. At the same time, the new version of VMware ESX also added 4-way Virtual SMP support and increased the virtual memory support of virtual machines to 16GB, a critical support feature for enterprises wanting to use virtual machines on high utilization production class systems. And finally, in December of 2007, VMware announced the latest version of VMware Infrastructure 3 which included VMware ESX 3.5 and VirtualCenter 2.5. This version provided new capabilities for increased levels of automation, improved overall infrastructure availability and higher performance for mission critical workloads.

ESX hosts virtual machines running a broad range of operating systems. To achieve such wide support, ESX emulates a generic virtual hardware platform. Each virtual machine leverages its own virtual hardware consisting of a single or multiprocessor system with an Intel 440BX motherboard including an NS338 SIO (Serial Input Output) chip and six virtual PCI slots. A Phoenix Bios 4.0 Release 6 acts as the virtual BIOS for the system. Depending on the host server's capacity, up to 64GB of memory can be given to a single virtual machine. Each virtual machine also has a virtual SVGA graphics card, up to four virtual SCSI controllers supporting fifteen devices per controller, up to two virtual 1.44 MB floppy drives, up to four virtual CD/DVD-ROM drives, four serial ports, three parallel ports, and up to four virtual network adapters. As discussed throughout the book, there are specific restrictions as to which physical hardware devices are supported by VMware ESX.

Today, VMware has the most powerful and mature platform available in the enterprise virtualization space. This was accomplished by focusing on performance and function above all else. With each release of VMware ESX, more and more enterprises are making the decision to implement virtualization in their production environments. VMware is steadily gaining traction in the mission critical and production enterprise data center space by providing a low-overhead, high-performance and mature solution with an ever increasing feature list.

ESX Platform Specifics

At the core of VMware ESX is a series of modules that provide capabilities to regulate CPU affinity, memory allocation and oversubscription, network bandwidth throttling, and I/O bandwidth control. These modules along with the capabilities offered with VMFS make up the VMware ESX base platform.

VMkernel

The VMkernel lies at the heart of the VMware ESX hypervisor, and future enhancements to the product will come from this important subsystem. The VMkernel is a high performance operating system that was developed by VMware and runs directly on the ESX host server. While it may look similar to a Linux kernel, it is not. Though there are some similarities. Like Linux, VMkernel loads various system modules, though over time this too has changed from one version of ESX to the next. ESX version 3 takes a more modular approach than previous builds which allows new devices to be added without requiring a recompile of the VMkernel. A key enhancement to the product is the addition of separate modules such as the vmkapimod which offers third-party solution providers the ability to create new tools for the product through a common application programming interface (API). Other modules have been removed over time, such as those needed for older and now considered obsolete hardware.

The VMkernel controls and manages most of the physical resources on the hardware, including the physical processors, memory, and storage and networking controllers. The VMkernel includes schedulers for CPU, memory, and disk access, and has full fledged storage and network stacks.

Console Operating System (COS)

The service console (COS) has been upgraded from being based on a variant of Red Hat Linux version 7.2 to being based on a variant of Red Hat Enterprise Linux 3, Update 8 (RHEL 3 U8). However, do not think that the COS is in any way a complete distribution of Linux. It is a limited distribution, and technically, not even Linux at all. VMkernel is what interacts with the system hardware; the COS is simply providing the execution environment for monitoring and administrating the ESX system. COS runs within a virtual machine and can be considered a management appliance. This feature has been removed from ESXi, as you will see later in this chapter.

NOTE

It is important to remember that the COS is based on Red Hat Linux, but that it is not Red Hat Linux. What that means is, you should never apply Red Hat Linux updates to the COS. The only patches and updates that should ever be applied to COS will come directly from VMware.

Virtual Machine File System (VMFS)

The Virtual Machine File System (VMFS) is a high performance cluster file system created by VMware as a solution to large file support and solves performance issues that haunt existing Linux based file systems. The VMFS file system addresses control, security, and management issues associated with virtual machine hard disk files. VMFS allows virtual hard disk files to be created contiguously by VMware ESX, which enhances access speeds from disk to virtualization platform. VMware VMFS has been optimized and certified for a number of local storage SCSI hard drives as well as a wide range of Fibre Channel and iSCSI SAN equipment.

Contrary to conventional file systems that only allow one server to have read-write access to the same file at a given time, VMFS can leverage shared storage systems to allow multiple instances of VMware ESX to concurrently read and write to the same storage. It uses a system of on-disk locking to ensure that a virtual machine is not powered on by multiple host servers at the same time.

The VMFS cluster file system is now capable of unique virtualization capabilities such as live migration of powered on virtual machines from one host server to another, clustering virtual machines across different physical servers, and automatic restart of a failed virtual machine on one physical server to another.

There are a few native Linux commands that do not work with or recognize the VMFS file system. When that is the case, VMware provides alternative commands that are compatible with the VMFS file system and may be used from the Service Console. As an example, VMware provides the 'vdf' command as a VMFS-compatible alternative to the Linux 'df' command. VMFS has become the premier virtual hard disk file system available within the virtualization community.

VMware VirtualCenter

VMware VirtualCenter is the central command and control console used in a VMware environment to configure, provision, and manage virtualized enterprise environments.

VirtualCenter was first released as 1.0 when VMware ESX Server was in the 2.0.1 release state, and VMware has since added even more features and functionality. At the time of this writing, VirtualCenter Version 2.5 is the current release.

Before getting into the details of VirtualCenter, it is worth mentioning something about database sizing for the management application. This seems to be one of the first questions that get asked when planning a VirtualCenter deployment. VMware has put together and released a tool for this called "The VMware VirtualCenter Database size calculator spreadsheet". The spreadsheet can be found online at http://www.vmware.com/support/vi3/doc/vc_db_calculator.xls. The calculator will estimate the size of the VirtualCenter database after it runs for a certain period of time. This estimate is calculated based on information you enter about your VMware Infrastructure 3 deployment, such as the number of hosts and virtual machines. There are two versions of the calculator—one for the VirtualCenter 2 releases prior to 2.0.1 Patch 2 and one for VirtualCenter 2.0.1 Patch 2 or later. So instead of going into too much detail here, I encourage you to download the spreadsheet and check it out for yourself.

Currently there are five components that make up VirtualCenter.

1. **VirtualCenter Management Server** is the central control point for all configuration, provisioning and management of the VMware environment.
2. **VirtualCenter Database** is the storage piece of the equation, used to store all the information about the physical server, resource pools as well as the virtual machines that are managed by VirtualCenter.
3. **Virtual Infrastructure Client** is the administrative client used to connect to and manage the VirtualCenter Management Server or the VMware ESX server directly.
4. **VirtualCenter Agent** is the ESX server agent used to connect to VirtualCenter on the VMware ESX server.

TIP

Good to know for troubleshooting: This is the vmware-vpxa service. You will sometimes find the need to restart that service as well as the mgmt-vmware service on the VMware ESX hosts.

---

5. **Virtual Infrastructure Web Access** allows virtual machine management and access to consoles without the use of the client. Note that this method is extremely limited in its functionality.

So now that we know what makes up VirtualCenter, what does this give us in the form of functionality? Let's get a quick overview of the features.

Core Features

Large-scale management

VirtualCenter is able to manage up to 200 hosts and 2000 virtual machines with a single VirtualCenter instance.

Centralized licensing model

VMware has given us the ability to manage all VMware software licenses with an embedded FlexNet licensing server and a single license file. You have your choice between a "host" based license model and a "server" based license model. And for the VMware ESX server itself, you must use the license server for any of the Enterprise License features like DRS, HA and or VMotion to name a few.

TIP

This tip works very well for Disaster Recovery and scripted installs of VMware ESX. You should have a host based license added to your ks.cfg for kickstart server builds. This way, once the machine has been built, it can immediately be started and run virtual machines. This is very helpful during a DR test and when your VirtualCenter is a virtual machine. You cannot start the virtual machines without a license server, so this will let you get the VirtualCenter virtual machine up and running as quickly as possible.

Deployment Wizard

VMware has made the task of creating a virtual machine very easy with an easy to use wizard to make every deployment unique in its environment.

Editable virtual machine templates

VMware has provided the ability to save virtual machines as a template stored on shared storage. This gives the ability to step configuration standards for your virtual machines. Templates also support virtual machine updating and patching.

Cloning of virtual machines

VMware has provided the ability to clone a virtual machine to make a full backup or deploy when a new server is needed. Having and/or creating a "Golden Image" will help speed up any deployments. To have a virtual machine fully loaded and fully patched ready to go will save countless hours of configuration and can lower deployments times to hours rather than days.

Live Migration (VMotion)

VMotion is the ability to migrate a live running virtual machine from one physical host to another with no impact to end users. The way this process works is the entire state of the virtual machine is encapsulated by a set of files stored on shared storage. The real key to this is VMware's VMFS file system. The file system is a "true" clustered file system which allows both the source and target VMware ESX server to access these files concurrently. What's left is the active memory as well as the execution state of the virtual machine which are transferred over a high speed network. This is truly the corner stone of VirtualCenter and the Virtual Infrastructure.

Distributed Resource Scheduler (DRS)

DRS will continually monitor your physical hosts in a VMware ESX cluster to maintain balanced utilization across the load on all servers by using VMotion technology to migrate virtual machines from host to host to maintain this balance. The setting is configurable with different available options from simply recommending a migration all the way to a fully aggressive automated migration policy.

Distributed Power Management (DPM)

VMware has taken DRS to another level with DPM. Although this is experimental with VirtualCenter version 2.5, DPM will consolidate workloads by monitoring the resource requirements and power consumption across a DRS Cluster and place unused hosts in a standby mode to reduce power consumption. When the work load increases, DPM will bring the powered-down hosts back online to ensure service level agreements can be met.

High Availability (HA)

VMware's HA will start all virtual machines on a failed node of a cluster onto the other members of the cluster. This is truly an easy to use and cost effective failover solution. In my testing, the first virtual machine will be back up and running in under 5 minutes. Your mileage may vary depending on the number of virtual machines as well as the setting and configuration of the virtual machines.

Features Available from Plug-ins

Integrated Physical to Virtual machine conversion or P2V with VMware Converter Plug-in

VMware has taken its Converter product and combined it into VirtualCenter. This functionality is new to VirtualCenter 2.5 and gives you the ability to manage multiple physical conversions to virtual machines using the VirtualCenter console. A simple right click and import machine is all it takes now.

Consolidation Plug-in

VMware has taken some of the Capacity Planner product functionality and built it into VirtualCenter in the form of a plug-in. This is new to VirtualCenter 2.5 and so is the ability to add plug-ins. (Plug-ins leave a lot to the imagination as to the direction things will go with adding functionality to VirtualCenter, especially with 3rd party applications.) Using a wizard, the consolidation plug-in will automatically discover physical servers and analyze their performance as well as trigger the conversion of the physical server to a virtual machine.

Update Manager Plug-in

VMware has released Update Manager as a plug-in. This is a new feature to VirtualCenter 2.5. Update manger will automate the scanning and patching of ESX servers as well as Microsoft and Linux virtual machines. The feature also reduces downtime through automatic snapshots prior to patching which leaves a rollback option. Integration of Update Manager and DRS will enable zero downtime when patching VMware ESX hosts. This has been a well sought out feature and VMware has had multiple feature requests for this option. It is really great to see VMware listen to the customer's requests and develop these tools.

Ability to Create Custom Plug-ins

At the time of this writing, several custom plug-ins have been created, including:

- **SvMotion**—Allows VMware administrators to invoke Storage VMotion (SvMotion) events.
- **Add Port Groups**—Enables the creation of multiple port groups of any type on any number of ESX servers and virtual switches at once.
- **RDP**—Allows for RDP from VMware Virtual Infrastructure client right click menu.

- **Console**—Adds an SSH-enabled tab named 'Console' when a host system is selected.
- **Invoke**—Allows third-party applications to be launched from within the VI 2.5 client using an existing, authenticated session cookie.

VirtualCenter—Physical or Virtual

Now that we have taken a look at some of the features in VirtualCenter, the next logical step is installation. So do we install VirtualCenter on a virtual machine or on a physical server? This is a question that comes up a lot in the VMware Community Forum.

> **TIP**
>
> Speaking of the Community Forum, it is worthwhile to say that this is a fantastic resource to ask questions and get feedback from your peers. The forums could be considered VMware's unofficial tier 1 support channel. If you have a problem with a VMware product, chances are you will get an answer or find out how to do something there faster than any other means available.

To virtualize VirtualCenter or not, that is the question. There is no right or wrong answer here and both answers have their own pros and cons.

One of the biggest reasons to use VirtualCenter in a virtual machine would be quite simply—High Availability. VirtualCenter is the configuration point for High Availability but is not required to make it work. If you have VirtualCenter as a virtual machine and the VMware ESX server that it is running on fails and crashes, VirtualCenter will go down but the High Availability option will take over and restart the downed virtual machines on the other hosts. You can give VirtualCenter the highest priority for the restart and know that it should come up first. The recovery time for VirtualCenter should be quick enough, depending on what type of alert system you have in place, before you have the opportunity to check on things. Another reason would be the ability to snapshot the virtual machine before any patches or upgrades are deployed, which will give you a fall back option. Another benefit to note: If you are using any type of SAN replication to another site that has VirtualCenter running in a virtual machine, this will mean that VirtualCenter will be replicated to the secondary site and will be immediately available.

On the opposite side of the argument, one of the biggest reasons to run VirtualCenter on a physical server to counter the HA option above is that HA does not cover all failures. For example if the backend storage was to fail, this would not be caught by HA unless the physical host server went down. In my experience, I have seen certain 'issues' show up where all VMware ESX hosts were down and to try and locate VirtualCenter across all the hosts in a cluster and get it started can be a daunting task for someone without good command line skills on the service console of the VMware ESX host. Another thought on running VirtualCenter in a virtual machine: The databases used for VirtualCenter, both SQL and Oracle, are transactional databases that sometimes have issues after hard crashes. A worst case scenario would be loss of transactions with the possibility of database corruption. One way to help overcome this would be to have local backup copies of the database to be able to restore if needed. While not a perfect solution, it would help if this situation were to arise.

VirtualCenter Location

Where to place VirtualCenter in the enterprise? This is a very easy question if you only have one datacenter or single central point for your environment. If you have multiple geographic locations operating with VMware ESX servers, your decision is a little more difficult. The main thing to really consider when making this decision is the available bandwidth between the site with VirtualCenter and the remote site with the VMware ESX servers. It is not the link size or the size of the pipe that really matters but the amount of available bandwidth between the sites. This is an important thing to remember, so say that with me one more time. "It is not the size of the pipe that matters but available bandwidth." This is key. Low available bandwidth between sites will cause sporadic and very frustrating issues in VirtualCenter. Disconnected ESX servers is one of the big issues along with sluggish or delayed response when issuing commands and slow updates on performance graphs and data. If your site has a T1 or smaller pipe between sites, you may want to consider multiple VirtualCenter servers. Setting up multiple VirtualCenter server environments is as easy as replicating what you have done in one site over again as needed.

VirtualCenter Authentication

VirtualCenter uses authentication of the Windows server it operates on. If the Windows server is not part of a domain, it will use local accounts to determine who has which permissions to perform operations in VirtualCenter. If the Windows server is part of a domain, VirtualCenter can either use local account or domain account authentication to assign rights in VirtualCenter. When configuring account access in a VirtualCenter installation that is part of a domain environment which has thousands of users, the client has been known to hang while searching through all of the accounts. An easy way to get around this is to create local groups on the Windows server, and then assign permissions to the local groups.

When logging into VirtualCenter through the VI Client, enter the name of the VirtualCenter server in the IP Address/Name box, followed by username and password in the User name and Password boxes respectively as shown in Figure 2.1.

Figure 2.1   Logging into VirtualCenter with VI Client.

TIP

Pass-through Authentication has finally been added to VirtualCenter 2.5. At the time of this writing, this is classified as experimental but is activated by default. To use this feature you will simply need to edit the shortcut used to launch VirtualCenter and then append this on the end after the quotes.

```
passthroughAuth -s vc_server_name
```

The default setting is for security to use Negotiate SSPI provider, however you can change that behavior to use Kerberos by adding the following inside the VirtualCenter vpxd.cfg file. Add the following within the

```
<sspiProtocol>Kerberos</sspiProtocol>
```

VMware ESXi

VMware ESXi, or 3i as it was once called, is the latest VMware ESX release for VMware. ESXi is an integrated version of VMware ESX which runs without a Service Console. The VMkernel, or VMvisor, runs on bare-metal with a footprint around 32MB. This is significantly smaller than a VMware ESX 3.5 installation. VMware ESXi has been called a few names ranging from "ESX Lite" to "VMware Embedded ESX Server" and until recently was officially named VMware ESX Server 3i.

It is rumored that ESXi came about from the personal work of a VMware employee. The story goes on to say that this employee crafted and maintained a LiveCD version of every new VMware ESX release and build. I guess one day someone said "hey, wouldn't it be cool if we did this..." Voila! A new product was born. Keep in mind, this is a rumor and should be treated as such, but it does leave you wondering.

Figure 2.2 Loading VMware Hypervisor.

VMware made the announcement about VMware ESXi during the virtualization conference—VMworld 2007. After the announcement was made, VMware started handing out 1GB Kingston memory sticks with a LiveUSB installation of ESXi to all attendees. VMware ESXi has just been released at the time of this writing and can now be installed with a CD (referred to as the installable release), or preinstalled on select Dell, Fujitsu, HP or IBM servers. In the near future, other OEMs will also be shipping servers with VMware ESXi preinstalled. When this happens, the OEMs will likely include hardware agents allowing hardware monitoring with VirtualCenter and/or another SNMP monitoring system.

What are the benefits of using VMware ESXi over VMware ESX 3.x? A significant difference between ESXi and ESX 3.x is the fact that VMware ESXi does not have a Service Console. Ok, that statement is not entirely true. It doesn't really drop the RHEL-based COS, instead it replaces it with a much smaller distribution called BusyBox which is tweaked and customized to provide a minimal set of services. The modifications that VMware introduced into ESXi along with the adoption of BusyBox allowed VMware to produce a small-footprint hypervisor which doesn't need installation. This works just like a LiveCD distribution which can boot from USB, CD or Solid State Drives (SSD). As mentioned above, an engineer was working on a LiveCD version of VMware ESX and this should help put all the pieces together on the birth of VMware ESXi. So without a full blown service console, VMware ESXi becomes a more secure release than VMware ESX 3.x. With all of the previous releases of VMware ESX, patches have primarily addressed the security vulnerabilities with the Service Console. But because ESXi has no Service Console, the number of security patches for VMware ESXi will be less frequent, resulting in far fewer downtimes caused by security patching. This plays a significant part in the less patching, longer uptimes mantra.

Another advantage is the time required to deploy VMware ESXi host servers. With ESXi being factory loaded, by simply configuring the IP address, adding the server to VirtualCenter, and completing configuration, ESXi hosts can deployed quickly, easily, and in record time. If installed from the CD, (See Figure 2.2) the

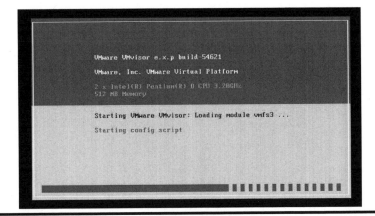

Figure 2.3   VMware ESXi Quick Boot Process.

install process is finished in minutes with very few interactions needed during the process. (See Figure 2.3)

New deployments as well as small and medium businesses that are looking to get into virtualization will see great benefit from VMware ESXi. Larger organizations that have been using Virtual Infrastructure for some time, may not adopt ESXi as quickly. This could be caused by the automated deployment and configuration techniques already developed for use with VMware ESX 3.x. With ESXi, Kickstart scripted builds, deployment via remote deployment tools, and other methods will have limited capabilities. Many VMware administrators use these methods to deploy, configure, patch, update, and modify an ESX installation. I personally have used custom scripts to perform certain operational tasks. I have used Altiris Deployment Server to install and patch all of my ESX 3.x hosts as well as push out any task or script to my hosts. A good example of an administrative task would be adding a LUN to the ESX servers. Because VirtualCenter scans the entire farm at once, I choose not to do this from VirtualCenter. In the past, this has caused the system to freeze or become unresponsive. Therefore, I push shell commands to my ESX hosts, in the form of a script, from my Altiris Rapid Deploy Server and run the script on all the VMware ESX servers at once. This type of custom scripting can save someone a great amount of time in doing administrative tasks that need to be done from the command line to multiple ESX servers. For reasons such as this, many companies with large scale virtualization deployments may not be ready to switch methodologies quite yet. When it becomes commonplace to deploy OEM systems with ESXi embedded, as well as have the hardware monitoring pieces in place, ESXi will have a better chance of adoption in the enterprise. Until then, I think most organizations will continue to operate with VMware ESX 3.x in production clusters for the time being.

An area that would be a great fit for VMware ESXi is in a disaster recovery site. This is because a disaster recovery site typically requires the ability to be brought online quickly and easily. In a cold site disaster recovery configuration, servers with

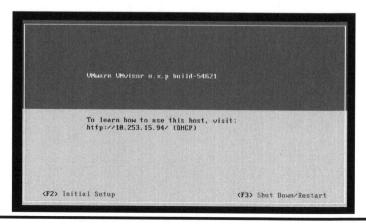

Figure 2.4 Default Settings Needed with VMware ESXi.

ESXi embedded could be brought up quickly and easily. In a hot site disaster recovery configuration, servers with ESXi installed, or embedded, require little maintenance due to the fact that patching is not required as often as VMware ESX 3.x.

A default installation of VMware ESXi will have a few default settings that will need to be addressed and configured initially as shown in Figure 2.4. First and foremost, the IP address should be configured. Secondly, from a security standpoint, the root account has no password assigned to it, so a root password should be assigned. VMware ESXi will assign itself a default Fully Qualified Domain Name (FQDN) of vmvisor.vmware.com. The hostname will need to be changed to match your domain settings before you add the ESXi server to your VMware VirtualCenter server. One important thing to remember is that without proper Domain Naming Service (DNS) settings, the advanced functions of VMware VirtualCenter (HA and DRS) will not function properly. With this release, an interesting thing to note is that the default network settings create only one virtual switch, or vSwitch0, and it only has two default ports:

1. VM Network (for the virtual machines)
2. Management Network Portgroup.

The service console on VMware ESX servers uses vswif0 for the IP settings. In VMware ESXi, the vswif0 settings are rolled in to the Management Network Portgroup and this replaces vswif0.

Summary

VMware ESX is the premier enterprise virtualization platform. For the last seven years, the product has evolved to become the most powerful, stable, and scalable commercial server virtualization platform on the market today. And its performance is considered by many to be the best of all of the commercial virtualization products available in today's market. VMware ESX provides strict control over all of the critical system resources, and it is this granular control combined with native SAN support that helps to provide a solution to a wide range of problems in the enterprise today.

VirtualCenter provides a central management point of control for the entire virtual infrastructure. VirtualCenter is the heart of a virtual infrastructure implementation. VirtualCenter takes care of the management, automation, resource optimization and high availability in the virtual environments. By providing the ability to run plug-ins, coupled with a framework for the way tools and programs are added to virtual infrastructure, VMware has embraced the school of thought that users can add appropriate tools, open-source or third-party, to better manage their environments. So far, these plug-ins have worked as advertised.

We have also gone over the options that are available when installing Virtual-Center and tried to answer whether we should install VirtualCenter on a physical box or in a virtual machine? And how do we best install VirtualCenter when we have different geographical locations to manage?

All in all, you should now have a good understanding of the basic components that make up VirtualCenter. Later in chapter 10 we will go into more details on the advanced features that are available in VirtualCenter.

VMware ESXi is the newest release of VMware's ESX server line. The primary differences between VMware ESX and ESXi are that ESXi does not have a Service Console and does not have vswif0. All other functionality is the same. ESXi is the most secure of its predecessors and looks to be the direction that VMware wants to take virtualization to in the future. One thing is for certain, we are still in the infancy stages of virtualization and the best is yet to come.

Chapter 3

VMware ESX Architecture

VMware ESX is an enterprise class x86 architecture virtualization platform. While there is a clear buzz around the term virtualization right now, the term and the technology is still new to many people. Virtualization isn't new. It has actually been around for more than 40 years. Virtualization is the act of hiding, or masking, resources to appear different than they actually are. This shouldn't be confused with multitasking or hyperthreading technologies. Multitasking allows one or more CPU(s) to manage a single operating system and one or more applications. Hyperthreading behaves like multitasking, with the exception that one or more CPU(s) behaves as if each individual CPU is multiple logical CPUs. Also shown in Figure 3.1, virtualization allows one or more physical CPU(s) to be represented as a number of virtual CPUs while at the same time creating an isolated set of hardware. In turn, a single physical system can appear to be one or more different virtual systems, each with their own set of virtual hardware.

There are three primary components that allow VMware ESX to provide the virtualization layer. These components include the physical host server, the Service

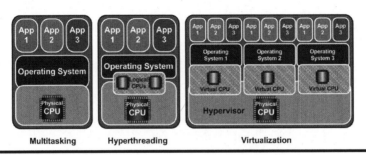

Figure 3.1 Multitasking, Hyperthreading and Virtualization.

Figure 3.2   Components of VMware ESX.

Console, and the VMkernel. Each component plays a vital role in the operation of the product called VMware ESX. Figure 3.2 provides a representation of an ESX host by depicting the physical host, the Service Console, and the VMkernel. The physical host is typically an enterprise-class server system, the Service Console is comprised of a modified installation of RedHat Enterprise Linux, and the VMkernel is a specialized kernel created by VMware for the purpose of virtualization.

Physical Host Server

The host server is the physical system that VMware ESX executes on. Because VMware ESX is designed to be a highly efficient virtualization platform, VMware has a stringent list of approved systems that are eligible to receive official support. The Hardware Compatibility List (HCL) primarily includes systems from OEM's like Dell, Hewlett-Packard, IBM and others. At the time of this writing, the current HCL for physical hosts can be found at this URL: **http://www.vmware.com/ pdf/vi35_systems_guide.pdf**. Each system model on the HCL is rigorously tested and certified by VMware to ensure that VMware ESX will operate properly. With each new release of VMware ESX, VMware re-evaluates the HCL to ensure all systems can properly run the platform. Additionally, as new server models are released by manufacturers, they are evaluated to determine their operational effectiveness in running ESX. As new versions and builds are released, older hardware that may have previously been on the HCL may no longer remain on the list. This list is maintained with great care. For VMware ESX to efficiently or effectively perform its task of virtualization, the physical host server must be able to provide ample CPU, memory, storage and networking resources.

CPU Resources

CPU resources are provided by physical systems having multiple processors with single, dual or quad processor cores. These cores provide the capabilities to execute the instructions of the VMware ESX operating system, known as the VMkernel, as well as the instructions from any of the virtual CPUs that the VMkernel presents to virtual machines. In some instances, there are systems listed on the HCL that are supported but only with specified processors. The HCL denotes any special cases for each type of host system and processor combination. VMware ESX 3.5 has a minimal requirement for processors with a clock speed of at least 1.5GHz. This is a minimum supported requirement, but not an actual limitation. As virtualization technologies have come to the forefront of the information technology sector, processor manufacturers have begun to play an important part in the capabilities of virtualization technologies. Virtualization enabled processors such as Intel-VT (Virtualization Technology) and AMD-V (AMD Virtualization) have stepped up to the plate to contribute much needed enhanced virtualization techniques.

Memory Resources

Memory resources are provided by configuring the amount of RAM commensurate with the amount of RAM the VMkernel is expected to present to the virtual machines as well as the RAM necessary to operate the VMkernel itself.

NOTE

Physical memory is the only resource that does not have explicit requirements on the HCL.

Many VMware administrators argue that the amount of physical RAM plays a crucial role in the performance of virtual machines. A good rule of thumb when configuring a physical system is to not fully populate the server with smaller sized memory modules. Doing so limits the ability to add more memory to the host server down the road when you need to gain a higher consolidation ratio. As an example, if you have the need for a 16GB server, and your physical host can accommodate up to 32GB, it might prove more beneficial to configure the system with four 4GB memory modules as opposed to using eight 2GB sticks. The former configuration would allow for future growth, while the latter would not accommodate any future memory expansion without replacement of the existing RAM. This should be thought out carefully, as often times, memory costs could prove to be quite expensive.

Storage Resources

The storage side of VMware ESX provides the location of where the virtual machine's virtual hard disk resides. Virtual disks can reside on local or remote storage, as long as the ESX host is aware of it. In a multi-host configuration, when leveraging VirtualCenter, storage must be shared across multiple ESX hosts simultaneously. Previous versions of VMware ESX only supported physically attached storage and Fibre Channel based Storage Area Network (SAN) storage. VMware ESX 3.5 can use local SCSI or even SATA physical storage, physically attached storage arrays, Fibre Channel based SAN storage, Internet Small Computer Systems Interface (iSCSI) based storage, or Network File System (NFS) based storage, as represented in Figure 3.3. Storage systems must also meet HCL requirements to be supported by VMware. At the time of this writing, the current HCL for storage devices can be found here:

■ Storage area networks, iSCSI storage, Network Attached Storage, and Serial Attached SCSI (SAS) arrays: **http://www.vmware.com/pdf/vi35_san_guide.pdf**

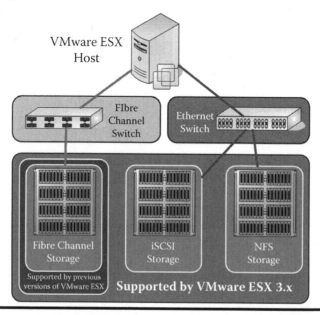

Figure 3.3   VMware ESX Storage.

■ Storage I/O devices, including SCSI controllers, Host Bus Adapters, iSCSI adapters, and more: http://www.vmware.com/pdf/vi35_io_guide.pdf

The VMware Technology Network community forums have several posts regarding different types of storage controllers that users have had success with but are not officially supported.

NOTE

VMware ESX may be installed on IDE hard disks, but the VMFS file system is not supported on IDE disks. Only Small Computer Systems Interface (SCSI) disks and some Serial ATA (SATA) disks are allowed to support the VMFS file system.

Storage presented to VMware ESX can be any combination of a single drive, multiple independent drives, or multiple drives configured in one or more arrays. The performance of disk storage can be tied to the type of connection to the storage (Fibre Channel, iSCSI or NFS), the types of drives (SCSI, SATA or Serial Attached SCSI), the speed of the drives (7200rpm, 10,000rpm or 15,000rpm), and the number of drives presented as a Logical Unit or LUN. Another good rule of thumb to follow is when creating arrays, the more drives you have in an array, generally equates to better performance. In short, "more spindles, more performance." It would be better to present a LUN created with twelve 146GB drives (for about 1.5TB in RAID 5) than it would be to present a LUN created with six 300GB drives (for about 1.4TB in RAID 5). With multiple virtual machines accessing virtual disks at the same time and on the same file system, it is easily seen how more spindles can make a difference in the guest's disk performance.

Network Resources

Given that VMware ESX has the ability for a single system to behave as more than one system; it would be somewhat of a waste if the ESX host could only allow those virtual systems access to a single network segment or Virtual Local Area Network (VLAN). Through the use of virtual switches, bound to physical adapters and their port group subcomponents, ESX virtual networking has the ability to allow different guests access to different network segments, VLANs and isolated internal networks.

Networking resources are provided by Ethernet adapters and other network equipment. Just as physical systems and storage systems have an HCL, there is also an I/O HCL as well. The network portion of the I/O HCL details a list of supported network adapters. The importance of network and other I/O requirements can often be seen immediately when using adapters that have not been certified. VMware ESX will often not know how to access network resources when attempting to use adapters that are not on the HCL.

In addition to Ethernet adapters, external switches in various configurations augment the ability of VMware ESX to perform the task of virtualizing the network component of a virtual machine. Physical adapters in the ESX host can be configured in several methods to provide redundancy, network flexibility, as well as better accommodate network traffic. The abilities of virtual networking will be discussed further in Chapter 8—Networking.

The Service Console

The Service Console, or Console Operating System, is very important to VMware ESX. It acts as an interface that allows administrator access to a VMware ESX host while at the physical console of the server, a boot loader for the ESX Server, and a management point for a VirtualCenter (VC) server. In the current release, the Service Console is based on RedHat Enterprise Linux 3 Update 8. Figure 3.4 shows the Service Console upon initial boot up of a VMware ESX host.

As an interface, the SC is a text based console that gives administrators the ability to configure operating parameters for the ESX Server, view system utilization statistics, accept instructions from the Remote Command Line Interface (CLI), as well as run local scripts and remote scripts that grant flexibility for the configuration and usage of ESX Server. The SC also runs a web based graphical user interface, shown in Figure 3.5, providing additional host system management.

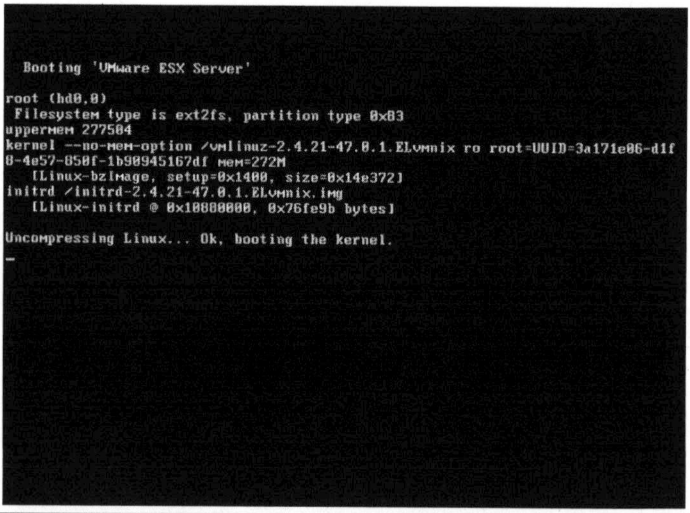

Figure 3.4   ESX Initial Boot.

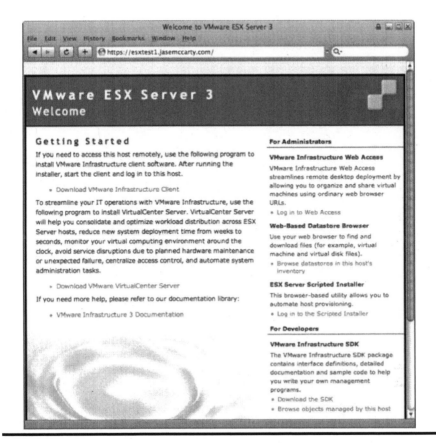

Figure 3.5   VMware Web Access.

These roles have been very important in the management of VMware ESX up until Virtual Infrastructure 3 was released. This is due to the fact that many of the settings could not be configured otherwise. This has changed with the release of the Virtual Infrastructure Client, now providing the ability to configure most, if not all of these settings.

The Service Console can be accessed using the physical keyboard, mouse, and monitor connected to the ESX host, or through the use of a terminal application, such as PuTTY, that supports the Secure Shell (SSH) protocol.

As a boot loader, the SC handles the initial boot process of ESX Server. When the host system initially starts, the SC is loaded. During the boot process, the SC hands off the role of operating system to the VMkernel. At this point, the SC behaves as a virtual machine itself, continuing to provide access as a management interface for VMware ESX.

In the management interface role, the SC works hand in hand with VC to enable the additional components of Virtual Infrastructure 3, including VMotion, VMware High Availability (HA), VMware Distributed Resource Scheduling

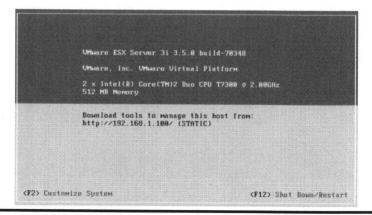

Figure 3.6   VMware ESXi Console.

(DRS), and VMware Consolidated Backup (VCB). By communicating through the VC agent that is installed when VMware ESX is added to a VC managed farm, the SC keeps VirtualCenter up-to-date for management, statistical data collection, and use of advanced features. In an event where the SC cannot communicate with the VC server, either because of connectivity or a VC agent failure, VMware ESX is determined to be offline and features such as VMware HA are initiated to ensure availability of the virtual machines in the Virtual Infrastructure environment.

With the release of VMware ESXi, a specialized build of VMware ESX designed to be run from an embedded installation on the physical host, the Service Console has somewhat been deprecated. Looking at the differences between the Service Console in VMware ESX and VMware ESXi, it would seem as though the Service Console has gone away. In fact, VMware ESXi does have a minimal Service Console, albeit, harder to obtain access to. The Service Console for VMware ESXi, much like the VMware ESX Service Console, is a modified Linux distribution. This distribution is based on the BusyBox project. The console for VMware ESXi can be seen in Figure 3.6. Additionally, the VMware ESXi installation is approximately 32MB, where the more mature VMware ESX installation requires several gigabytes for installation. In a similar fashion to the Service Console of VMware ESX, the minimal console for VMware ESXi interacts with VirtualCenter, the RCLI and the VMware Software Development Kits (SDKs).

The VMkernel

The VMkernel is hypervisor code, coupled with device driver modules, and designed to provide the virtualization layer. Because the VMkernel takes over the operation of the physical host, it could be called the main operating system for ESX. It is actually a microkernel, handling complex scheduling and execution of

CPU, memory, disk and network functions for virtual machines and is referred to as a guest and the VMware ESX itself.

All physical resources are controlled by the VMkernel. Through share based priorities, the VMkernel provides resources to the SC and guests. That being said, if there are four guests running on an ESX host server each with 1000 CPU shares allocated, along with 1000 CPU shares allocated to the SC, each guest and the SC has a 1 in 5 opportunity to access CPU resources. This is because of the total CPU shares allocated, which in this case, is 5000. With each guest and the SC configured equally, they each have the same opportunity to consume CPU resources. If one of the guests were configured with 2000 CPU shares, then the remaining 3 guests and the SC have a 1 in 6 opportunity for CPU cycles, while the guest with more shares allocated has a 2 in 6 priority. Share priority is also configured for memory, disk and network resources.

In addition to resource allocation per share configuration, the VMkernel allows for resource reservations and limits of CPU and memory resources. By configuring a CPU reservation of 1GHz to a guest, that guest is guaranteed 1GHz worth of CPU cycles. On the same token, the VMkernel can allocate a limit of 1GHz worth of CPU cycles. Advanced CPU scheduling is provided by a rate based proportional share scheduler referred to as the VMware ESX Scheduler. As more guests are added to an ESX server, the likelihood a guest will have to wait for CPU resources increases. This can be referred to as Virtual Machine Ready Time, or the time a guest will have to wait before it can be scheduled for CPU resource allocation. Many factors can determine the Ready Time, including total CPU utilization, number of guests, types of processes running in the guests, and number of vCPUs a guest has configured. It is easy to see how the total CPU utilization and number of guests are factored in, but how do the types of processes and numbers of vCPUs play a factor? If a process in a guest executes and ends, Ready Time can be low; but if a process immediately spawns another process, the Ready Time could potentially be high. Also, if a guest has 2 or 4 vCPUs configured, a number of physical cores equal to the number of vCPUs have to be available for scheduling.

The VMkernel has a very unique feature that allows for over commitment of memory resources. By utilizing a technique referred to as Transparent Page Sharing, the VMkernel will keep a single copy of memory instructions that several guests have in common, rather than a copy for each guest. An example to describe this would be, if 10 guests all had the same information running in their memory space, only a single copy would be loaded into physical memory, and each of the guests' memory "points" to the common information physically loaded in memory. To the guest, this process is transparent. However, if the memory page changes for a single guest, a copy of the original is made and then presented to the guest where the memory page changed. This works very well when many guests are running the same operating system and have the same applications or services running.

The VMkernel accesses the physical host's network devices through device modules, based on Linux device drivers. Network access is provided by the VMkernel to the SC, the guests, and the VMkernel itself. To the SC, connectivity is provided to give administrators and VirtualCenter access to manage the ESX server. To guests, network access is provided through virtual switches and virtual network interface cards (NICs). The virtual switches act in virtually the same manner as physical switches external to the ESX server. These virtual switches provide various features that many enterprise level physical switches have, including the 802.1q standard, or VLAN Tagging and outgoing traffic shaping capabilities. The virtual NIC provided to a guest initially starts out as an AMD Lance based Ethernet device. Through installation of VMware Tools in the guest, this gets upgraded to a VMware Accelerated Ethernet adapter, a paravirtualized adapter that is aware that it is in a virtual environment. Because this virtual adapter is aware of the virtualization layer, it can operate more efficiently and much more quickly. In 64-bit guests, the default virtual adapter looks like an Intel e1000 Ethernet adapter, much in the same way the AMD Lance adapter looks to a 32-bit virtual machine. This adapter type can be used in both 32-bit and 64-bit environments.

The VMkernel accesses the physical host's storage, as well as external storage through device modules. Disk resources are provided to guests either through virtual disk files (*.vmdk) or through raw device mappings (RDM). Virtual machine disk files (*.vmdk) can be stored on a local VMFS partition, a Fibre Channel based SAN with LUNs formatted as VMFS file systems, iSCSI based storage, or NFS based storage. The VMFS file system was created to allow multiple ESX hosts the ability to simultaneously mount the same file system. This plays an important role in the ability to migrate virtual machines easily from one VMware ESX host to another.

Summary

The primary components of the VMware ESX architecture are the physical hardware, the Service Console and the VMkernel. Each of these components plays a significant part to the success of VMware ESX and Virtual Infrastructure 3. The core component, the VMkernel, could not be as successful as it is without the appropriate hardware and the Service Console playing their parts.

Chapter 4

Installing VMware ESX Server

VMware ESX is a hypervisor virtualization technology, and as such installs on "bare-metal". That means, unlike some other virtualization platforms, VMware ESX is its own operating system with its own kernel. Therefore, you don't install the technology on top of another host operating system like Linux or Windows; you simply install it on the server itself.

The installation of VMware ESX is really quite simple, and shouldn't be feared. In fact, if you've ever installed a Linux distribution like Red Hat before, it should look somewhat familiar to you. And it doesn't take very long either; the installation should take less than 30 minutes depending on the hardware involved.

The difficulty isn't in the actual software installation; it's in the planning phase. It is essential to have a well-developed deployment plan in place to successfully build a production system using server virtualization technology. Before the project is implemented, a solid understanding of the project is required. This understanding is realized by learning the issues and considerations specific to server virtualization, defining the use case, obtaining the specific requirements, and planning the deployment. By taking the time to properly plan and document the project, the implementation will have a much higher degree of success and much less risk. This chapter covers many of the considerations which affect the design and implementation of VMware ESX. It is important to be aware of the many issues regarding hardware compatibility, software licensing, capacity, scalability, and many other factors which affect decisions about hardware, software, and outside services.

As an example, we don't want to find out after the fact that the hardware we have available to us isn't compatible with VMware ESX. Or worst, after a "successful" installation and implementation, we find out down the road when a problem arises that the hardware we have been using isn't supported by VMware, and therefore, is outside of the scope of our VMware support agreement.

Planning for Deployment

Hardware

Selecting the hardware necessary for a server virtualization deployment may seem like an easy task at first. But, after digging into the details, it soon becomes evident that there are many factors at work. It isn't quite as easy as selecting the hardware in an all physical datacenter.

The difficulty lies in balancing the cost, capabilities and compatibility, referred to as the 3 Cs. Cost and required capabilities should be documented in the Use Case and Requirements Documents. Compatibility is a derivative of the requirements put forth by your virtualization platform, in this case, VMware ESX. Before attempting to select your server hardware, it is important to reference VMware's hardware compatibility guide for the version of ESX that you are installing. It can be easy to take your server architecture into the wrong direction by losing focus on any one of the 3 Cs.

For example, an older host server with two single-core processors, 2GB of memory and 100GB of hard disk storage space could be purchased for less than US$1,500.00. This solution would not be very useful as it could probably support no more than two or three virtual machines, even though it is very inexpensive. On the other hand, host servers with eight processor cores, 64GB of memory, and 1TB of hard disk storage might support forty or more virtual machines at a cost of less than US$25,000. Older processors are also missing the important hardware virtualization instructions found in Intel-VT and AMD-V processors. The virtualization instructions in newer processors will ultimately offer more capabilities to the virtualization environment, further justifying their cost.

For the reasons illustrated above, it makes sense to try and balance out cost versus capability needs in regards to server hardware. In most scenarios, two-way (dual-core processors) or four-way (dual-core processors) servers with 8GB of memory will probably be good choices from both cost and performance perspectives. This will change over time as processor advancements such as multi-core processors and hardware-level virtualization support built into the processor continue to take shape.

It is equally important to select server hardware that is compatible with VMware ESX. Careful attention must be exercised to ensure that all hardware components are compatible and device drivers are available. This includes chipset drivers, disk controller drivers, network adapters, SAN host bus adapters, etc. VMware provides a number of hardware compatibility guides online that cover all of the different components and peripherals. It is important to consult these guides before making a purchase or before identifying and earmarking existing equipment for the project. And make sure you are verifying it against the version of VMware ESX that you are installing. Different components are added and dropped over time, so make sure you have the most recent guide available for your particular build.

Host Server Usage

It is highly recommended that you dedicate your ESX server to the role of a virtualization host server. This is usually implicit with VMware ESX; however, you do have the ability to install other applications on your ESX host server. Be mindful, anything that you add to the host server will ultimately affect your server's overall performance, and it will steal resources away from ESX and from your virtual machines. It may also be the difference between a virtual machine staying put on its physical server or being migrated to another server with VMotion because of a DRS event.

Software Licenses

Understanding the pitfalls of software licensing on your ESX server virtualization deployment is very important and can be one of the most complex aspects of a deployment. The rise of mainstream virtualization technology, such as x86 server virtualization, is causing confusion today regarding operating system and software licensing. Virtualization technology is causing a major paradigm shift in software licensing schemes, for better or worse. Most software vendors have not yet attempted to adjust their licensing schemes to account for their software running inside of virtual machines. Some vendors are not even aware of how server virtualization might impact their current licensing schemes, not accounting for the architectural and philosophical changes that are brought about by virtualization technology.

Because of this lack of visibility into virtualization, there are some interpretations that must be made in order to stay in compliance with software licenses. It is highly recommended to contact the software company and to request an exception or written interpretation as to how their licensing scheme is affected or not affected by the fact that their software will be running inside virtual machines. However, this may not always be practical. When it is not practical, there are some simple things that can be done to attempt to stay in compliance in most situations.

Below is a list of several common licensing scenarios and how to adapt them to virtualization.

■ **Instance-based licensing**: Instance-based licensing is the most common type of software licensing scheme. Each time the software is installed, it requires a license. The consumer will purchase a fixed number of licenses (or seats) and the software may legally be installed on the same number of computers, whether physical or virtual. This is one of the easiest to manage licensing schemes and it works the same way on virtual machines as it does with physical computers. These licenses are usually worded in such a way that little to no interpretation is necessary when considering virtualization.

■ **Computer-based licensing**: Computer-based licensing allows software to be installed more than once on a single computer, possibly even limitless instances, but only requires one license per computer. In some cases, it may be interpreted that some computer-based licensing schemes may allow the software to be installed an unlimited amount of times within multiple virtual machines on a given host and only have to acquire one license per host server. Care must be taken, and it is highly advisable to either contact the manufacturer for clarification or to treat each virtual machine as a separate computer in regards to the terms of the license to ensure that licensing compliance is properly met.

■ **Processor-based licensing:** Processor-based licensing schemes incur a cost for each processor or a different cost based upon the number of processors installed in the computer. Depending upon the exact verbiage of the license agreement, the license may only apply to the number of physical processors installed in the computer or only to the number of processors available to the virtual machine. The licensing costs could also apply once per physical server or virtual server depending on how the license is written. This scenario is one of the most confusing of all licensing schemes as it could work in favor of the vendor or the consumer depending on the interpretation of the license. The recommended and easiest method to use to stay in compliance with processor-based licensing is to purchase a processor license for each virtual processor used by each virtual machine. Although this may seem expensive or aggressive in terms of licensing, it will almost always guarantee licensing compliance with the software vendor.

■ **Fixed user-based licensing:** Some software is licensed by an amount of fixed or named users that will access the software. In this licensing scheme, one license is purchased for each exact user of the software, regardless of whether they are all using the software at the same time or not. This licensing scheme works the same way in virtual machines as it does on physical computers.

■ **Concurrent user-based licensing:** In the concurrent user-based licensing scheme, software licenses are required for the total number of simultaneous users connecting to or using the software. This licensing scheme is much more flexible than the fixed user-based licensing scheme. Concurrent user-based licensing works the same way in virtualization as it does on physical computers. One aspect of this type of licensing which tends to vary among software vendors is how the license controls the number of installed instances. Some software vendors may allow the software to be installed only once and may also require a separate instance-based license in addition to user licenses while other vendors may allow the software to be installed many times as long as the total concurrent user limit is not exceeded.

■ **Device connection-based licensing:** In device connection-based licensing schemes, a license is required for every device which connects to the software. This is usually found in enterprise server applications. The term device usually refers to any user, computer, or other device or account which connects to the software. The verbiage on most device connection-based licenses will almost always be either vague enough or complete enough to include virtual machines or virtual devices. Device connection license schemes should be treated the same way under virtualization as is would be on physical computers, whether virtual machines act in the client or server role in relation to the software.

The list above is a sample of the most common licensing schemes. It does not attempt to cover every scheme in existence because there are simply too many variations and they often change frequently. It's a good idea to read and understand the licensing scheme for each piece of your software that will be installed on your virtual machines. It is also advisable to audit the software licenses on a quarterly or semi-annual basis to check for changes in the licensing schemes. As virtualization continues to develop and grow, more software vendors will become aware of the issues around licensing and virtualization and will adjust accordingly. A good rule of thumb to remember is that treating virtual machines as equals to physical computers in regards to software licensing usually avoids any issues.

Supported Versus Unsupported Guest Operating Systems

The issue of running guest operating systems, which are not officially supported by the server virtualization platform vendor sparks a lot of controversy. It is important to understand the implications of using software such as server virtualization in unsupported configurations, especially when considering doing this in a production system. Depending on an organization's level of comfort with the officially unsupported guest operating system and the virtualization platform and depending on the use case of the server virtualization implementation, it may be well justified by the organization to absorb the amount of risk associated in using an unsupported configuration.

VMware ESX currently has a large list of supported guest operating systems. But what does having "official support" for a guest operating system really mean? It doesn't necessarily mean that an unsupported guest operating system won't install or run properly in a virtual machine. In fact, I've installed a few of them myself over the years out of necessity, and they seemed to work just fine. What this does mean however is that VMware will not be able to provide assistance in the advent of a malfunction, bug, or other issue that might arise. And VMware won't assume responsibility or risk in these cases either, nor will they generally spend any time attempting to support such a configuration, even if the problem truly is caused by ESX. In addition, an unsupported guest operating system may also perform poorly or be without certain capabilities because of the lack of VMware Tools. Depending on your use case for using VMware ESX (perhaps this is a development or testing environment), the lack of support or the poor performance may not be a huge deterrent.

Support from Software Vendors

Virtualization is a technology that has been around for quite some time, yet it's only now becoming considered mainstream. Because of this, many people in the information technology industry, including many software vendors, are not yet virtualization savvy. Support issues can arise from installing applications in virtual machines when the software vendor has little to no virtualization experience. Some software vendors may refuse to support the application if it is installed in a virtual machine. Others may ask you to reproduce the problem on a physical server.

As more people continue to virtualize with VMware, software vendors will have to play catch-up and support their products within virtual machines. This will probably become a necessity as the software vendors' competition could use their support of virtualization as marketing leverage. The outcome is a positive and natural evolution of the industry which will further catapult VMware's growth in the datacenter.

Unexpected Server Growth

A common side effect that often takes place with implementing virtualization is the unexpected server growth caused by unplanned virtual machines. In some ways, this can be thought of as "virtual server sprawl". Virtualization makes it very easy to deploy new servers in a very short amount of time. This is not necessarily bad unless it negatively impacts the existing virtual machines. Unexpected server growth not only impacts the production system, but it can also increase operating system and software licensing costs. The key here is to make sure you follow similar processes and procedures that are in place for your physical environment.

Virtual Machine Density

The number of virtual machines residing on a single host server is referred to as virtual machine density, or VM density. When a high VM density is achieved, overall costs are generally lowered by sharing and better utilizing the host server's resources. Many factors must be considered to properly estimate VM density.

- The number of processors in each host server
- The amount of available memory in each host server
- The amount of available disk storage
- The guest operating system and applications installed on each virtual machine
- The number of virtual processors configured for each virtual machine
- The amount of memory allocated to each virtual machine
- The size of all virtual hard disks assigned to each virtual machine
- The amount of idle processor consumption of each virtual machine
- The expected utilization of each virtual machine
- The acceptable performance of each virtual machine
- The expected usage of each virtual machine

The number of processors installed in each host server defines the maximum amount of processing power and parallelism capabilities. A general rule of thumb is that the more physical processors installed the more virtual machines that can be created. In reality, this is only true to a certain point, especially when considering very generic virtual machines with low utilization and low performance metrics.

The amount of available memory in each host server is one of the most important considerations of VM density. Memory is one of the scarcest and most expensive resources in the entire system. The larger the memory footprint of each virtual machine—the lower will be the VM density. When planning your virtualization environment, it is a good idea to obtain as much physical memory as possible.

The amount of available disk storage is another consideration of VM density. With local storage, there must be enough disk storage to account for VMware ESX, paging or swap files, log files, any applications installed on the host server, and finally, enough storage space to accommodate each virtual machine's configuration files and virtual hard disk files. You will also need disk space for any virtual machine snapshots or suspend files. If the system is using SAN storage, each LUN must be sized appropriately based on the considerations mentioned above.

The guest operating system and applications installed on each virtual machine must be considered as well as it must have enough virtual resources present for proper support. Typically, a well-tuned Linux operating system will require less memory and disk resources than most Windows operating systems. Knowing exactly what operating system, edition, version, service pack level, and what applications will be installed in each virtual machine can help gauge the amount of memory and disk space required.

The number of virtual processors configured for each virtual machine will also need to be considered. Virtual machines with more processing needs can be configured with two or four processors rather than just one. However, placing too many dual processor virtual machines on a single host with two processors, for example, will likely cause a processor resource bottleneck on the physical server that will in turn impact the performance of the other virtual machines on that same host.

The amount of memory allocated to each virtual machine will impact VM density in conjunction with the amount of memory available on each host server. Generally, each virtual machine should only be configured with just enough memory to perform its intended task. Performance considerations may alter the amount of memory needed, depending on the applications installed in the virtual machine.

The size of all virtual hard disks of each virtual machine must be considered in conjunction with the amount of available hard disk space. A good balance between having enough disk space in the virtual machine to accommodate log file growth and application data storage and having a surplus of disk space is the ideal goal.

The amount of idle processor consumption of each virtual machine is a consideration unique to virtualization. It is important to realize, powered on virtual machines that are idle still consume resources. When you have a very high VM density of more than 40:1, this could prove significant enough to cause issues.

The expected utilization of each virtual machine is one of the more complex and important factors when considering VM density. A high number of virtual machines each having a fairly low rate of utilization (20 percent or less) will be good candidates for being placed on the same host server in order to achieve high VM density. It is also a good idea to spread out virtual machines with heavier utilization across as many host servers as possible and combine these with low utilization virtual machines in order to achieve better VM densities and general performance. VMware ESX 3.5 includes resource pooling, DRS and VMotion to automatically figure out this once manual, complicated task.

Data and System Backup Considerations

Adding new systems into existing data centers will always have an impact on existing data center management systems and the data backup systems are no exception. Virtualization tends to greatly amplify this impact by potentially adding another level of complexity and larger than usual demand on existing data backup systems and strategies. In some cases, virtualization may not easily fit into existing data and system backup processes. The traditional concerns are the costs imposed by possibly needing additional backup system agents to install on the host server or the virtual machines, the storage capacity of the backup system, the backup time capacity of the backup system, new backup system software needs, and costs incurred by the need for additional persistent media and offsite storage. Besides the traditional backup issues, virtualization can impose two added dimensions of back up: backing up the host server and backing up the virtual machines which reside on that host.

In addition to the core operating system, the virtual machine configuration and log files should also be backed up. Virtual machines should be backed up as well, and there are several different strategies regarding virtual machine backup that can have a huge impact on storage capacity, costs, and time. When considering virtual machine back up, there are two major methodologies that are commonly used. One method is to back up the virtual machine hard disk files on a scheduled basis. These files tend to be very large, usually ranging from 2GB to over 100GB in size. It can be very costly, in both time and money, to back these files up on a daily basis. Another method is to back up the virtual machine using the same methods used with physical servers. In this scenario, the operating system and data residing within the virtual machine are usually backed up daily using the same mechanisms that are used for physical servers. This method provides a good balance between the cost of backups and the ease of restoration.

NOTE

VMware is well aware of the back up concerns within the virtualization community, which is why the company created VMware Consolidated Backup (VCB). Unlike other virtualization solutions, it is possible within a VMware ESX environment to back up virtual machine disk files without having to power down the virtual machine.

Monitoring Considerations

Most established datacenters often have a centralized server monitoring system in place which monitors the health and status of servers and applications. Once server virtualization becomes a part of the datacenter, it will likely affect the existing server monitoring system. The server monitoring system currently in use may not have any understanding or capabilities to monitor VMware ESX or virtual machines. If it can, the existing monitoring solution may require additional licenses (increasing the cost) as the virtual server farm comes online and then grows over time (unless kept in check with processes and procedures—remember "virtual server sprawl"?). It is a good idea to be aware of this issue and to plan ahead for the increased costs of any additional server monitoring licenses or the need to find a new monitoring solution to handle your VMware environment.

Network Considerations

VMware ESX will have an impact on those existing networks to which the host servers and virtual machines are connected. Virtualization host servers have a higher potential need for more Ethernet adapters over their physical server counterparts. This in turn directly impacts the number of available physical switch ports that will be needed. And this may require additional physical switches be purchased and installed, so this will need to be factored into your project planning. Existing network infrastructure may be sufficient for a physical environment, however in a virtual world, it may not perform well. If your physical server still has 10/100 network adapters connected to 10/100 switches, you might consider migrating and upgrading to Gig-E switches and network adapters, and at the same time, make sure you have Cat-6 network cabling to support the upgraded network infrastructure. Remember, your physical server will now support multiple servers, multiple operating systems and multiple applications. A 10/100 Mb/s connection will probably no longer be sufficient.

Performance Considerations

Performance can be very difficult to estimate or measure in advance when planning a new server virtualization deployment. It is always better to make conservative performance estimates, especially if performance is a sensitive issue. To properly size for performance, real world testing and benchmarking must be performed. Real world testing and benchmarking refers to creating a test environment that is identical to that of the planned production environment with the exception of the scale. The hardware and software must be installed and configured exactly as in a production system in order to obtain useful performance metrics. It is highly recommended that evaluation equipment be acquired, even for short evaluation-only terms, such as 30 days, so that in-house testing and benchmarking can be completed. For some organizations, this may not be possible. Obtaining third-party white papers with similar benchmarking using similar equipment and server virtualization platforms may be the only option for some organizations on which to base their planning. In this case, many assumptions are being made that could invariably be wrong; therefore, there is much higher risk in using this option of gauging the performance of the use case.

Ensuring adequate performance is often important because if the applications running on the virtual machines do not perform well, the end users of those applications may deem the deployment or the virtualization technology a failure, even when the systems are executing as planned. If applications are planned to be migrated from an existing physical server environment to a VMware environment, performance testing is imperative in order to ensure that the final production configuration of the virtualized system meets or exceeds the existing expected performance levels.

Security Considerations

Security is a very important consideration in the deployment plan. Aside from the additional costs that could be incurred from the needs for additional security software licenses such as anti-virus client licenses for each virtual machine, there are other considerations that could affect the overall architecture of the system.

The exposure of any host servers or virtual machines to the Internet is one of the most primary security concerns. It is highly recommended that host servers and management software do not get placed on an Internet-facing connection. Host servers should be placed behind a firewall on an internal network and shouldn't be placed in a DMZ or directly connected to the Internet. The reason for the recommendation is that if a host server is compromised, all of the virtual machines on that host can also be compromised. Just because things are virtualized doesn't mean that good old fashioned perimeter security and access control architectures and best practices should be ignored. If host servers need to be managed remotely, a reliable VPN connection should be used.

If a virtual machine is compromised, for instance, because of an unpatched guest operating system being placed directly on the Internet, it may affect the host server and any other virtual machine on the same network. In this case, the compromised virtual machine can be used to launch attacks elsewhere on the network as well as the Internet, if outbound Internet access exists. Depending on the virtual machine's resource configuration within the host server, the attacker could cause the virtual machine to execute attacks causing the CPU and memory utilization of the virtual machine to spike for extended periods of time, thereby eating up valuable resources from the host server that may be needed by other virtual machines. The result would be a performance issue realized on the host server, on other virtual machines on that host server, and also cause unnecessary VMotions to take place.

Without good user security put in place, it is also important to realize that anyone capable of accessing the host server may be able to affect the virtual machines that live on that host server. They may not have direct access to log into those virtual machines, but they might be able to make changes to VMware, modify virtual machine files or configurations, or even restart or power down the host server or the virtual machines.

Use Case

The use case is the critical first step in building a solid foundation for a successful VMware ESX deployment. It defines how and why a particular technology and solution, in this case VMware ESX and virtualization, will be used. Most projects do not follow a formal process for creating a use case and this can cause many problems throughout the deployment. Creating the Use Case Document ensures alignment of stake holders in the project, business and technical, which ensures that a common goal and vision is understood and agreed upon by all. It can also be used to show key business stakeholders that a problem exists and to propose the intended solution. The Use Case Document also serves as the foundation of the Requirements Document, which is explained later.

The Use Case Document should identify the specific business and technical stakeholders, describe in detail the problem being addressed, the proposed solution to the problem, and other details of the proposed solution such as impacts, costs, and returns.

Use Case Document Outline

1. **Document the stakeholders**
    a. **Identify the End Users:** The end users are business stakeholders which must interface with or are impacted by the proposed solution. End users can also be affected by the problems and may have the best insight on the issues which need to be addressed.
    b. **Identify the Project Owner:** The project owner is the primary business stakeholder which has the overall authority to approve the project and its costs. The project owner usually sets the high-level goals and timelines.
    c. **Identify the Project Manager:** The project manager is the primary business stakeholder which manages the day-to-day implementation of the project from a business standpoint, collecting requirements, ensuring that timelines are kept on track, that milestones are met, and that costs are kept within budget. The project manager usually reports to the project owner and directly interfaces with the system architect, lead system engineer, and the implementation team.
    d. **Identify the System Architect:** The system architect is the primary technical stakeholder charged with the overall design of the solution. The system architect must make major technical decisions, such as what hardware, software, and outside services will be used and how the overall solution will be constructed.
    e. **Identify the Lead System Engineer:** The lead system engineer is the primary technical stakeholder charged with the overall technical leadership and decision making during the implementation. The lead system engineer is usually responsible for ordering the hardware, software, and services, and delegating tasks to the rest of the implementation team. In some cases, the same person can fill the system architect and lead system engineer roles.
    f. **Identify the Implementation Team:** The implementation team consists of technical stakeholders responsible for carrying out the implementation. The lead system engineer is almost always also a member of the implementation team. The implementation team carries out all technical tasks related to the completion of the project, including installing hardware, software, and directing outside services.

2. **Document the problem addressed in detail**
   a. Describe the current situation
   b. Identify the cause of the problem
   c. Describe the current systems and technologies in place, which are associated with the problem or the solution
   d. Describe the current processes in place which are associated with the problem or the solution

3. **Document the proposed solution**
   a. Describe the solution—this is the goal and vision
   b. Describe the changes the solution will impart to existing systems and processes

4. **Document the details of the solution**
   a. Describe the impact on existing systems and processes the solution will impart
   b. Describe all items that need to be purchased including hardware, software licenses, and services
   c. Describe the risks
   d. Describe the costs
   e. Describe the Return On Investment (ROI)

When creating the Use Case Document, it is important to involve all of the stakeholders. Interviewing the stakeholders is a good method of gathering the initial information for the document and to get an understanding of each stakeholder's perceptions regarding the project. It is also very important to understand the problem driving the project from both the business and technical point-of-views to ensure that the proposed solution is able to meet the requirements and work within the constraints of both. Addressing the problem with a proposed solution will ultimately cause changes to be made to existing systems and processes. Below is a sample list of interview questions which will help gather important information which will be used to build the Use Case Document.

- What is driving the necessity of the changes?
- What is the desired outcome of the changes?
- What is the expected life expectancy of the proposed solution?
- What existing systems will be impacted by the changes?
  - Administration and Management
  - Data and System Backup
  - Disaster Recovery
  - Intranet
  - Monitoring
  - Networking
  - Security
  - Storage

- What existing processes or job functions will be impacted by the changes?
  - Business
  - Development
  - Education/Training
  - Helpdesk/Support Staff
  - System Administration
  - Testing/QA
- What business or technical problems might be anticipated with the changes?
- What business constraints may impact the proposed solution?
  - Budget
  - Time
  - Human Resources
- What technical constraints may impact the proposed solution?
  - Hardware limitations
  - Limited data center floor space
  - Network infrastructure limitations
  - Operating system restrictions
  - Inadequate skill sets and knowledge

Once the Use Case Document has been created, it can be used as a tool to obtain approval for the project or mark the start of the project. The primary stakeholders should have a meeting to focus on communicating the goal and overall vision. The project manager, system architect, and lead system engineer can then proceed to create the Requirements Document.

Requirements

All successful projects are generally governed by a set of rules used to define what exact needs must be fulfilled, the constraints of the project, and the success criteria. These rules are the project's requirements. The Requirements Document sets the overall scope of the project in terms of budget and time at a high level. It details the needs of the project and the success criteria, a set of rules which determine if the project was successful after its completion.

Once a project officially begins, the Requirements Document should be created. The Project Manager is usually responsible for the creation of the Requirements Document, although it is not uncommon for the System Architect and Lead System Engineer roles to have direct input into the document. The Use Case Document contains all of the initial information needed to start building the Requirements Document. It is also a good idea to include the Use Case Document into the Requirements Document. The Requirements Document must provide detailed information regarding the problem and the solution being implemented. However, it does not contain information about how to implement the exact solution. It will serve as an input to the Deployment Plan Document.

Deployment Plan

The deployment plan, also referred to as the project plan, is used to manage the flow of the project, maintaining the project schedule and milestones. Based upon the Requirements Document, the Deployment Plan Document is used to track the project through completion. The deployment plan should also include all of the major and detailed steps of the project including the ordering of equipment, installing and configuring the equipment and the VMware ESX software, building of virtual machine images, and conducting all other aspects of the deployment. The deployment plan should also include detailed networking and server layout diagrams.

Planning Complete—Ready to Begin

With planning out of the way, you are ready to begin your VMware ESX installation. Before you can install the virtualization software, you should be aware of the product's requirements.

VMware ESX 3.5 Hardware System Requirements

While VMware ESX is regarded as being the highest performing virtualization platform on the market, it is also the most restrictive when it comes to server hardware requirements. Because of the highly optimized nature of VMware ESX, it is natural to have a more stringent set of requirements. The requirements are very important and very different from other virtualization platforms and care must be taken to review this section very carefully before making large-scale or costly decisions regarding system components, such as physical server hardware.

Basic Server Hardware Requirements: :

- At least two physical processors: Intel Xeon 1500 MHz and later, AMD Opteron processors in 32-bit mode, or Intel Viiv or AMD A64 x2 dual-core processors
- 1GB of memory minimum (but with 4GB recommended as the real minimum)
- One or more Ethernet network adapters (supports Broadcom NetXtreme 570x gigabit controllers or Intel PRO/100/1000 adapters)
- At least one SCSI controller, SCSI RAID controller, or Fibre Channel adapter (check the VMware hardware compatibility list for all supported controllers)

- At least one SCSI disk, SCSI RAID logical disk, Fibre Channel LUN or RAID LUN with unpartitioned space. In a minimum configuration, this disk or RAID is shared between the service console and the virtual machines. This is far from optimal. This minimum configuration will probably lead to disk I/O bottlenecks.
- For hardware iSCSI, a disk attached to an iSCSI controller such as the QLogic qla405x.
- New with ESX 3.5, SATA support with a disk connected through supported dual SAS-SATA controllers that are using SAS drivers.

In addition to the basic server hardware requirements listed above, not all server hardware makes and models are supported. Because VMware ESX does not run on top of a host operating system such as Linux or Windows, it requires ESX server-specific hardware drivers. These drivers are typically only available from VMware and its community source partners, but most are distributed with ESX. VMware produces up-to-date compatibility guides which provide very granular hardware compatibility information for servers, SCSI controllers, RAID controllers, Fibre Channel HBAs, SAN devices, and network adapters. The three most important compatibility guides are listed below.

- **Systems Compatibility Guide:** VMware ESX is tested for compatibility with a variety of major guest operating systems running in virtual machines. Additionally, the product is tested for compatibility with currently shipping platforms from the major server manufacturers in pre-release testing. This guide includes information about servers, guest operating systems and VMotion processor compatibility requirements.
- **I/O Compatibility Guide:** VMware ESX software delivers high performance I/O for PCI-based SCSI, RAID, Fibre Channel, and Ethernet controllers. To achieve high performance, the devices are accessed directly through device drivers in the ESX host. Make sure to verify compatibility for the specific device with the supported version of VMware ESX. This information is critical when designing the server configuration that will be used in a new ESX implementation. The information in this guide should be used along with the server information provided in the Systems Compatibility guide.
- **Storage/SAN Compatibility Guide:** VMware ESX has been tested and deployed in a variety of storage area network (SAN) environments. The guide provides information on the qualified SAN components including storage arrays and host bus adapters (HBAs) for use with VMware ESX. In addition to the supported makes and models of supported SAN equipment, the guide also provides information regarding the compatible uses of certain features when SAN technology is used in an ESX system, including clustering, multi-pathing, and booting from SAN support.

As of this writing, the VMware compatibility guides are available on VMware's Web site using the following URL: http://www.vmware.com/resources/ techresources/ cat/119.

NOTE

Aside from the server hardware requirements, at least one workstation computer is required to perform the final configuration and management of the ESX server upon completion of the basic installation procedures. The workstation computer requires network connectivity and a Web browser, such as Microsoft Internet Explorer, which is used to access the ESX server's Web-based interface.

VMware ESX 3.5 Installation

The basic installation of VMware ESX 3.5 is covered in this chapter. Details such as the physical server's BIOS settings, a discussion on hardware drivers for ESX, and the ESX installation on a bare-metal server with screenshots are presented. This section will give insight and will set expectations for those system engineers that have never before installed the VMware product.

Preparing the Host Server

The host server requires minimal preparation before ESX can be installed. The basic preparation includes ensuring that the server is set up and installed in its proper location, such as a server rack in the data center, and that it is cabled properly and has power. All server components should be installed at or before this stage, including processors, memory, SCSI controllers, RAID controllers, Fibre Channel HBAs, SCSI disks, network adapters, and any external storage devices. All network adapters should be cabled and patched into the proper switch ports. External storage devices should be properly cabled to the server, have all of its disks installed, and should be powered on. Fibre Channel HBAs should be properly cabled to the correct switch.

Once the server hardware is fully set up, it should be powered on and have the following items configured:

- Update the server's firmware
- Configure the server's BIOS
  - Configure the CD/DVD-ROM device as a bootable device if using for installation
  - Enable/Disable HyperThreading as necessary

- Configure the SCSI BIOS for all SCSI controllers
- Configure the RAID arrays and logical drives for all RAID controllers
- Configure the BIOS for Fibre Channel HBAs, if necessary

Preparing the Host Operating System

Because VMware ESX is a hypervisor-style virtualization platform, it does not install or run within an existing operating system. Instead, it provides its own optimized kernel and is installed directly onto physical server hardware, often referred to as a bare-metal installation. There is no host operating system to be configured with VMware ESX. Once the server hardware has been properly configured, the installation process can begin.

Preparing to Install VMware ESX

Before starting the installation process, the following items and information should be readily available:

- Make sure you have the VMware ESX installation CD-ROM media or ISO image available (verify your media is valid and error free by validating the MD5SUM value).
- Know where you want the boot disk located.
- Determine your file system layout.
- Have on hand your valid or registered license information for VMware ESX and its components.
- Know the host name for the new server.
- Have ready the TCP/IP configuration information for the new server:
  - IP Address
  - Subnet Mask
  - Gateway
  - DNS Server IP Address(es)
  - Fully qualified domain name of the server

VMware ESX supports several different installation options. There are two installation modes which can be used: the graphical installation mode and the text mode installer. The graphics installation mode uses a graphic user interface and the keyboard and mouse to perform the installation. This installation mode is supported by most up-to-date server hardware. The text mode installer is a down-level install which uses a character-based display during the installation. The text mode installer is primarily used if the server hardware does not have a graphics chipset that is compatible with the ESX installer. The choice of the installer mode does not affect the end-product of the installation, only the installation itself.

Installing VMware ESX

TIP

If you are not planning on booting from SAN, it is wise to disconnect the system from the SAN or iSCSI server. If you aren't booting from SAN, having it connected during the installation process may cause unwanted and unexpected results during boot of the ESX host once the installation is complete. It can also prevent the accidental erasing of the SAN disks during the installation process.

NOTE

The installation engine being used is Anaconda, which is the same installation engine that is used with Red Hat Linux. Although slightly modified (much like the ESX console itself), it also supports installation from CD-ROM, floppy or Pre-Execution Environment (PXE). This is helpful to know when scripting the installation.

Installing VMware ESX Locally

1. Power on the host server with the VMware ESX CD-ROM installation media in the CD/DVD-ROM drive. (You can also use the ISO image if you have some type of ILO device on your system to leverage remote installation). If during the POST sequence you are prompted to press any key to boot from CD-ROM, do so. The server will boot from the CD-ROM and the installation process will begin.

2. Installation boot options are shown in Figure 4.1. Choose the default installation options by pressing the Enter key. This will launch the graphical

Figure 4.1   Installation Boot Options.

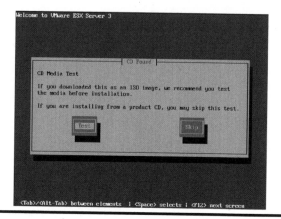

Figure 4.2   CD Media Test Screen.

installer. You can also select the "text" installation as well if your system is having difficulty displaying the graphical installation process (either because of your server's display or perhaps you are using ILO). Waiting will automatically select the graphical installation mode. The installer will begin booting and the screen shown in Figure 4.2 will be displayed.

3. You can either choose to test the media or skip this check. If you followed the advice above, you would have already tested the media with MD5SUM, so you should be able to skip the media test here. Choose Skip.

4. The Welcome screen is now displayed (See Figure 4.3). At this point, the installation information gathering process is about to begin. Click the Next button to proceed.

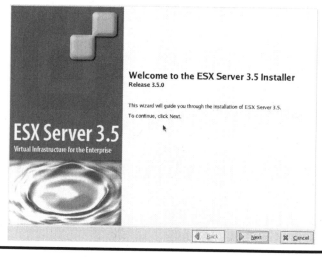

Figure 4.3   VMware ESX 3.5 Welcome Screen.

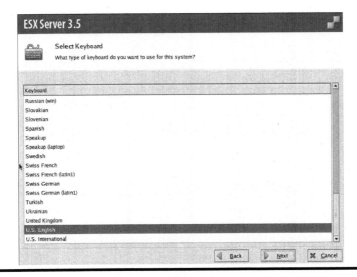

Figure 4.4   Keyboard Configuration Option.

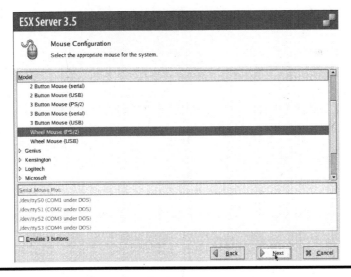

Figure 4.5   Mouse Configuration Option.

5. At the Keyboard Configuration screen (See Figure 4.4), select the proper keyboard type from the keyboard model list and then select Next to continue.

6. At the Mouse Configuration screen (See Figure 4.5), select the proper mouse type from the list. Selecting Wheel Mouse (PS2), the default, should be fine. ESX does not run in a graphical X-Window format, so this option will be used for the Anaconda installation process only. After you select the mouse, click Next to continue.

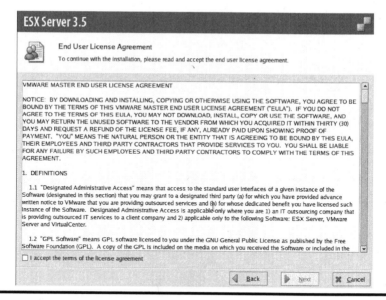

Figure 4.6 VMware End User License Agreement.

NOTE

If you are installing over a previous VMware ESX installation, you will be prompted with a choice of upgrading or a new installation. If you are installing from a clean environment, you won't receive this option.

---

7. On the End User License Agreement (EULA) screen (See Figure 4.6), read the agreement and then once you are comfortable with it, check the field labeled "I accept" and then click Next.

NOTE

A warning may appear stating that the partition table was unreadable (See Figure 4.7). Since this is a new environment, we know that this is because it is blank. However, if you didn't disconnect your SAN as requested above, it is important to make sure that the system isn't identifying the wrong partition space. This will erase data on a known good drive. Since we followed the steps above and know this is a clean drive, we can proceed. If you receive this message, click Yes to continue.

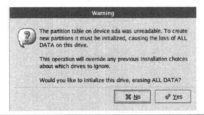

Figure 4.7   Partition Table Warning Popup.

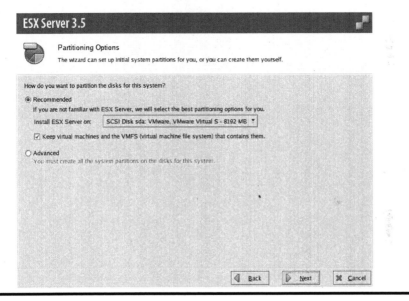

Figure 4.8   Disk Partitioning Options.

8. At the Partitioning Options screen (See Figure 4.8), you can choose either Recommended or Advanced. For most installations, you should probably choose Recommended. As you get comfortable partitioning, you can choose Advanced if you want to manually change or modify the recommended partitioning table. For now, let's select Recommended. Then click Next.

NOTE

A change from VMware ESX Server 3.0.x to 3.5, with 3.5, the default of "keep virtual machines and the VMFS" is checked. In 3.0, this was not checked by default.

TIP

As you continue to advance with your ESX environment, you will learn what works and what is necessary in your partitioning schema for your organization. You can check the VMware Community Forums for more advice on different options here. However, you will probably find that you want to increase some of these default settings:

a. Swap—I typically oversubscribe here to err on the side of caution. This is the location where the Service Console swaps files if memory is low. I typically set this around 1500MB.

b. Root or /—The location where operating system and configuration files are copied. If the root partition fills up, you will have performance problems or worst. I typically increase the default value to 5120MB.

c. /var and /var/log—These are the locations that log files are stored. Again, you don't want these locations to fill up. I usually change this setting to 2048MB and 7168MB respectively.

d. /tmp—Since the early days, I've always created a separate temp directory. I assign it more space than needed, typically 2048MB.

e. /opt—VMware Community Forum members have stated that this location can become filled with logging data and can fill up rapidly. I have since started adding this partition and assign it a value of 2048MB.

f. /vmimages—This is a carry over from the VMware ESX Server 2.x days. This location would typically store Template Images or ISO files, but most now store these on network storage rather than locally. I still use it for backward compatibility and for quick storage access. The size will vary, however I typically assign it between 16 and 32GB. It depends on if you plan on storing images here or not, and if so, what types, what size and how much overall space is available.

9. After choosing a partitioning method and accepting or updating the partition tables, you will receive a popup warning (See Figure 4.9) that notifies you that by continuing, all partitions except VMFS partitions will be deleted (as long as you accepted the default in an earlier step). Click Yes to continue.

10. On the Partition Disks screen, verify that your information is correct and then click New. This will begin the process of creating the partitions.

11. On the Advanced Options screen (See Figure 4.10), you can normally just click Next. However, the screen allows you to choose from which device the ESX server will boot. For many, the default of booting from the internal drive should be fine. Click Next to continue.

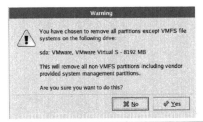

Figure 4.9   Removing Partitions Warning Popup.

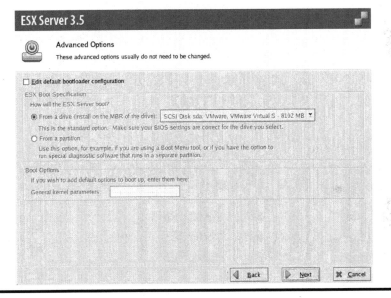

Figure 4.10   Bootloader Advanced Options.

NOTE

The "Edit default bootloader configuration" check box is new with ESX 3.5. In 3.0, the ability to select one of the radio buttons was active by default. In most cases, the master boot record (MBR) should be located on the same LUN that you selected in the partition table. This was a good modification on VMware's part, and it will hopefully keep people from incorrectly installing the MBR in the wrong location and causing boot problems.

12. At the Network Configuration screen (See Figure 4.11), select your network interface card used by your service console. Earlier, we said to identify and note your network information. This is where you need it.

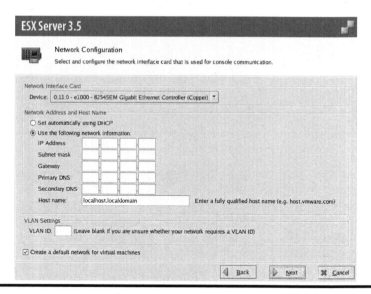

Figure 4.11   Network Configuration Screen.

a.   It is much easier to enter your IP information now, as opposed to choosing DHCP and then trying to change it later. Enter the IP Address, Subnet Mask, Gateway, Primary and Secondary DNS and fully qualified domain name (FQDN) for your host name. It is important to use a FQDN here because it is required for the HA feature of ESX to work properly, and it is required for the VMware License Server.

b.   If you are using VLAN Tagging on the network interface for the service console, you need to enter the VLAN ID that the Service Console IP Address is using. Otherwise, leave it blank.

c.   If you are separating the network traffic of the Service Console from the virtual machine network, make sure you uncheck the "Create a default network for virtual machines" check box. Leaving it checked will allow the two networks to co-exist.

13. At the Time Zone Configuration screen, you can choose from selecting your time zone from the Map, Location or UTC Offset. Whichever method you choose, make sure you select the correct time. Your virtual machines will sync to the host server, and so you want to make sure you don't have any problems in your environment because of a time issue.

14. At the Set Root Password screen (See Figure 4.12), choose a password for the root account and type it in again to confirm. Make sure you select a difficult password, because the root account is the super user or highest privileged administrator account on the host server. You should create other users that will get actively used once the environment is setup.

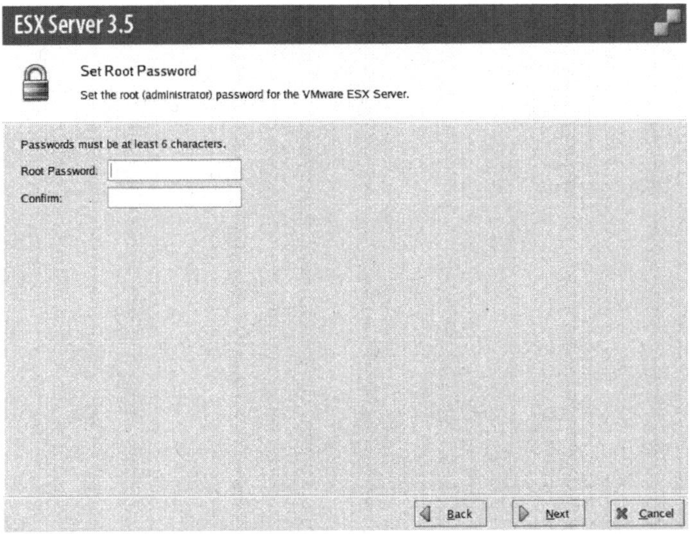

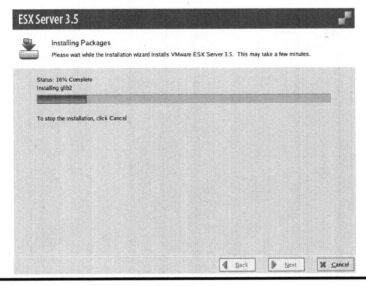

Figure 4.12   Set Root Password Screen.

Figure 4.13   Installation Status Bar.

15. The next screen, About to Install, shows you a summary of the choices that you made during the installation process. You can review these settings, and once you are ready, you can select Next to start the installation.

16. During the installation process, you can watch the packages get installed on your system and monitor its status from the status bars and percentage (See Figure 4.13). Once complete, click Finish and you have officially installed

your VMware ESX host server. When complete, the CD-ROM should eject automatically from the server. If you are using an ISO image, make sure to disconnect it from the system.

Automating Installations

Automated installations can be a huge time saver. We think of VMware ESX as an appliance that can be rebuilt in a flash when something goes wrong. At three o'clock in the morning, knowing that anyone can rebuild a host server gives me a nice warm and fuzzy feeling and allows me to sleep well at night. Right now, I have a custom automated install that will fully configure an ESX server so that the only thing I have left to do is add the server to my VirtuaCenter instance.

There are two main parts to consider when automating the installation of VMware ESX. The first part is the general install, which uses the kickstart installation method. Using kickstart, a system administrator can use a single file, ks.cfg by default, containing the answers to all the questions that would normally be asked during a typical installation.

- Language selection
- Network configuration and distribution source selection
- Keyboard selection
- Boot loader installation
- Disk partitioning and filesystem creation
- Mouse selection
- Timezone selection
- Password for root

There is a ton of information about kickstart and automated builds on the Internet, so we aren't going to try and reinvent the wheel here. If you connect via a web browser to an ESX host, you will see an option to "Log in to the Scripted Installer" as shown in Figure 4.14. The scripted installer is disabled by default, and the instruction to enable this can be found in the VMware Installation Guide, located at http://www.vmware.com/pdf/vi3_installation_guide.pdf.

TIP

On any ESX host server, look for the file /root/anaconda-ks.cfg. This contains the settings used to create the ESX server that you are looking at, and you can use this file to rebuild the server or use it as a baseline to create the ks.cfg files for another automated install.

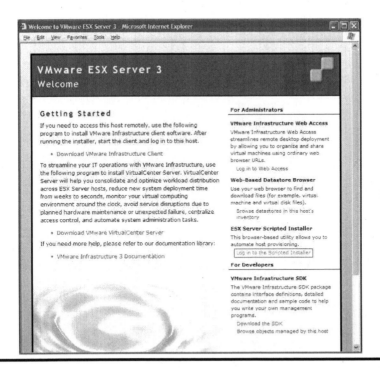

Figure 4.14   Log in to the Scripted Installer.

The real bread and butter of any installation are the %post of the kickstart configuration file or post install scripts. First, we need to mention the limitations with the %post section of the kickstart builds. The %post section is run before the last reboot of the installation. The VMkernel is not loaded at this stage, so no VMkernel commands can be used here. Figure 4.15 has a list of commands that would be considered off limits during the post because they rely on VMkernel to be up and running.

Those are a lot of commands to be excluded from running in the %post section of the build. But we have another trick up our sleeve, and that is the ability to create a script in the %post section and launch this script with rc.local. The /etc/rc.d/rc.local is a file which runs at the end of all the multi-user boot levels, and which we can use to launch scripts or applications. As a best practice, make a copy of this file before you make any changes. This gives you the ability to put the original rc.local back into place once you are finished with your task or process. An example of this would look something like Figure 4.16.

We don't want to turn the rest of this chapter into a scripting lesson, but it seems important to present two different methods here so that you can see a finished product and be able to reverse engineer as needed in order to bring something into your own environment.

Commands that should be considered off limit		
esxcfg-advcfg	esxcfg-init	esxcfg-resgrp
esxcfg-auth	esxcfg-linuxnet	esxcfg-route
esxcfg-boot	esxcfg-module	esxcfg-swiscsi
esxcfg-configcheck	esxcfg-mpath	esxcfg-upgrade
esxcfg-dumppart	esxcfg-nas	esxcfg-vmhbadevs
esxcfg-firewall	esxcfg-nics	esxcfg-vmknic
esxcfg-hwiscsi	esxcfg-pciid	esxcfg-vswif
esxcfg-info	esxcfg-rescan	esxcfg-vswitch

Figure 4.15   Off Limit VMkernel Commands.

A modified rc.local for scripting
save a copy of rc. local
cp /etc/rc.d/rc.local /etc/rc.d/rc.local.sav
add install.sh to rc.local
cat >> /etc/rc.d/rc.local << EOF
cd /tmp/install
/tmp/install/install.sh
EOF
And inside the insall.sh would be the command to reset rc.local back to the original
Reset rc.local to original
mv -f /etc/rc.d/rc.local.sav /etc/rc.d/rc.local

Figure 4.16   Modified rc.local File for Automated Installations.

This is a ks.cfg file that builds an ESX server and also builds the post installation scripts that can be used during the initial boot. This configuration file was built and contributed by Jason Boche (aka jasonboche from the VMware Community Forums).

```
Here is my kickstart script for automating ESX. It uses
ftp server for source files and does the following:

 1. Creates vmkernal portgroup and enables vmotion
 2. Populates host file
 3. Populates resolv.conf
 4. Populates syslog.conf
 5. Creates all vswitches COS,VMotion and VMNetwork
 6. Configures firewall
 7. Installs insight manager agents and installs trusted
certificate
 8. Sets console memory to 512MB
 9. Configures ntp services
 10. Enable root login thru ssh
###############################################

# This file is used for VMware ESX Server Scripted
Install Deployment

# Installation Method
url --url ftp://10.x.x.x/kickstart/

# root Password
rootpw --iscrypted $1$/NZm0rle$nmc.O2RBMzG/esAgGD.ABC
#$1$Rihg62Vt$ndyTLuNbedcUEq.aBc1Qf/

# Authconfig
auth --enableshadow --enablemd5

# BootLoader (The user has to use grub by default)
bootloader --location=mbr

# Timezone
timezone America/Phoenix

# X windowing System
skipx

# Install or Upgrade
install

# Text Mode
text

# Network install type
network --device=eth4 --bootproto static --ip 10.x.x.x --
netmask 255.255.0.0 --gateway 10.x.x.x --nameserver 10.
x.x.x --hostname servername.widget.domain.com --
addvmportgroup=0 --vlanid=0
```

```
# Language
lang en_US

# Langauge Support
langsupport --default en_US

# Keyboard
keyboard us

# Mouse
mouse none

# Reboot after install ?
reboot

# Firewall settings
firewall --disabled

# Clear Partitions
clearpart --all --drives=cciss/c0d0 --initlabel

# Partitioning HP Only
part /boot --fstype ext3 --size 100 --ondisk=cciss/c0d0
--asprimary
part / --fstype ext3 --size 10240 --ondisk=cciss/c0d0
--asprimary
part swap --size 544 --ondisk=cciss/c0d0 --asprimary
part
/var/log --fstype ext3 --size 2048 --ondisk=cciss/c0d0
part /home --fstype ext3 --size 1024 --ondisk=cciss/c0d0
part /tmp --fstype ext3 --size 1024 --ondisk=cciss/c0d0

# VMware Specific Commands
vmaccepteula
vmlicense --mode=server --server=VC.Licensing.Server.
Hostname --edition=esxFull

%packages
@base
%vmlicense_text

%post

####################################################
cat > /tmp/esxcfg.sh <<\EOF3
#!/bin/sh
# Configure ESX Server
```

```
########################################
#Set console memory to 512M
########################################
/bin/sed -i -e 's/272/512/' /etc/vmware/esx.conf
/bin/sed -i -e 's/272M/512M/' /boot/grub/grub.conf
/bin/sed -i -e 's/277504/523264/' /boot/grub/grub.conf

########################################
# Configure VSwitches WIP
########################################
#Removes VSwitch0 Pnics#
esxcfg-vswitch vSwitch0 -U vmnic0
esxcfg-vswitch -A COS vSwitch0
esxcfg-vswif -p COS vswif0
esxcfg-vswitch -D "Service Console" vSwitch0
#Add Pnics 4 and 5 to VSwitch0#
esxcfg-vswitch vSwitch0 -L vmnic4
esxcfg-vswitch vSwitch0 -L vmnic5
#Create Vswitch1 and add pnics 0 and 3 to it#
esxcfg-vswitch -a vSwitch1
esxcfg-vswitch -A VMotion vSwitch1
esxcfg-vswitch vSwitch1 -L vmnic0
esxcfg-vswitch vSwitch1 -L vmnic3
#create vmkernal portgroup and enable vmotion capability
esxcfg-vmknic -a VMotion -i 192.168.X.X -n 255.255.255.0
esxcfg-route 192.168.X.X
sleep 30
service mgmt-vmware restart
sleep 30
vimsh -n -e "/hostsvc/vmotion/vnic_set portgroup3"
#Create Vswitch1 and add pnics 1 and 2 to it#
esxcfg-vswitch -a vSwitch2
esxcfg-vswitch vSwitch2 -L vmnic1
esxcfg-vswitch vSwitch2 -L vmnic2
#Add portgroup VMotion to vSwitch1 and set vlan disabled#
#esxcfg-vswitch vSwitch1 -A "VMotion"
#esxcfg-vswitch vSwitch1 -p "VMotion" -v 0
#Add portgroup VMNetwork to vSwitch2 and set vlan
disabled#
esxcfg-vswitch vSwitch2 -A "VMNetwork"
esxcfg-vswitch vSwitch2 -p "VMNetwork" -v 0

########################################
# where to get time when starting
/bin/echo "DNSserver.widget.microsoft.com" >>/etc/ntp/step-tickers
/bin/echo "DNSserver.widget.microsoft.com" >>
/etc/ntp/step-tickers
/bin/echo "DNSserver.widget.microsoft.com" >>/etc/ntp/step-tickers
```

```
/bin/echo "DNSserver.widget.microsoft.com" >>/etc/ntp/step-tickers
/bin/echo "DNSserver.widget.microsoft.com" >>/etc/ntp/step-tickers
/bin/echo "1.widget.microsoft.com" >> /etc/ntp/step-tickers
/bin/echo "2.widget.microsoft.com" >> /etc/ntp/step-tickers
/bin/echo "3.widget.microsoft.com" >> /etc/ntp/step-tickers
/bin/echo "4.widget.microsoft.com" >> /etc/ntp/step-tickers
/bin/echo "5.widget.microsoft.com" >> /etc/ntp/step-tickers
/bin/echo "widget.microsoft.com" >> /etc/ntp/step-tickers

# /etc/ntp.conf
/bin/cp /etc/ntp.conf /etc/ntp.conf.orig
/bin/cat /dev/null>/etc/ntp.conf
/bin/cat <<EOF >>/etc/ntp.conf
# Prohibit general access to this service.
restrict default ignore

# the administrative functions.
restrict 127.0.0.1

# permit the source to query or modify the service on
this system.

restrict 10.x.x.x mask 255.255.255.255 kod nomodify
notrap noquery
nopeer
server 10.x.x.x

restrict 10.x.x.x mask 255.255.255.255 kod nomodify
notrap noquery
nopeer
server 10.x.x.x

restrict 10.x.x.x mask 255.255.255.255 kod nomodify
notrap noquery
nopeer
server 10.x.x.x

restrict 10.x.x.x mask 255.255.255.255 kod nomodify
notrap noquery
nopeer
server 10.x.x.x

restrict 10.x.x.x mask 255.255.255.255 kod nomodify
notrap noquery
nopeer
server 10.x.x.x
```

```
# fudge 127.127.1.0 stratum 10

#
driftfile /etc/ntp/drift

# authenticate yes

# keys /etc/ntp/keys

EOF

#######################################
# Configure hosts GOOD
#######################################
# /etc/hosts
/bin/cat /dev/null>/etc/hosts
/bin/cat <<EOF >>/etc/hosts
# that require network functionality will fail.
127.0.0.1 localhost.localdomain localhost
10.x.x.x servername.widget.microsoft.com servername
10.x.x.x SEREVRNAME.widget.microsoft.com SEREVRNAME
10.x.x.x SEREVRNAME.widget.microsoft.com SEREVRNAME
10.x.x.x servername.widget.microsoft.com servername
10.x.x.x SERVERNAME
10.x.x.x servername
10.x.x.x 1.widget.microsoft.com
10.x.x.x 2.widget.microsoft.com
10.x.x.x 3.widget.microsoft.com
10.x.x.x 4.widget.microsoft.com
10.x.x.x 5.widget.microsoft.com
widget.microsoft.com

EOF

#######################################
# Firewall configuration
#######################################
# We need to enable ntpClient, sshClient, snmpd, HP SIM,
SSH Server,Syslog
esxcfg-firewall -e ntpClient
esxcfg-firewall -e sshClient
esxcfg-firewall -e snmpd
esxcfg-firewall -e sshServer
esxcfg-firewall -e CIMSLP
esxcfg-firewall -e LicenseClient
esxcfg-firewall -e CIMHttpServer
```

```
esxcfg-firewall -e CIMHttpsServer
esxcfg-firewall -e vpxHeartbeats
esxcfg-firewall -e ftpClient
esxcfg-firewall -o 2381,tcp,in,hpim
esxcfg-firewall -o 280,tcp,out,sim-cert
esxcfg-firewall -o 514,udp,out,Syslog

#######################################
# NTP Hardware Sync
#######################################
/sbin/chkconfig --level 345 ntpd on
/etc/init.d/ntpd start
/sbin/hwclock --systohc

#######################################
# Enable root access thru SSH
#######################################
# WARNING: This is not the most secure course of action!
sed -e 's/PermitRootLogin no/PermitRootLogin yes/' /etc/
ssh/sshd_config > /etc/ssh/sshd_config.new
mv -f /etc/ssh/sshd_config.new /etc/ssh/sshd_config
service sshd restart

#######################################
# Secondary Resolv.conf entry
#######################################
/bin/cat /dev/null>/etc/resolv.conf
echo "nameserver 10.x.x.x" >> /etc/resolv.conf
echo "nameserver 10.x.x.x" >> /etc/resolv.conf
echo "search widget.microsoft.com microsoft.com" >> /etc/
resolv.conf

#######################################
# Ftp urlgrabber.py to allow ESX patching script to
execute GOOD
#######################################
#!/bin/sh
esxcfg-firewall -allowOutgoing
ftp -n ftpserver.widget.microsoft.com.IP << "EOF"
quote user anonymous
quote pass anonymous
get urlgrabber.py /tmp/urlgrabber.py
quit
EOF

esxcfg-firewall -blockOutgoing
cp /usr/share/yum/urlgrabber.py /usr/share/yum/
urlgrabber.ks
cp /tmp/urlgrabber.py /usr/share/yum/urlgrabber.py
rm /tmp/urlgrabber.py
```

```
#########################################
#Syslog.conf modification for syslog logging to 10.x.x.x
#########################################
# /etc/syslog.conf
/bin/cp /etc/syslog.conf /etc/syslog.conf.ks
/bin/cat /dev/null>/etc/syslog.conf
/bin/cat <<EOF >>/etc/syslog.conf
# Logging much else clutters up the screen.
#kern.* /dev/console

# Don't log private authentication, cron, or vmkernel
messages!
*.info;mail.none;authpriv.none;cron.none;local6.
none;local5.none /var/log/messages
*.info;mail.none;authpriv.none;cron.none;local6.
none;local5.none @10.x.x.x
# The authpriv file has restricted access.
authpriv.* /var/log/secure

# Log all the mail messages in one place.
mail.* /var/log/maillog

# Log cron stuff
cron.* /var/log/cron

# Everybody gets emergency messages
*.emerg *

# Save news errors of level crit and higher in a special
file.
uucp,news.crit /var/log/spooler

# Save boot messages also to boot.log
local7.* /var/log/boot.log
local7.* @10.x.x.x

#send all local6.info messages to special summary log
only.
#loclocal6.info;local6.!notice /var/log/vmksummary
#loclocal6.info;local6.!notice @10.x.x.x

#send all vmkernel .warning messages to warnings logs.
local6.warning /var/log/vmkwarning
local6.warning @10.x.x.x

#send all local6.notice and higher messages to vmkernel
log.
local6.notice /var/log/vmkernel
```

```
#send all userworld proxy messages to proxy log
local5.* /var/log/vmkproxy

#send all storage monitor related messages to
storageMonitor log
local4.* /var/log/storageMonitor
local4.* @10.x.x.x
EOF

###########################################
#Install IM agents
###########################################
esxcfg-firewall -allowOutgoing
ftp -n ftpserver.widget.microsoft.com.IP << "EOF"
quote user anonymous
quote pass anonymous
binary
get /imagent/hpmgmt-7.7.0-vmware3x.tar /tmp/hpmgmt-7.7.0-
vmware3x.tar
get /imagent/hpmgmt.conf /tmp/hpmgmt.conf
get /imagent/insightmanagertrustedcertificatename.pem /
tmp/insightmanagertrustedcertificatename.pem
quit
EOF
export PATH=$PATH:/tmp
cd /tmp
chmod +x hpmgmt-7.7.0-vmware3x.tar
tar -xzvf hpmgmt-7.7.0-vmware3x.tar
cp /tmp/hpmgmt.conf /tmp/hpmgmt/770/hpmgmt.conf
cd /tmp/hpmgmt/770
./installvm770.sh --silent --inputfile /tmp/hpmgmt/770/
hpmgmt.conf
rm -f -r /tmp/hpmgmt
rm -f /tmp/hpmgmt-7.7.0-vmware3x.tar
rm -f /tmp/hpmgmt.conf
cp /tmp/insightmanagertrustedcertificatename.pem /opt/hp/
hpsmh/certs/insightmanagertrustedcertificatename.pem
rm -f /tmp/insightmanagertrustedcertificatename.pem
esxcfg-firewall -blockOutgoing
EOF3
# make configuration script executable
chmod +x /tmp/esxcfg.sh

#######################################################
# save a copy of rc.local
cp /etc/rc.d/rc.local /etc/rc.d/rc.local.sav
# add esxcfg.sh to rc.local
cat >> /etc/rc.d/rc.local <<EOF
cd /tmp
/tmp/esxcfg.sh
EOF>
```

In this next example, the post installation script and some pre-configured files are pushed out to the ESX host servers in a single directory. The pre-configured files are then copied and put into place during the script. Notice at the bottom of the script the call for the different sections that can be turned on and off as needed.

```sh
#!/bin/sh
echo "VMWare ESX Post Install Script" > /root/PostInstall/
PostInstall.log
#######################
# Server Configuration Variables
SRVCFG=ServerName
SCIP=Service Console IP
VMIP=vMotionIP
DGW=Default gateway
VMKGW=vMotion Gateway
#######################
setPath()
{
 echo "Setting PATH...."
 sleep 5

PATH=/usr/local/sbin:/usr/local/bin:/sbin:/bin:/usr/sbin:
/usr/bin:/usr/X11R6/bin
}

setSCmem()
{
 echo "Setting Service Console memory to 512MB" #>> /root/
PostInstall/PostInstall.log
 mv -f /etc/vmware/esx.conf /tmp/esx.conf.bak
 sed -e 's/boot\/memSize = \"272\"/boot\/memSize =
\"512\"/g' /tmp/esx.conf.bak >>
/etc/vmware/esx.conf
 mv -f /boot/grub/grub.conf /tmp/grub.conf.bak

sed
-e 's/uppermem 277504/uppermem 523264/g' -e 's/mem=272M/
mem=512M/g'
/tmp/grub.conf.bak >> /boot/grub/grub.conf
 echo "Service Console memory has been set to 512mb" #>>
/root/PostInstall/PostInstall.log
}

openFirewall()
{
 /usr/sbin/esxcfg-firewall --allowIncoming
 /usr/sbin/esxcfg-firewall --allowOutgoing
}
```

```
hpinsight()
{
 echo "First step unpack and install the HP Agents" >>
/root/PostInstall/PostInstall.log
 cd /root
 tar -zxvf hpmgmt-7.7.0-vmware3x.tgz
 ./hpmgmt/770/installvm770.sh --silent --inputfile ./
hpmgmt.conf
 echo "Post Install -- HP Insight Agents installed" >>
/root/PostInstall/PostInstall.log
}

addKerberos()
{
 echo "Next we will install the RPM's for Kerberos and
LDAP" >>
/root/PostInstall/PostInstall.log
 rpm -ivh /root/PostInstall/OpenLDAP/krb5-workstation-
1.2.7-47.i386.rpm --nodeps
 rpm -ivh /root/PostInstall/OpenLDAP/cyrus-sasl-gssapi-
2.1.15-10.i386.rpm
 rpm -ivh /root/PostInstall/OpenLDAP/pam_krb5-2.2.11-1.
i386.rpm
 rpm -ivh /root/PostInstall/OpenLDAP/samba-common-3.0.25-
2.i386.rpm
 rpm -ivh /root/PostInstall/OpenLDAP/samba-client-3.0.25-
2.i386.rpm
 echo "krb5-workstation has been installed" >> /root/
PostInstall/PostInstall.log
}

addDir()
{
 echo "We need to make certain directories for vm-diag
scripts and kerberos" >>
/root/PostInstall/PostInstall.log
 mkdir -p /var/kerberos/krb5kdc
 mkdir -p /usr/vm-diag
 mkdir -p /usr/vm-diag/logs
 echo "Needed directories have been created" >>
/root/PostInstall/PostInstall.log
}

addCopyFiles()
{
 echo "Here where we copy over specific preconfigured
files" >>
/root/PostInstall/PostInstall.log
```

```
cp -f /root/PostInstall/ntp.conf /etc/ntp.conf
cp -f /root/PostInstall/step-tickers/etc/ntp/step-tickers
cp -f /root/PostInstall/krb5kdc/kdc.conf /var/kerberos/
krb5kdc/kdc.conf
cp -f /root/PostInstall/snmp/snmpd.conf /etc/snmp/snmpd.
conf
cp -f /root/PostInstall/ldap.conf /etc/openldap/ldap.
conf
cp -f /root/PostInstall/cacert.cer /etc/openldap/cacert.
cer
cp -f /etc/vmware/hostd/authorization.xml /etc/vmware/
hostd/authorization.xml.bak
cp -f /root/PostInstall/authorization.xml /etc/vmware/
hostd/authorization.xml
cp -f /root/PostInstall/inq /usr/sbin/inq
chmod a+x /usr/sbin/inq
chmod a+x /root/PostInstall/vm_mapping.pl
chmod a+x /root/PostInstall/vmfs_mapping.pl
echo "Pre-Configuration files have been copied over" >>
/root/PostInstall/PostInstall.log
}

setSSHRoot()
{
echo "Allowing root to login via SSH..." >> /root/
PostInstall/PostInstall.log
mv /etc/ssh/sshd_config /etc/ssh/sshd_config.old
sed -e "s/PermitRootLogin no/PermitRootLogin yes/g" /
etc/ssh/sshd_config.old >
/etc/ssh/sshd_config
rm -f /etc/ssh/sshd_config.old
/etc/init.d/ sshd restart
echo "$scriptName - Set root to login via SSH" >> /root/
PostInstall/PostInstall.log
}

setSNMP()
{
echo "Copy over the snmp configuration files and restart
service" >>
/root/PostInstall/PostInstall.log
cp -f ./snmp/snmpd.conf /etc/snmp/snmpd.conf
service snmpd restart
service sshd restart
echo "SNMP has been configured" >> /root/PostInstall/
PostInstall.log
}
```

```
setUsers()
{
  echo "Adding default users..." >> /root/PostInstall/
PostInstall.log
  groupadd VMAdmin
  /usr/sbin/useradd -c "VMAdmin" -G VMAdmin -p password
  echo "Default users have neem created" >> /root/
PostInstall/PostInstall.log
}

setLDAPSearch()
{
  echo "Starting configuration of LDAP Search Script" >>
/root/PostInstall/PostInstall.log
  cp /root/PostInstall/LDAP /etc/cron.hourly/LDAP
  chmod a+x /etc/cron.hourly/LDAP
  /etc/cron.hourly/LDAP
  /etc/cron.hourly/LDAP
  echo "LDAP Search Script has been configured and the
script has been run" >>
/root/PostInstall/PostInstall.log
}

setConsoleNIC()
{
echo "Deleting current network configuration" >> /root/
PostInstall/PostInstall.log
/usr/sbin/esxcfg-vswitch vSwitch0 -D "VM Network"
/usr/sbin/esxcfg-vswitch -U vmnic0 vSwitch0
/usr/sbin/esxcfg-vswitch -U vmnic1 vSwitch0
/usr/sbin/esxcfg-vswif -d vswif0
/usr/sbin/esxcfg-vswitch -d vSwitch0
service mgmt-vmware restart
echo "Reconfiguring Service Console NIC..." >> /root/
PostInstall/PostInstall.log
cp /etc/vmware/esx.conf /tmp/post/esx.conf.bak
/usr/sbin/esxcfg-vswitch -a vSwitch0
/usr/sbin/esxcfg-vswitch vSwitch0 -L vmnic0
/usr/sbin/esxcfg-vswitch vSwitch0 -L vmnic1
/usr/sbin/esxcfg-vswitch -A "Service Console" vSwitch0
/usr/sbin/esxcfg-vswitch vSwitch0 -p "Service Console" -v
0
/usr/sbin/esxcfg-vswif -a vswif0 -p "Service Console" -i
$SCIP -n 255.255.255.0
route add default gw $DGW
echo "GATEWAY=$DGW" >> /etc/sysconfig/network
```

```
/usr/sbin/esxcfg-vswitch -U vmnic0 vSwitch0
/usr/sbin/esxcfg-vswitch -U vmnic1 vSwitch0
/usr/sbin/esxcfg-vswitch vSwitch0 -L vmnic0
/usr/sbin/esxcfg-vswitch vSwitch0 -L vmnic1
service mgmt-vmware restart
sleep 20
vimsh -n -e "hostsvc/net/vswitch_setpolicy --
nicorderpolicy-active vmnic0 vSwitch0"
vimsh -n -e "hostsvc/net/vswitch_setpolicy --
nicorderpolicy-active vmnic0,vmnic1
vSwitch0"
}

setVMotion()
{
echo "Setting up vMotion..." >> /root/PostInstall/
PostInstall.log
# Setup your VMkernel and Virtual Machine networking:
# EXAMPLE: Add VMotion portgroup
#/usr/sbin/esxcfg-vswitch --add --pg=VMotion vSwitch0
#/usr/sbin/esxcfg-vmknic --add --ip %#!computer@lic_os_
user% --netmask 255.255.255.0
VMotion
# EXAMPLE: Setup the VMkernel IP Stack default gateway
# GW address can be obtained from the Windows licensing
organization field during
token replacement
#/usr/sbin/esxcfg-route %#!computer@lic_os_org%
/usr/sbin/esxcfg-vswitch vSwitch0 -A vMotion
/usr/sbin/esxcfg-vswitch vSwitch0 -p vMotion
/usr/sbin/esxcfg-vmknic -a vMotion -i $VMIP -n
255.255.255.0
/usr/sbin/esxcfg-route $VMKGW
service mgmt-vmware restart
sleep 40
# vimsh -n -e "/hostsvc/vmotion/vnic_set portgroup4" #
Command for 3.0.2 and earlier
vimsh -n -e "/hostsvc/vmotion/vnic_set vmk0" # Used for
ESX3.5 and higher
}

setVMNet()
{
echo "Setting up FH LAN Switch and Network..." >> /root/
PostInstall/PostInstall.log
/usr/sbin/esxcfg-vswitch -a vSwitch1
```

```
/usr/sbin/esxcfg-vswitch vSwitch1 -L vmnic6
/usr/sbin/esxcfg-vswitch vSwitch1 -L vmnic7
/usr/sbin/esxcfg-vswitch vSwitch1 -A "VM_Network"
/usr/sbin/esxcfg-vswitch vSwitch1 -p "VM_Network"
service mgmt-vmware restart
sleep 20
vimsh -n -e "hostsvc/net/vswitch_setpolicy --
nicorderpolicy-active vmnic6 vSwitch1"
vimsh -n -e "hostsvc/net/vswitch_setpolicy --
nicorderpolicy-active vmnic6,vmnic7
vSwitch1"
}

setCSS()
{
echo "Setting up CSS Switch and Network..." >> /root/
PostInstall/PostInstall.log
/usr/sbin/esxcfg-vswitch -a vSwitch2
/usr/sbin/esxcfg-vswitch vSwitch2 -L vmnic4
/usr/sbin/esxcfg-vswitch vSwitch2 -L vmnic5
/usr/sbin/esxcfg-nics -s 100 -d full vmnic4
/usr/sbin/esxcfg-nics -s 100 -d full vmnic5
/usr/sbin/esxcfg-vswitch vSwitch2 -A "VLAN_111_CSS"
/usr/sbin/esxcfg-vswitch vSwitch2 -p "VLAN_111_CSS"
service mgmt-vmware restart
sleep 20
vimsh -n -e "hostsvc/net/vswitch_setpolicy --
nicorderpolicy-active vmnic4 vSwitch2"
vimsh -n -e "hostsvc/net/vswitch_setpolicy --
nicorderpolicy-active vmnic4,vmnic5
vSwitch2"
}

setDMZ()
{
echo "Setting up DMZ Switch and Network..." >> /root/
PostInstall/PostInstall.log
/usr/sbin/esxcfg-vswitch -a vSwitch3
/usr/sbin/esxcfg-vswitch vSwitch3 -L vmnic2
/usr/sbin/esxcfg-nics -s 100 -d full vmnic2
/usr/sbin/esxcfg-vswitch vSwitch3 -A "DMZ"
/usr/sbin/esxcfg-vswitch vSwitch3 -p "DMZ"
}
```

```
setProdNet()
{
# EXAMPLE: Create production vSwitch using remaining
physical NICs and default
portgroup(s)
/usr/sbin/esxcfg-vswitch --add vswitch1
export VMNICS=`esxcfg-nics --list | sed -e '1d' -e '/
vmnic0/d' | awk '{print $1}'`
for i in $VMNICS; do esxcfg-vswitch --link=$i vswitch1;
done
/usr/sbin/esxcfg-vswitch --add-pg=FH_Network vswitch1
# or
#/usr/sbin/esxcfg-vswitch --vlan=1 -p defaultProd
prodSwitch
/usr/sbin/esxcfg-vswitch -U vmnic2 vSwitch1
/usr/sbin/esxcfg-vswitch -U vmnic3 vSwitch1
/usr/sbin/esxcfg-vswitch vSwitch1 -L vmnic2
/usr/sbin/esxcfg-vswitch vSwitch2 -L vmnic3
service mgmt-vmware restart
sleep 20
vimsh -n -e "hostsvc/net/vswitch_setpolicy --
nicorderpolicy-active vmnic2 vSwitch1"
vimsh -n -e "hostsvc/net/vswitch_setpolicy --
nicorderpolicy-active vmnic2,vmnic3
vSwitch1"
}

setLocalNet()
{
# EXAMPLE: Create private vSwitch and default portgroup
#/usr/sbin/esxcfg-vswitch --add privateSwitch
#/usr/sbin/esxcfg-vswitch --add-pg=defaultPrivate
privateSwitch
# or
#/usr/sbin/esxcfg-vswitch --vlan=11 -p defaultPrivate
privateSwitch
#/usr/sbin/esxcfg-vswitch --add Local
/usr/sbin/esxcfg-vswitch --add --pg=Local vSwitch4
/usr/sbin/esxcfg-vswitch vSwitch4 -A Local
/usr/sbin/esxcfg-vswitch vSwitch4 -p Local
service mgmt-vmware restart
}

setNextGen()
{
echo "Setting up FH LAN Switch and Network..." >> /root/
PostInstall/PostInstall.log
```

```
/usr/sbin/esxcfg-vswitch -a vSwitch5
/usr/sbin/esxcfg-vswitch vSwitch1 -L vmnic2
/usr/sbin/esxcfg-vswitch vSwitch1 -L vmnic1
/usr/sbin/esxcfg-vswitch vSwitch1 -A "NGen"
/usr/sbin/esxcfg-vswitch vSwitch1 -p "NGen"
service mgmt-vmware restart
sleep 20
vimsh -n -e "hostsvc/net/vswitch_setpolicy --
nicorderpolicy-active vmnic2 vSwitch5"
vimsh -n -e "hostsvc/net/vswitch_setpolicy --
nicorderpolicy-active vmnic2,vmnic1
vSwitch5"
}

setVMFS()
{
 echo "Creating VMFS partition name to computer name" >>
/root/PostInstall/PostInstall.log
 export VMFS_PARTITION=`fdisk -l /dev/cciss/c0d0 | grep
fb | sed -e
"s/\/dev\/cciss\/c0d0p\(.\).*/\1/"`
 vmkfstools -C vmfs3 -S $SRVCFG-VMFS
vmhba0:0:0:$VMFS_PARTITION
 echo "Local VMFS Volume has been renamed" >> /root/
PostInstall/PostInstall.log
}

setNameResolution()
{
 echo "Adding DNS Entries for DNS resolution" >> /root/
PostInstall/PostInstall.log
 echo "# Built by automated post install script" > /etc/
resolv.conf
 echo "search flhosp.net" >> /etc/resolv.conf
 echo "nameserver X.X.X.X" >> /etc/resolv.conf
 echo "nameserver X.X.X.X" >> /etc/resolv.conf
 echo "nameserver X.X.X.X" >> /etc/resolv.conf
 mv -f /etc/hosts /etc/hosts.bak
}

setESXcfg()
{
 echo "Configure esxcfg-auth..." >> /root/PostInstall/
PostInstall.log
 esxcfg-auth --enablead --addomain domain.com --addc
domain.com --enablekrb5
```

```
esxcfg-auth --passmaxdays=0
 echo "ESX Authentication Configuration Completed" >>
/root/PostInstall/PostInstall.log
}

setAuthd()
{
 echo "Updating vmware-authd to allow AD logons" >>
/root/PostInstall/PostInstall.log
 echo "#%PAM-1.0" > /etc/pam.d/vmware-authd
 echo "# Built by automated post install script" >> /etc/
pam.d/vmware-authd
 echo "auth sufficient /lib/security/pam_unix_auth.so
shadow nullok" >>
/etc/pam.d/vmware-authd
 echo "auth sufficient /lib/security/pam_krb5.so use_
first_pass" >>
/etc/pam.d/vmware-authd
 echo "auth sufficient /lib/security/pam_ldap.so" >> /etc/
pam.d/vmware-authd
 echo "account required /lib/security/pam_unix_acct.so"
>> /etc/pam.d/vmware-authd
 echo "account sufficient /lib/security/pam_ldap.so" >> /
etc/pam.d/vmware-authd
 echo "vmware-authd has been updated" >> /root/
PostInstall/PostInstall.log
}

setFirewall()
{
 echo "Configuring Firewall Ports...." >> /root/
PostInstall/PostInstall.log
 echo "Configuring Firewall Ports...." >> /root/
PostInstall/PostInstall.log
 /usr/sbin/esxcfg-firewall --openPort
88,tcp,out,KerberosClient
 /usr/sbin/esxcfg-firewall --openPort
88,udp,out,KerberosClient
 /usr/sbin/esxcfg-firewall --openPort
464,tcp,out,KerberosPasswordChange
 /usr/sbin/esxcfg-firewall --openPort
749,tcp,out,KerberosAdm
 #/usr/sbin/esxcfg-firewall --enableService LicenseClient
 #/usr/sbin/esxcfg-firewall --enableService sshServer
 #/usr/sbin/esxcfg-firewall --enableService vpxHeartbeats
 /usr/sbin/esxcfg-firewall --openport 389,tcp,out,in,LDAP
 /usr/sbin/esxcfg-firewall --openport
636,tcp,out,in,OpenSSL
```

```
--krb5realm= domain.com --krb5kdc= domain.com
--enableldapauth
--ldapserver= domain.com --ldapbasedn=DC=domain,DC=com

 /usr/sbin/esxcfg-firewall --openPort 2381,tcp,in,hpim
 /usr/sbin/esxcfg-firewall --openPort 2381,tcp,out,hpim
 /usr/sbin/esxcfg-firewall --openPort 231,udp,in,out,ntpd
 /usr/sbin/esxcfg-firewall --openport
280,tcp,out,sim-cert
 /usr/sbin/esxcfg-firewall --enableService snmpd
 /usr/sbin/esxcfg-firewall --enableService ntpClient
 /usr/sbin/esxcfg-firewall --enableService CIMHttpsServer
 /usr/sbin/esxcfg-firewall --enableService CIMHttpServer
 /usr/sbin/esxcfg-firewall --enableService CIMSLP
 /usr/sbin/esxcfg-firewall --enableService hpim
 echo "Firewall has been configured" >> /root/
PostInstall/PostInstall.log
}

setPerfScript()
{
 echo "Now to set up performace scripts" >> /root/
PostInstall/PostInstall.log
 cd /root/PostInstall
 cp /root/PostInstall/vm-diag/rotatemem /etc/cron.daily/
rotatemem

cp
/root/PostInstall/vm-diag/checkmem /usr/vm-diag/checkmem

cp
/root/PostInstall/vm-diag/memcheck /usr/vm-diag/memcheck
 cp /root/PostInstall/vm-diag/meminfo-munge.pl /usr/vm-
diag/meminfo-munge.pl
 cp /root/PostInstall/vm-diag/meminfo-munge.sh /usr/vm-
diag/meminfo-munge.sh

cp
/root/PostInstall/vm-diag/memrotate /usr/vm-diag/memrotate
 cp /root/PostInstall/vm-diag/ps-munge.pl /usr/vm-diag/
ps-munge.pl
 cp /root/PostInstall/vm-diag/ps-munge.sh /usr/vm-diag/
ps-munge.sh
 # A last forced copy of the ldap.conf file as a good
measure
 cp -f /root/PostInstall/ldap.conf
/etc/openldap/ldap.conf
 chmod a+x /etc/cron.daily/vm_backup
 chmod a+x /etc/cron.daily/rotatemem
```

```
chmod a+x /usr/vm-diag/checkmem
 chmod a+x /usr/vm-diag/memcheck
 chmod a+x /usr/vm-diag/meminfo-munge.pl
 chmod a+x /usr/vm-diag/meminfo-munge.sh
 chmod a+x /usr/vm-diag/memrotate
 chmod a+x /usr/vm-diag/ps-munge.pl
 chmod a+x /usr/vm-diag/ps-munge.sh
 crontab crontab.txt
 echo "Performance scripts have been installed" >> /root/
PostInstall/PostInstall.log
}

setNTP()
{
 echo "turn on ntpd and start service" >> /root/
PostInstall/PostInstall.log
 chkconfig --level 345 ntpd on
 chown ntp:ntp /etc/ntp
 service ntpd restart
 hwclock --systohc
 echo "NTP has been configured and started" >> /root/
PostInstall/PostInstall.log
}

setSSHBANNER()
{
 echo "Setting SSH Security Logon Banner Text..."
 echo $bannertxt1 > /etc/ssh/banner
 echo " " >>/etc/ssh/banner
 echo $bannertxt2 >> /etc/ssh/banner
 echo " " >> /etc/ssh/banner
 echo $bannertxt3 >> /etc/ssh/banner
 echo " " >> /etc/ssh/banner
 echo $bannertxt4 >> /etc/ssh/banner
 echo "banner /etc/ssh/banner" >> /etc/ssh/sshd_config
 echo "$scriptName - Configured SSH Banner text" >> /root/
PostInstall/PostInstall.log
}

FWEnabled()
{
 /usr/sbin/esxcfg-firewall --blockIncoming
 /usr/sbin/esxcfg-firewall --blockOutgoing
 echo "Post Install Done" >> /root/PostInstall/
PostInstall.log
 echo "Firewall has been enabled" >> /root/PostInstall/
PostInstall.log
}
```

```
SoftMaxDirty()
{
echo 15 > /proc/vmware/config/BufferCache/SoftMaxDirty
}

TurnOnHostLicense()
{
 echo "Changing License Type from unlicensed to ESX
Standard" >>
/root/PostInstall/PostInstall.log
 mv -f /etc/vmware/license.cfg /etc/vmware/license.cfg.
bak
 sed -e 's/EDITION=/EDITION=esxFull/g' /etc/vmware/
license.cfg.bak >>
/etc/vmware/license.cfg
 service mgmt-vmware restart
 echo "License Type has been changed to ESX Standard"
}

NoHyperthread()
{
 echo "Disabling Hyperthreading on ESX Host" >> /root/
PostInstall/PostInstall.log
 echo '/vmkernel/hyperthreading = "FALSE"' >> /etc/vmware/
esx.conf
 echo "Hyperthreading is disabled" >> /root/PostInstall/
PostInstall.log
}

SANConfig()
{
esxcfg-advcfg -s 0 /Disk/UseDeviceReset
service mgmt-vmware restart
}

NoVMFS2()
{
#Modification to prevent vmfs2 module from loading to
improve LUN and volume scan
speed and improve overall performance:
echo "Setting VMFS2 not to load" >> /root/PostInstall/
PostInstall.log
mv /etc/init.d/vmware /etc/init.d/vmware.old
sed -e "s/echo \"vmfs2 vmfs2\"/\#echo \"vmfs2 vmfs2\"/g"
/etc/init.d/vmware.old >
/etc/init.d/vmware
chmod 744 /etc/init.d/vmware
}
```

```
SetWinbind()
{
echo "Starting configuration on winbind" >> /root/
PostInstall/PostInstall.log
esxcfg-firewall -o 445,tcp,out,MicrosoftDS
esxcfg-firewall -o 445,udp,out,MicrosoftDS
esxcfg-firewall -o 464,udp,out,kpasswd
rpm -ivh /root/PostInstall/OpenLDAP/krb5-1.3.4-10.src.rpm
echo "-:ALL EXCEPT wheel FHAdmin <Group>:ALL" >> /etc/
security/access.conf
cp -f /root/PostInstall/nsswitch.conf /etc/nsswitch.conf
cp -f /root/PostInstall/smb.conf /etc/samba/smb.conf
cp -f /root/PostInstall/pam.d/system-auth
cp -f /root/PostInstall/pam.d/login
cp -f /root/PostInstall/pam.d/sshd
cp -f /root/PostInstall/krb5.conf /etc/krb5.conf
service winbind start
chkconfig winbind on
echo "Starting configuration on winbind" >> /root/
PostInstall/PostInstall.log
}

HBABalance()
{
PREVIOUS="vmhba1"
echo "Starting HBA Balance....." >> /root/PostInstall/
PostInstall.log
 # Execute new config
 for LUN in $(esxcfg-vmhbadevs | tail +2 | awk '{print
$1}')
 do
 CURRENT=$(esxcfg-mpath -q --lun=${LUN} | grep FC | grep
"preferred" | awk
'{print $4}' | awk -F ":" '{print $1}')
 if [[ ${CURRENT} = ${PREVIOUS} ]]
 then
 NEW=$(esxcfg-mpath -q --lun=${LUN} | grep FC | grep -v
"preferred" |
awk '{print $4}' | awk -F ":" '{print $1}')
 NEWPATH=$(esxcfg-mpath -q --lun=${LUN} | grep FC | grep
-v "preferred"
| awk '{print $4}')
 esxcfg-mpath --lun=${LUN} --path=${NEWPATH} --preferred
 PREVIOUS=${NEW}
 else
 PREVIOUS=${CURRENT}
 fi
 done
```

```
echo >> /root/PostInstall/PostInstall.log
 echo "****** NEW HBA CONFIG *****" >> /root/PostInstall/
PostInstall.log
 echo >> /root/PostInstall/PostInstall.log
 for LUN in $(esxcfg-vmhbadevs | tail +2 | awk '{print
$1}')
 do
 esxcfg-mpath -q --lun=${LUN} | grep FC
 echo >> /root/PostInstall/PostInstall.log
 done
 echo >> /root/PostInstall/PostInstall.log
 echo "****** \"active\" flag will be moved after disk
activity *****" >>
/root/PostInstall/PostInstall.log
 echo >> /root/PostInstall/PostInstall.log
echo "Finished HBA Balance....." >> /root/PostInstall/
PostInstall.log
}

#
# MAIN PROGRAM - ENTER HERE...
#

scriptName="ESX Post Install Script" >> /root/
PostInstall/PostInstall.log
dateTime=`date '+%c'` >> /root/PostInstall/PostInstall.
log

bannertxt1="Legal warning test line 1."
bannertxt2="Legal warning test line 2."
bannertxt3="Legal warning test line 3."
bannertxt4="Legal warning test line 4."

echo "$scriptName - started" >> /root/PostInstall/
PostInstall.log

echo "Starting $scriptName..." >> /root/PostInstall/
PostInstall.log
setPath
setSCmem
openFirewall
#hpinsight
addKerberos
addDir
addCopyFiles
setSSHRoot
setSNMP
setUsers
```

```
setLDAPSearch
setVMFS
setNameResolution
setESXcfg
setAuthd
setFirewall
setPerfScript
setNTP
SoftMaxDirty
TurnOnHostLicense
NoHyperthread
setConsoleNIC
setVMotion
#setFHNet
#setCSS
#setDMZ
setNextGen
setProdNet
setLocalNet
SANConfig
NoVMFS2
HBABalance
SetWinbind
#FWEnabled
echo "$scriptName - ended" >> /root/PostInstall/
PostInstall.log
reboot
exit 0
```

Again, this section is not meant to be a scripting lesson, but we wanted to present you with some real world examples that you can take back with you to your enterprise in order to make your life and job easier. After all, isn't that what automation is all about?

Summary

During the planning stages of a server virtualization deployment, a large amount of information must be gathered. In addition, there are a number of server virtualization-specific considerations to be aware of. It is important to be aware of the technical considerations and how they affect the choices that are made. The information presented in this chapter can be leveraged into making a server virtualization deployment a success.

VMware ESX is generally installed using the methods described above. The text mode installer configures the same data using a character-based user interface instead of a VGA graphical user interface. The installation process can generally be completed in less than 30 minutes when the proper preparation has been made. And this can be done even faster when using a hands-off method by automating the installation.

Chapter 5

Virtual Machines

Virtual Machine Concepts

Virtual machines (VMs), also called guests, are virtual systems residing in a VMware ESX environment that operates on a single piece of hardware that leverages virtualization in order to operate more than a single operating system at a time. VMware accomplishes this process through the use of a hypervisor technology.

The hypervisor gives a single physical system, or host server, the ability to distribute resources to one or more virtual systems at a single time. When a new virtual machine is created and then subsequently powered on, a virtual world is created as a process running on the VMware ESX host. Figure 5.1 represents how the hypervisor model works. The outermost square represents the physical hardware. VMware ESX is then loaded on the physical hardware (known as a bare-metal installation). VMware ESX then presents virtual hardware, a virtual CPU, memory, storage, and network adapter, to a virtual machine. A guest operating system is installed and runs on or within the virtual machine world.

It is a common operational practice to separate applications, services, or databases on different systems to ensure isolation. As a result, often times a physical server may only utilize 5 to 10% of the available resources it has available. From an operations standpoint, this is very good for reasons including isolation, separation of maintenance and patching and the like. From a business standpoint, this doesn't make much sense as you normally wouldn't purchase 100 items when you are only going to use 5 or 10 of them. As you can see in Figure 5.2, virtualization can bring together both schools of thought. When the group of servers on the left is underutilized, a VMware ESX host can provide a similar layer of isolation but with

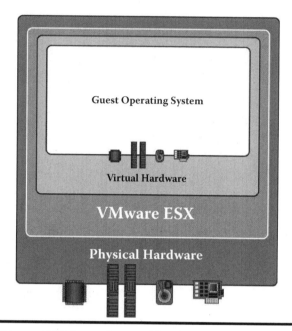

Figure 5.1   VMware ESX Hypervisor Architecture.

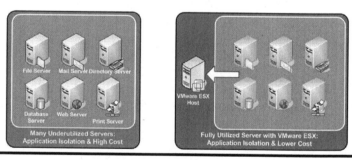

Figure 5.2   Application Isolation and Server Utilization.

a higher level of utilization, and a better return on investment of the physical hardware. Virtualization provides good technical practice by better utilizing resources and it provides good business sense by better utilizing the equipment purchased.

Virtual Machines

The hypervisor provides a virtual, encapsulated hardware layer to the guests. This virtual hardware is comprised of a configuration file, some virtual disk files, and various other files that include configuration data such as non-volatile RAM (NVRAM).

Virtual machines provide many benefits in comparison to physical machines. Because virtual machines consist of configuration files and virtual disk files, they can easily be copied, easily backed up, or easily migrated from one physical system to another. On the other hand, to make a copy of a physical system, the use of some type of imaging software is needed. Once an image is captured from one physical system, it can be deployed to many other physical systems. However the best success in restoring the image occurs when restoring it to a similar, if not an exact duplicate piece of hardware. But because the virtual machine hardware is encapsulated, the hardware characteristics of the physical system, with the exception of the processor, do not come into play.

The virtual hardware presented allows the guests to run operating systems in the same fashion as operating systems running on physical hardware. The virtual hardware provided to guests includes a virtual Intel 440BX motherboard with a NS338 SIO chip, a Phoenix BIOS, up to four virtual CPUs, virtual RAM, virtual network controllers, virtual disk controllers (only SCSI is supported for storage in VMware ESX while IDE and SCSI are both supported in other VMware products), floppy devices, serial and parallel ports. Because the Intel 440BX chipset has limited support for devices, there are some configuration maximums. At the time of this writing, these maximums are as follows for VMware ESX:

- 4 SCSI controllers per virtual machine
- 15 Devices per SCSI controller
- 60 Devices per virtual machine (Windows) 60 Devices per virtual machine (Linux)
- 2TB SCSI disk space
- 4 virtual CPUs per virtual machine
- 65532MB of RAM per virtual machine
- 4 NICs per virtual machine
- 4 IDE devices per virtual machine
- 2 floppy devices per virtual machine
- 3 parallel ports per virtual machine
- 4 serial ports per virtual machine
- 65532MB space for virtual machine swap file
- 6 total virtual PCI devices
- 10 remote consoles to a virtual machine

NOTE

The virtual graphics card does not support all of the current technologies that physical graphics cards do, so some 3D and specialized graphics functions are not available in a virtual machine. An example of this is that Microsoft Vista's Aero Glass cannot run natively in a virtual machine.

Because the virtual hardware is, for the most part, constant, this allows for a very significant ability. If a virtual machine is created on one system vendor's platform, that system can be moved, copied, migrated, or restored on a completely different platform from another vendor. Virtual hardware will change from the guest operating system's perspective when CPU changes are realized. An example of this would occur when a system created on an Intel-based host is moved, copied, or restored to an AMD-based host. Most Windows operating systems do not have a significant issue with this, but it is a known issue with many Linux distributions. When Linux distributions are initially installed, many optimizations that are specific to the type of processor are installed in the guest. This issue is not isolated to a virtual machine. Additionally, when a virtual machine is copied, deployed, or moved, a new MAC address can be created for the virtual NIC, giving the appearance of a virtual hardware change. In cases like this, technologies such as Microsoft's activation process can be retriggered even by such a simple set of changes to the virtual hardware.

In the physical world, it is a very difficult process to move a system from one piece of hardware to a different piece of hardware and still retain the ability to function properly. This is especially true when the two pieces of hardware are from different vendors. In the VMware guest world, because guests are virtualized and their virtual hardware remains the same for the most part, it is very easy to move a guest from one vendor's system to another.

Not everything is sunshine and roses. Virtual machines do have shortfalls in that they cannot see the underlying hardware of the physical host server. And because of that, virtual machines in a VMware ESX environment cannot leverage devices such as specific controllers, specific graphics cards, USB devices or other such specialized devices.

Guest Operating Systems

To the guest operating system, the only hardware it sees is the virtual hardware presented by VMware ESX. Under VMware ESX, guests can operate a wide variety of operating systems. Depending on which operating system is to be run, the virtual machine should be configured for the appropriate type and version. By configuring the operating system type, VMware ESX can better optimize the way it interacts with the guest. Different types of operating systems would include Microsoft Windows, Linux, Novell Netware, Solaris or Other. To be more precise, VMware ESX supports several different versions of each of these operating systems. As seen in Figure 5.3, not all Windows operating systems are supported in VMware ESX 3.5. The figure shows that there is no support for Windows 3.x, Windows 9x or Windows ME. Another version of Windows that is no longer supported in the latest version of VMware ESX is Windows Server 2003 Web Edition.

When configuring the operating system type and version, not all operating system versions are available. VMware painstakingly tests and certifies different

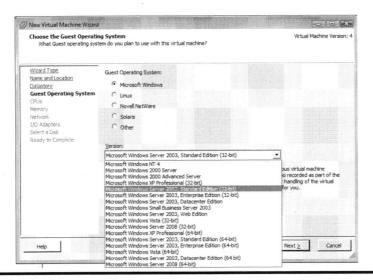

Figure 5.3   Supported Guest Operating Systems.

operating systems before providing them as an option in the configuration of a virtual machine.

Power State Options

Power on, power off, suspend, resume, and reset are the five power state options available to a virtual machine. Each of these states is different in how it impacts the VMware ESX host server and the guest operating systems. Each state also has different options with regard to configuring a virtual machine.

When a guest is powered on, the shares that it has been allocated, as well as the limits and reservations assigned are in full effect and add to the overall load and resource scheduling that VMware ESX has to perform. Configuration of virtual machines while powered on is not allowed, and as a result, the Virtual Infrastructure Client disables most hardware editing options in the Virtual Machine Configuration menu. The one hardware modification allowed is the ability to add additional hard disks. Resource shares can be modified while the guest is running, giving an administrator flexibility to adjust the properties for the guest accordingly. When a virtual machine is powered on, it cannot be migrated to another VMware ESX host unless one of the advanced features such as VMotion, HA or DRS are in place and ready to handle the migration.

When guests are powered off, they release the resources they were consuming back to VMware ESX. And while the virtual machine is powered off, changes are allowed to be made to the guest. Configuration changes such as changing the amount of memory allocated to the virtual machine and the like are also available. Guest shares can be modified in the off state, much like the on state, but they do not affect the host until the guest is powered on again. While a virtual machine is powered off, it may be migrated to another VMware ESX host in the farm without the requirement of any advanced features.

Virtual Machines that are suspended are treated a little differently than those that are powered on or powered off. Suspended virtual machines are similar to powered on virtual machines in the fact that they cannot have changes made to their virtual hardware. And they are like powered off virtual machines in that they can be migrated without the need for advanced features. One difference that sets suspended virtual machines apart is the fact that their memory is saved to disk, much like when an operating system saves its memory to disk when it goes into hibernation. This places the virtual machine in a frozen state and keeps the guest from consuming any resources.

To return a suspended guest to normal operation, the resume operation is performed. This powers on the virtual machine and restores the saved memory from disk to the virtual machine's live memory state. Once powered on, the guest operates as it did before it was suspended.

The reset operation will perform a reset of the virtual machine. If the guest operating system supports automatic shutdown, it will shutdown the guest and then restart it, providing the VMware Tools are installed. If VMware Tools are not installed or the guest operating system doesn't support automatic shutdown, this operation will reset the guest in the same fashion as pressing a reset button on a physical system. In this situation, the guest is not gracefully rebooted.

Snapshots and Virtual Disk Modes

Snapshots allow virtual disks to be configured as read-only, and any changes made to the virtual disk are stored in a separate disk file. One of the limitations of using snapshots is that they cannot be used when raw device mappings (RDMs) are used. Additionally, when virtual disks are in independent mode, snapshots are not allowed. Snapshots provide the ability for a virtual disk to be restored to a previous point in time, which can be very useful when testing patches, testing applications or doing some other repetitive type of testing or designing tasks.

In snapshot mode, when the virtual machine is powered off, the option to revert to snapshot will delete the difference disk and all changes are lost. If a snapshot is deleted, the changes will be applied to the virtual disk, committing any changes that are made. Snapshots are enabled by default on all disks that are not explicitly set to independent disk mode and aren't raw device mappings. The Snapshot Manager utility gives administrators the ability to manage virtual machine snapshots. This interface, as shown in Figure 5.4, shows any snapshots for the selected virtual machine as well as any descriptions for those snapshots. Using the "Go to" function, a snapshot can be selected, and the guest will be restored to the state of that snapshot. As mentioned, when deleting a snapshot, the changes will be applied to the virtual disk.

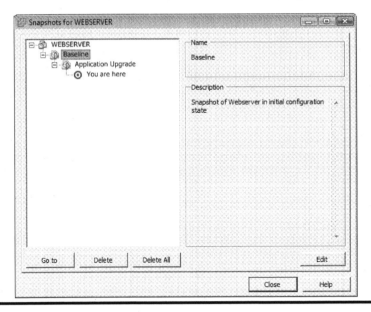

Figure 5.4   Snapshot Manager.

When a virtual disk is configured in independent disk mode, snapshots are not allowed. However, some of the same features offered through snapshot mode are still made available, depending on the independent disk mode configuration selected. If the independent disk is configured as persistent, changes are immediately written to the virtual disk. Persistent mode operates very similar to the normal mode of a virtual disk, but at the loss of snapshot capabilities. If the independent disk is configured as non-persistent, changes to the virtual disk are discarded when the virtual machine is powered off. Because non-persistent mode discards changes to the disk, the virtual machine will have the same operating system state each time the guest is powered on.

Depending on the operation desired, each of these disk modes can provide vital flexibility to the operation and use of a virtual machine.

VMware Tools

VMware Tools are a set of applications, services and system drivers that allow the guest operating system to communicate with VMware ESX. VMware Tools are designed to run on supported guest operating systems, but in some cases, they can run on unsupported guest operating systems as well. Additionally, the version of the guest tools is also very important. If a guest has been migrated from a VMware ESX 2.5 host to an ESX 3.5 host, the build version of the Tools is different and relative to the virtual machine hardware version. That being said, when upgrading ESX hosts, it is very important to upgrade the VMware Tools as well.

With VMware Tools in place, VMware ESX can better manage the guest environment. Also, VMware Tools provide for better graphics and network performance for the guest operating systems as well. In some guest operating systems, better mouse performance is also provided. When a guest has VMware Tools installed, additional features are made available through the Virtual Infrastructure Client such as copy and paste and drag and drop capabilities.

Because guests do not run with a dedicated CPU as in a physical system, time sync is somewhat different in a virtual machine. If a virtual machine's internal clock does not keep time correctly, it is said to have "drift". If enabled in the VMware Tools configuration, time synchronization with the VMware ESX host server is possible, allowing VMware Tools to keep the guest's time from drifting.

When a power state change is initiated, the tools interact with the guest operating system and run scripts to either power off or suspend the virtual machine. If a guest does not have VMware Tools installed, it is not possible to cleanly shutdown a virtual machine from the Virtual Infrastructure Client. In this case, it is only possible to power off the guest from the Virtual Infrastructure Client. If connected through a remote console to the guest operating system, a user could initiate shutdown to cleanly power off the guest. But when VMware Tools are installed, the guest can be given a shutdown command through the Virtual Infrastructure Client or through VirtualCenter, making it unnecessary to open a remote console to manually shutdown the virtual machine from within the guest operating system.

VMware Tools also provide the ability to connect and disconnect virtual devices and shrink the virtual disk file. Connecting and disconnecting virtual devices can be used to load data or enable network connections. In VMware ESX, the ability to shrink the virtual disk file can only be realized if the virtual disk was created using a non-default "thin-provisioned" method where the virtual disk does not occupy as much space as it has been allowed to grow to.

Creating a Virtual Machine

To begin to leverage the virtualization capabilities of VMware ESX, virtual machines must be created. The creation process can take place a number of different ways. Virtual machines can be created by using a wizard to manually create a VM, they can be imported into VMware ESX, they can be a cloned from an existing VM, or they can be deployed from a Template.

Using the New Virtual Machine Wizard is going to be the most likely starting place for virtual machine creation. When using the wizard, either typical or custom paths can be taken as shown in Figure 5.5. The typical path provides a basic configuration with the ability to choose the name, location, location of virtual disk, operating system type and version, number of processors, amount of memory, number of NICs and where they are connected to, and virtual disk size. The custom path adds to the typical path by allowing for the type of SCSI controller to be used,

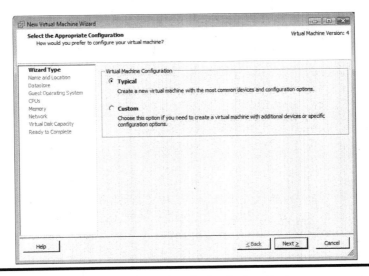

Figure 5.5 New Virtual Machine Wizard—Typical or Custom.

whether to create a disk, use an existing disk, use no disk at all, choose the disk mode, and which SCSI node to connect the disk to.

Importing a virtual machine can be accomplished using the Virtual Appliance—Import option. Appliances can be imported from local disks, a URL, or from the VMTN Website. For an appliance to be imported, it must be in the Open Virtual Machine Format (OVF). The VMware Converter Enterprise module in VirtualCenter can also migrate virtual machines that were created in other VMware products to the OVF format.

VMware Converter can also import a physical system or virtual machine to VMware ESX. This process is referred to as a Physical to Virtual (P2V) or Virtual to Virtual (V2V) conversion. VMware Converter has different options to create a virtual machine on VMware ESX. Physical or virtual systems can be imported by using an agent or a boot CD. The Converter Agent and boot CD work in the same manner, by making a copy of the system on the VMware ESX, while adding appropriate driver and configuration information for proper boot up of the new guest. Without these additions, the guest would likely not boot. VMware Converter can also import virtual machines of several different types into VMware ESX. Additional formats that VMware Converter supports include Microsoft Virtual PC guests and Symantec Ghost images.

Often times, to prevent having to perform the routine steps of installing, configuring, patching, and hardening a virtual machine, cloning can be used to speed up the process. With much of the initial setup work completed in a working guest, cloning can provide a very quick and easy way to make many similar virtual machines with identical configurations. Some settings can be modified for the destination virtual machine, but the internal operating system configuration is identical

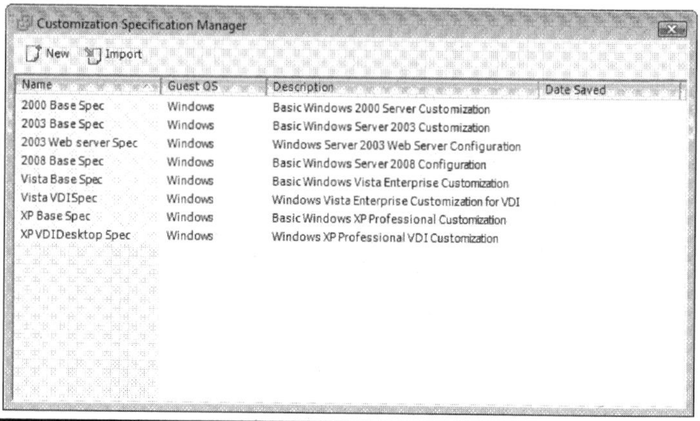

Figure 5.6   Customization Specification Manager.

to the source guest. As most networks do not allow identical systems to be on the network simultaneously, VMware has provided the ability to customize a destination guest to ensure that they are different and meet minimum requirements for being unique. VirtualCenter's customization wizard allows the ability to customize things such as the computer name, IP address, Windows Security Identifier (SID), and other options for destination virtual machines. As customizations are created, they may be saved for later use. In the VI Client, when connected to VirtualCenter, the Customization Specification Manager can be selected from the Edit pull down menu. The Customization Specification Manager is the central point of control for customization specifications. Each of the saved customization specifications are contained in this interface, as seen in Figure 5.6. Modifying these specifications, as well as making copies, is easily accommodated through this management tool. Additionally, previously generated Microsoft sysprep.inf configuration files can be directly imported to create new customization specifications. To be able to use these specifications for the deployment of Windows based guests, Microsoft's deployment tools for Windows XP, Windows 2000, and Windows Server 2003 are required. These must be downloaded and extracted to the appropriate location for VirtualCenter to be able to leverage this capability. Windows Vista guests and Windows Server 2008 guests do not require any additional files for customization.

TIP

Windows Server 2008 guests, by default, are not allowed to be customized with VMware ESX 3.5 Update 1. By changing a Windows Server 2008 guest version in the guest configuration to Windows Vista, it is possible to customize a Windows Server 2008 guest. When the customization has been completed, change the guest version back to Windows Server 2008.

Virtual machines can also be deployed from Templates. Templates are similar to virtual machines in configuration, but they are different in the fact that they cannot be powered on, and through compression techniques, they can take up less space than that of a normal virtual machine. Before a Template becomes a Template, it is a virtual machine. Once a virtual machine has been configured as desired, it can be converted into a Template. Because Templates cannot be powered on, their guest operating system configuration cannot be changed. When making a copy of a virtual machine from a Template, the process is similar to the cloning process of an existing virtual machine.

Installing a Guest Operating System

When creating a virtual machine using the New Virtual Machine Wizard, the resulting virtual machine will not yet have an operating system installed in the guest. Think of this guest as a bare, brand new system.

Installing a guest operating system typically requires booting from a CD or DVD ROM. VMware ESX, through the Virtual Infrastructure Client or through VirtualCenter, allows the use of a CD or DVD ROM loaded into the CD or DVD ROM drive on the host VMware ESX, through a client side CD or DVD ROM drive, or a datastore mounted ISO file. An ISO file is a copy of a CD or DVD ROM in a file format, rather than a physical disc. Using an ISO is preferred to using physical media since hard drives are faster than optical media drives.

When the virtual machine is powered on, the virtual CD/DVD ROM drive operates exactly as a physical CD/DVD ROM drive would on a physical system. From the standpoint of the user installing the operating system, it is treated the same. Installation of the guest operating system is performed in the same manner as it would be on a physical system.

Not all operating systems recognize the virtual hardware presented by VMware ESX. In some cases, such as when installing Windows 2000 Server or Windows XP Professional on VMware ESX, a floppy disk with appropriate SCSI drivers must be loaded. VMware makes these drivers available on their Website in the form of a virtual floppy disk file. By saving the virtual floppy disk file (.flp) on an accessible datastore and then attaching it to the guests' virtual floppy disk drive, it will be possible to add additional drivers during the installation process.

Installing VMware Tools

VMware provides the VMware Tools software package for each of the guest operating systems supported by VMware ESX. These tools and its included drivers are loaded on the VMware ESX host server in ISO format.

NOTE

For a virtual machine to be able to install the VMware Tools, it will have to have a CD-ROM drive configured in its virtual hardware configuration. Without a CD-ROM configured, the guest has no mount point for the VMware Tools virtual CD.

VMware Tools can be installed from within the VI Client, from within the VI Client Guest Console, or from the vmware-vmupgrade command-line executable. Using the VI Client or guest console, the tools can be installed interactively or automatically. When clicking on Install/Upgrade VMware Tools, a dialog box allows the choice of either type of installation. An interactive installation is the same as putting a CD-ROM in a workstation, letting AutoRun launch the setup, and answering the questions that are presented. The automatic installation works much like a silent installation used to push software remotely through scripting. When choosing the automatic installation, there is also a dialog box available to add additional options when installing the tools. The options include:

- "-u user" A username with valid credentials
- "-p password" The user's password
- "-n vmname" The display name of the virtual machine to have tools installed/upgraded
- "-h host" Attempt install/upgrade tools on all virtual machines on a specified host
- "-m maxpowerons" On a specified host, only power on this number of guests at a time
- "-o port" Specify a different port if the standard 902 is not used due to special configuration
- "-t maxpowerontime" Set the max time a guest is allowed to run if the guest does not automatically power off after a successful install/upgrade.
- "-s" Does not install/upgrade the tools, but upgrades the virtual hardware
- "-q" Perform the install/upgrade silently, displaying no status messages

The third option for installing or upgrading VMware Tools is using the vmware-vmupgrade command-line executable. This can be found in the C:\Program Files\ VMware\Infrastructure\VirtualCenter Server\ directory. The vmware-vmupgrade command is used with the above options to install or upgrade the tools to one or more guests.

In earlier versions of VMware ESX, the tools installation was invoked using the VMware Remote Console. When VirtualCenter 1.x was released, it provided the option to install or upgrade the tools using either the console or selecting the Install/Upgrade VMware Tools option on the actions menu for a guest. VirtualCenter 2.0 added the ability to automatically install the tools without the interaction of the guest, and VirtualCenter 2.5 has added to that capability. There is a new setting in a guest configuration (under Options/VMware Tools) to "Check and upgrade Tools before each power-on". For years, many administrators and users of the VMware VMTN Community Forums have expressed the need to have the ability to upgrade tools on many different guests with limited interaction. This was addressed in VirtualCenter 2.0 but with a shortfall—administrators had to manually invoke a tools upgrade process. With the additional capability of having the guest check the tools version for itself, administrators should never have to worry about upgrading VMware Tools again.

Summary

For the most part, virtual machines operate exactly the same way as physical machines. In some cases, virtual machines do not have the same capabilities as physical machines. In an ESX environment, virtual machines lack the ability to use specialized devices and cannot use USB devices natively.

These shortfalls are not without their advantages, as virtual machines can do many things that physical systems cannot. Physical systems cannot use snapshots or other differencing disk techniques. They also cannot be migrated easily from one system platform or vendor to another. And they cannot be created, imported, cloned, or deployed in the fashion virtual machines can.

Chapter 6

Interacting with VMware ESX

In most environments, servers aren't typically utilized as workstations. That being said, work by an administrator is not, for the most part, performed directly on a VMware ESX host. Different types of servers have different types of interfaces used to configure the applications and services running. An example of this would include using different native components, such as using the computer management snap-in for local or remote configurations of Windows systems. Through the console GUI, Windows servers can also be used as a workstation. Meanwhile, VMware ESX is not designed to be used as a workstation; however, one common method of thought is that it should be treated as an appliance.

VMware has provided several different ways to configure, manage, and leverage VMware ESX. Each of the different interfaces used to work with VMware ESX is tailored to the type of work to be performed. Some of these are for direct user interaction, while others provide a programming interface giving the ability to execute managed code against an ESX server or a VirtualCenter server. These interfaces include the VI Client, the Web Client, the VMware Remote Console (VMRC), the Console Operating System (COS), VI Software Development Kit (VI SDK), and the Common Information Module (CIM) SDK.

To use each of these interfaces, appropriate credentials are required. When connecting directly to VMware ESX, authentication is checked against local accounts located in the Console Operating System. It is possible to configure an ESX host to use Lightweight Directory Authentication Protocol (LDAP), and subsequently Microsoft Windows Active Directory, but this functionality is not included by default. Authentication in VirtualCenter is handled using Microsoft Windows based credentials. If the VirtualCenter server is not part of a domain, local accounts and local groups can be used. If the VirtualCenter server is part of a Windows Active Directory domain, domain users and domain groups can also be used for authentication.

VI Client

The most prevalent component used to manage ESX and VirtualCenter is the Virtual Infrastructure Client, or VI Client. It is a Windows client application that has the ability to manage an ESX server directly, or connect to VirtualCenter to manage a complete VI environment. Just as early versions of Windows brought a GUI to the masses, the VI Client has brought VMware ESX management and configuration to the masses as well. The VI Client can be seen connected to VirtualCenter in Figure 6.1. In previous releases of ESX, many advanced features had to be configured either through the web based MUI, or through the Linux based Service Console. Windows administrators without Linux experience could find the Service Console difficult to navigate. The VI Client originally came about to manage VirtualCenter 1.x. It gave administrators the ability to create, delete, clone, deploy, customize, and manage virtual machines, as well as migrate virtual machines with

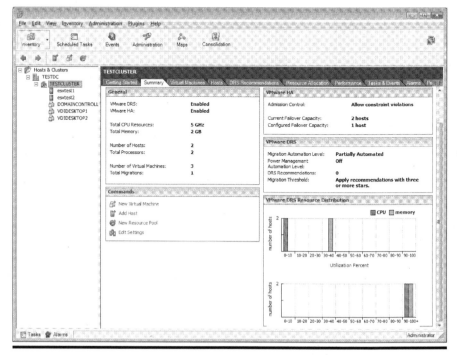

Figure 6.1   VI Client Connected to VirtualCenter.

Getting Started

If you need to access this host remotely, use the following program to install VMware Infrastructure client software. After running the installer, start the client and log in to this host.

- Download VMware Infrastructure Client

To streamline your IT operations with VMware Infrastructure, use the

Downloads		
VMware-viclient.exe		
17.0 of 54.3 MB (10.3 MB/sec) — 3 seconds remaining		

Clear	1 Download

If you need more help, please refer to our documentation library:

- VMware Infrastructure 3 Documentation

Figure 6.2   Download VMware Infrastructure Client.

VMotion technology. With two different interfaces for VMware ESX and an application for VirtualCenter, configuration and management of a VI environment could prove problematic. To address this, VMware added many new controls in the 2.0 and 2.5 VI Clients when managing ESX 3.0 and ESX 3.5 hosts.

The client can be downloaded either from the VMware site, from bundled media, or from an ESX server. To download the client from an ESX server, simply enter the IP address or hostname of the VMware ESX host in the address bar of a web browser, and click Download VMware Infrastructure Client. This is shown in Figure 6.2. There are some minimum requirements that must be satisfied before being able to run the VI Client. These requirements include some minimum hardware specifications, along with a list of supported operating systems that the client will run on. At the time of this writing, the VI Client is only designed to work on various Windows 32-bit operating systems. The previous version of the VI Client would install on some 64-bit operating systems, but this was not officially supported. VMware has stated that it will have a version of the VI Client that will be supported on several 64-bit operating systems sometime in 2008.

If the Microsoft .NET Framework 2.0 is not installed, the VI Client installer will automatically install it before it continues with the base client installation. The Microsoft .NET 2.0 Framework is a required component for the VI Client to operate, and cannot be omitted.

As shown in Figure 6.3, launching the VI Client will prompt for the IP address of an ESX host or VirtualCenter server, or its FQDN, along with a username and password. The VI Client is similar to other Windows based applications in that it has a common feel to it, giving it the ability to be easily used by just about anyone with experience using Windows applications. It contains the standard drop down menus found on most Windows applications, several dedicated action and view

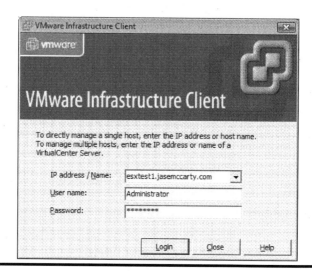

Figure 6.3   VMware Infrastructure Client Authentication.

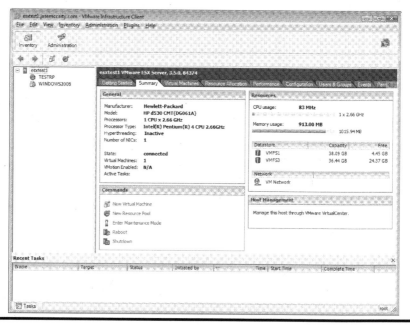

Figure 6.4   VI Client Connected to ESX Host.

buttons, and two panes that show either the ESX server or VirtualCenter farm, with objects on the left and inventory and property information on the right. The information displayed when connected to ESX is different than when connected to VirtualCenter. An illustration of VI Client connected to a VMware ESX host can be seen in Figure 6.4.

NOTE

When connected to VirtualCenter, many more options become available, as the VirtualCenter server provides additional features not available to a stand-alone ESX server.

There are several functional areas of the VI Client. When connecting to a VMware ESX host, these areas include Inventory and Scheduled Tasks. When connecting to VirtualCenter, additional areas are made available, including Events, Administration and Maps. Each of these areas allow for configuration of the host and guest systems.

Inventory

When working in the VI Client, most configuration and management is done when the Inventory area is selected. With the Inventory button selected, the different panes of the VI Client window behave differently. The left pane, by default, shows a list of ESX hosts and Clusters, including Resource Pools. The left pane can also display Virtual Machines, Networks, or Datastores, depending on which Inventory option is selected. As different hosts, clusters, resource pools, virtual machines, networks, and datastores are selected in the left pane, the options in the right pane change according to object type. The right pane can have several different layout types, and often include tabs for different types of functions or information summary. Some of the typical tabs include items such as:

- **Summary**: A general summarization of the selected object
- **Virtual Machines**: A list of virtual machines that are part of the object's hierarchy
- **Hosts**: A list of the hosts that are part of the object's hierarchy
- **DRS Recommendations**: Recommendations for DRS operations
- **Resource Allocation**: A list of the current resource allocations, and the ability to change resource allocation settings
- **Performance**: Current and historical performance metrics for the object, and its subcomponents
- **Configuration**: Used to configure all host level settings
- **Tasks & Events**: A list of events that have occurred for the object, or its subcomponents.
- **Alarms**: Displays the current alarm state of the object, or subcomponents, as well as the ability to configure custom alerting sequences
- **Console**: The local console of a virtual machine
- **Permissions**: Shows the current applied permissions for the object tree, as well as the ability to add and manage additional object level permissions

■ **Maps**: Provides a topological representation of how all hosts, guests, networks, or datastores are connected to each other.

Scheduled Tasks

This area displays the scheduled tasks list and allows for creation or modification of existing scheduled tasks. Adding a scheduled task is easy by using the New option, while modifying a task can be accomplished by choosing Properties. Information displayed includes name of the task, a short description, the last time the task was run, and when it is to be run again. There are many different types of tasks that can be scheduled. They include:

■ **Change the power state of a virtual machine**: power on, power off, shut down suspend, reset a guest
■ **Clone a virtual machine**: make a copy of a guest, with or without customization
■ **Deploy a virtual machine**: deploy a guest from a template
■ **Move a virtual machine with VMotion**: move a guest from one host to another
■ **Relocate a virtual machine**: move a guest to a different cluster, host, datastore, or resource pool
■ **Create a virtual machine**: create a new virtual machine
■ **Make a snapshot of a virtual machine**: create a guest snapshot
■ **Add a host**: add a host to a datacenter
■ **Export a virtual machine**: using the VMware Converter plug-in
■ **Scan for updates**: using the VMware Update Manager plug-in
■ **Remediate**: using the VMware Update Manager
■ **Import a virtual machine**: using the VMware Converter plug-in

Events

This area displays a list of all events that VirtualCenter has logged, with an additional pane to display the details of a specific event. A search feature gives the ability to filter events on particular search criteria, making it easier to find events that match times, description, type, target, task, or user. With all of this information available, it is easier to look at the historical events, leading up to, or after a point in time.

Administration

The Administration area provides an interface for information and configuration of roles, sessions, licenses, and system logs. The roles tab keeps all of the configuration settings for the role based access, and adds the flexibility to create custom permissions. The sessions tab displays all VirtualCenter sessions, including who and how long they were connected. A nice addition to this would include the IP address of the connected session. The licenses tab shows information provided by the VMware License Server in order to show the number of licenses in use, rather than having to launch and then browse the VMware License Server itself. The system log's tab shows VirtualCenter logging at a debugging level to allow an administrator to see a more detailed level of what is happening in VirtualCenter.

Maps

The Maps button accesses the VirtualCenter interactive topology maps, which can be seen in Figure 6.5. This area of VirtualCenter is not used for any configuration, but rather to display the topology of VMware ESX hosts, virtual machines, virtual networks, and datastores. The topology maps provide a visual image of how each of the different pieces are connected to one another, making it an effective tool when troubleshooting connectivity, as well as configuration abilities, given the current configuration of a VI3 environment.

Additional Buttons

When plug-ins for VirtualCenter are installed, additional information for these plug-ins can also be shown in the right pane, depending on how the plug-in was implemented. VMware Update Manager and the VMware Capacity Planner

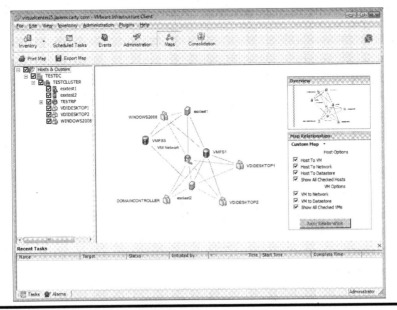

Figure 6.5 Virtual Infrastructure Client Maps.

(Consolidation) are two additional buttons that are added when these components are installed.

Web Client

In previous versions of ESX, there was a web interface referred to as the MUI. This is now referred to as VMware Virtual Infrastructure Web Access. Web Access does not include all the functions of the previous MUI, as it was primarily used to configure and monitor an ESX server, and to provide a launching point for the VMware Remote Console. This new interface allows for basic functions of virtual machine power control, management, event logging, and an embedded remote console. Because Web Access runs locally on each ESX server, only credentials local to the connected ESX host can be used. Opening a web browser and entering https://esxservername/ui/ in the address bar and entering valid credentials for the ESX server will begin the process.

Upon initial login, a list of guests on the ESX host is displayed on the left hand side, shown in Figure 6.6. When a guest has been selected, clicking on one

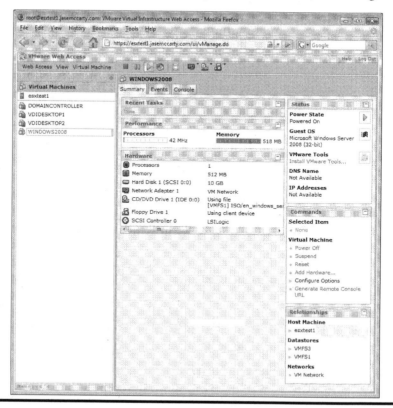

Figure 6.6 VMware Virtual Infrastructure Web Access.

of the guests' names will reveal the configuration and some utilization information for that guest in the Summary tab. The power off, suspend, power on, and reset buttons will modify the power state of the VM. The right hand pane includes different sub areas, including recent tasks, performance gauges, guest hardware configuration, guest status, and command functions. The Recent Tasks area shows information, but not limited to guest power state changes and reconfiguration. The Performance area shows guest CPU and memory utilization. The Hardware area displays the current virtual hardware configured for the guest. The Status area shows power state, guest OS (as configured), VMware Tools status, DNS name, and guest IP address. The Commands area has options to change the power state of the VM, add additional hardware to the guest, change configuration options, and generate a remote console URL. The Relationships area shows which ESX host the system is running on, which datastores the guest has virtual disks on, and which virtual network(s) the guest is configured to use. Additional tabs include the Events and Console tabs. The Events tab shows informational and warning messages pertaining to guest reconfiguration, power operations, and the like, including by who and when the event occurred. The Console tab provides a console window into the guest, giving the logged on user direct access to the virtual machine.

The web client is not as robust of an interface as the VI Client, but it does give a minimal amount of access when the VI Client is not available or cannot be used due to the operating system of the workstation being connected from.

VMware Remote Console (VMRC)

In early VMware ESX releases, the VMware Remote Console was used to connect through the MUI interface to the console of a guest system. When Virtual-Center 1.x was released, the remote console was integrated into VirtualCenter. In an ESX 2.x and VirtualCenter 1.x environment, it was possible to use either the VMware Remote Console or the embedded remote console in VirtualCenter to connect to guest systems. When ESX 3.0 and VirtualCenter 2.0 were released, the MUI went away because the VI Client had the ability to manage both ESX and VirtualCenter. As a result, the VMware Remote Console appeared to have gone away. As the MUI in previous versions of ESX allowed the ability to configure and manage guests through a web interface, the new VMware Web Access interface provided this ability as well. As a result, the VMware Remote Console changed from being a client side installed application to being a browser based plug-in. As can be seen in Figure 6.7, the VMRC is embedded in the VMware Web Access web user interface, or can be used by clicking on a link generated from a guest's Commands area in the Summary tab of a VMware Web Access user interface. When using the VMRC, depending on a user's rights as well as the options in the generated link, different abilities are offered with regard to the guest that the VMRC is connecting to. One benefit of using a URL to connect to a guest is the fact that a very small plug-in is required rather than the heavier VI Client with its

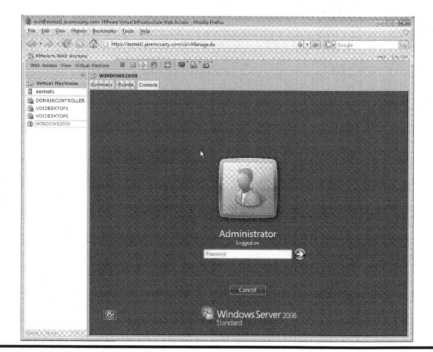

Figure 6.7   VMware Remote Console.

Microsoft .NET prerequisites. The two biggest drawbacks of using the VMRC are the fact that the level of guest control and configuration is limited and that when a guest moves from one ESX host to another in the farm, the generated URL is no longer valid.

Given the ease of use, coupled with the limited footprint, the VMRC can be very useful in the right environment.

Service Console (COS)

The Console Operating System, also referred to as the Service Console, allows administrators the ability to log in directly to a VMware ESX server. The Service Console runs a modified version of RedHat Enterprise Linux 3 Update 8. Not all of the features and commands available to a RHEL 3 U8 installation are available, but additional VMware ESX only commands have been added to the installation. These commands have been added to give administrators the ability to directly configure and manage the VMware ESX installation.

When at the physical console of VMware ESX, the only interface that can be seen is the Service Console. To log into the Service Console, an administrator must have valid credentials. By default, credentials for the server are configured locally. That being said, credentials that are valid for VirtualCenter most often are not valid on a VMware ESX host. With VirtualCenter using Windows based local or domain accounts and VMware ESX using local Service Console accounts, it is necessary to have multiple sets of credentials to manage both. Upon initial installation and configuration of VMware ESX, there is no functionality to use a common set of credentials.

To perform most operations in the Service Console, one must have elevated permissions. The primary user with elevated permissions is the administrative account called "root". The root account has full privileges in the Service Console. Access to the Service Console is not limited to the physical console of a VMware ESX host. The Secure Shell (SSH) protocol allows for remote console access to a VMware ESX host. However, the default security configuration of the ESX host specifically denies the root account remote access to the Service Console. For an administrator to remotely connect to the console of a host, one of two things will have to happen. The preferred method is to add additional user accounts to the Service Console and then change to the root account (using the command "su" to substitute user) to become root when necessary to perform administrative functions. This method allows for better security as well as better auditing when many users know the root password. A second method for remote access to the console is to modify the SSH service (SSH daemon) to allow remote connections by the root account. For obvious security reasons, this is not the preferred method.

Because the Service Console is a non-graphical interface, as shown in Figure 6.8, some of the functions that other interfaces provide are not available. For example, it is not possible to view the console of a guest while in the Service Console. Although the Service Console is limited by not being a graphical interface, it does provide for some very important functionality. As mentioned earlier, the Service Console has a set of VMware ESX specific commands installed. There are commands that are specific to the configuration of VMware ESX settings, like network configuration, firewall configuration, configuration of the VMkernel, VMware Consolidated Backup (VCB) commands, and more that give an administrator significant abilities in the Service Console. The command set is not limited though to VMware ESX host functions and settings. Additional commands allow for the starting, stopping, and modification of guests. While modifications to a guest configuration can be made through the VI Client, direct access to the Virtual Machine Configuration File (.vmx) can be edited using a text editor in the Service Console. UNIX and

Figure 6.8   VMware Service Console.

Linux administrators that are familiar with "vi" (visual editor) will be reassured to find that it is included in the Service Console. Administrators not familiar with vi can also use "nano" (a keyboard oriented editor) to modify .vmx or other configuration files.

The Service Console also provides a communications point for VMware ESX and VirtualCenter. The Service Console accepts remote commands. An example of this is the ability to invoke Storage VMotion through the use of the Remote Command Line Utility. The Remote Command Line Utility interacts with the Service Console by sending commands for the SC to act upon. Another new utility, currently in a Beta release, is the VMware VI Toolkit for Windows which provides Windows PowerShell scripting to pass commands to and from the Service Console to invoke actions. This new addition to the list of available interfaces has significant potential given that many Windows administrators have seen much success with the use of Windows PowerShell. The Service Console plays an important management role, given the ability to interact with additional management applications.

The Service Console is an important part of managing a VMware ESX host. This can easily be seen when a host has gone offline and there is no working network connectivity to the host. In situations such as this, a VMware ESX administrator must have knowledge of the location of configuration files and be fluent in the operation of commands in the Service Console.

VI SDK

The Virtual Infrastructure Software Development Kit (VI SDK) gives developers a way to interface with the Virtual Infrastructure Application Programming Interface (VI API). Developers can write applications that "call" the VI API, giving the ability to perform operations that are normally only available in a VMware client or interface. The VI API gives developers the flexibility to integrate the VMware architecture into other business applications or services. Several years ago, there existed some open-source code called the "VM Order Hotline". This Web-based application allowed a user to fill out a couple of web forms and then have a new VM customized and deployed. This Web application used the VI SDK and tied into the Virtual Infrastructure through API calls in order to deploy and customize the requested guest. The VI SDK provides documentation and sample code to get a developer started with writing code to directly manage ESX or a VirtualCenter server. By providing this interface into the Virtual Infrastructure, VMware has given developers additional flexibility to create their own applications which often times provide functionality that VirtualCenter or ESX server do not have. Another example of using the VI SDK is the Virtual MAC Tool. A developer compiled .NET code that would allow an administrator to change the MAC address on any powered off virtual machine in a Virtual Infrastructure farm.

One of the greatest benefits of providing administrators and developers with such a vessel is the fact that often time's developers can significantly enhance the capabilities that are found within the Virtual Infrastructure environment. The examples above show some usefulness of this, but a much better example would be the SVMotion plug-in application developed for VirtualCenter. When VMware originally introduced Storage VMotion (as DMotion) in the ESX 3.0 and VirtualCenter 2.0 release, it was a process that happened in the background. Through the use of developed plug-ins such as the Storage VMotion plug-in, a graphical interface was provided to perform Storage VMotion. This works well if the syntax is correct, but it can prove difficult to master. The SVMotion plug-in for VirtualCenter uses the VI SDK to communicate with the VI environment in order to determine the locations of virtual disks on datastores as well as find the available disk space on the datastores. The Remote Command Line utility does not provide the flexibility that the SVMotion plug-in does, thereby making an administrator's job that much easier. Had VMware not provided the VI SDK, tools such as this would not be possible.

CIM

VMware ESX also supports programmatic access via the Common Information Model (CIM) using the CIM SDK. What is the CIM? It is a common standard information model for the management of systems, networks, applications, and services. CIM also provides for the addition of vendor specific CIM extensions.

Utilizing CIM based communication and the CIM SDK, VMware has made it easier for system vendors and application providers to use common standards to control and work with VMware ESX. The current implementation of the CIM SDK primarily exposes the storage components of a VMware ESX host and any virtual machines. With VMware ESX supporting this piece of the Common Information Model, OEMs such as HP, Dell, IBM, and others have the ability to better manage an ESX host, as well as guest, storage configuration. This adds for better interoperability with OEM management and configuration software, like IBM Director for example. By allowing OEMs to talk directly to VMware ESX for storage management and configuration, it makes it very easy for OEMs to integrate Virtual Infrastructure into their management environment.

Summary

As an administrator, there are some interfaces that can directly access the Virtual Infrastructure environment, and there are others that work behind the scenes. Each interface, whether visually interactive or not, play an important part in the overall use, configuration, and management of VMware ESX and VirtualCenter.

Chapter 7

Console Operating System Explained

What is the Console Operating System?

The Console Operating System (COS), also called the Service Console (SC), is the component of VMware ESX that loads the VMkernel at system startup, while providing management functions during the operation of the VMkernel.

When exposed to VMware ESX for the very first time, people erroneously believe that VMware ESX runs "on top of Linux." In fact, the VMkernel is derived from Linux, but is not actually Linux. Confused? Don't be. This is a common misconception, and it comes from the fact that when booting up a VMware ESX host server, the primary console interface is a Linux type operating system.

When booting ESX, a GRUB loader menu is presented, as in Figure 7.1. The actual boot process shown in Figure 7.2 appears very similar to the booting of a Linux system. As the Console Operating System loads, it hands off control of the physical host server to the VMkernel. At that point, the COS transitions itself into a virtual machine. Even after the COS has transferred ownership of physical resources to the VMkernel, it may still appear as if it is the "loaded" operating system, but the VMkernel is in fact the one in control.

So if the VMkernel is in control, then why would we still need the Console Operating System? That's a good question. Most of the operational life of an ESX host is while it is up and running, and not during the initial boot up state. The COS serves a dual role with the boot portion being a small, albeit significant part. The COS is also used to manage and monitor VMware ESX.

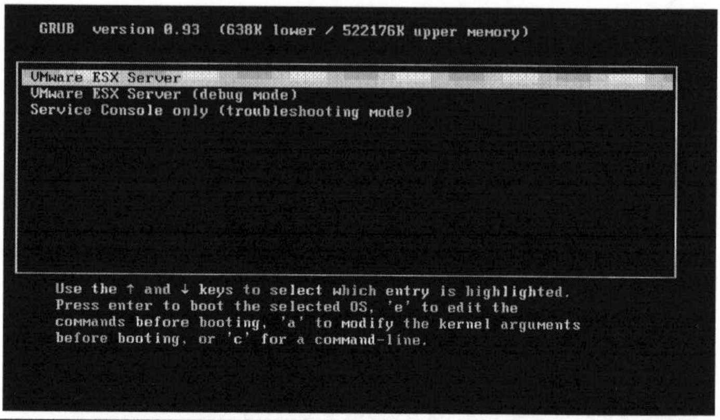

```
GRUB  version 0.93  (638K lower / 522176K upper memory)

 VMware ESX Server
 VMware ESX Server (debug mode)
 Service Console only (troubleshooting mode)




      Use the ↑ and ↓ keys to select which entry is highlighted.
      Press enter to boot the selected OS, 'e' to edit the
      commands before booting, 'a' to modify the kernel arguments
      before booting, or 'c' for a command-line.
```

Figure 7.1   VMware ESX GRUB Loader.

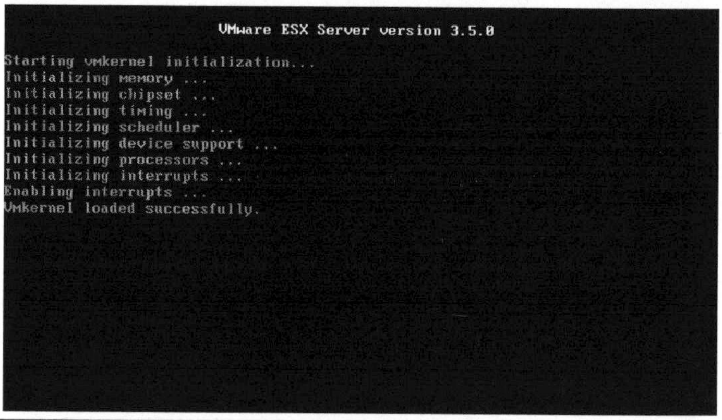

```
                    VMware ESX Server version 3.5.0
Starting vmkernel initialization...
Initializing memory ...
Initializing chipset ...
Initializing timing ...
Initializing scheduler ...
Initializing device support ...
Initializing processors ...
Initializing interrupts ...
Enabling interrupts ...
Vmkernel loaded successfully.
```

Figure 7.2   VMware ESX Boot Process.

The COS has a relatively small operating system footprint. In previous versions of VMware ESX, a distribution of Red Hat 7.2 was the basis for the Service Console's operating system. As with any operating system, newer releases provide better support for hardware, more efficient execution of instructions, greater program compatibility, better security, and additional features. Because Red Hat's original 7.2 distribution was released in October of 2001, when it came time to release VMware's latest and greatest version of ESX, it was important to provide a newer Console Operating System to provide for better hardware support, efficiency, security, and ability to work with newer management agents and other third-party applications. The current version of the Console Operating System is based on the Red Hat Enterprise Linux 3—Update 8 (RHEL3-U8) distribution, released in July of 2006.

With the COS being built on a Linux distribution, user interaction is very similar to that of an everyday version of Linux. Much like Linux, most of the COS file locations are the same with some additions for VMware specific commands and services. The folder structure off the root of the file system for the most part looks identical to a Linux installation. Administrators that have had experience with Linux can easily navigate around the Service Console because it looks and acts very familiar to them.

Even though the COS has ties to the Red Hat Enterprise Linux 3 distribution, administrators should not treat it the same. The COS is designed for the purpose of booting and managing the VMkernel, and as a result, it does not share all of the same commands or services available to a RHEL3 installation. It is a very strenuously recommended practice to not install graphical window managers like KDE and GNOME in the COS installation. Keeping the installation to a minimum is typically best. Adding overhead of additional, non-VMware provided applications can have a significant impact on the performance of the COS, resulting in a wide variety of undesirable results.

Having ties to Linux is not without benefits though. Every major OEM vendor has management agents for RHEL3, and subsequently, can test and certify their agents to run on VMware ESX. Whether it is IBM's Director or Dell's OpenManage monitoring platform, they have the ability to monitor the ESX server much in the same way as they monitor a Linux server. The new VMware CIM SDK will allow OEMs and 3rd-party vendors the ability to monitor components of VMware ESX, and perhaps more so VMware ESXi, without having to use a local agent running in the COS. When security issues arise, updates and patches for Red Hat Enterprise Linux 3 should not be applied to the COS, as they could potentially cause issues or break other functionality. Instead, VMware provides all updates and patches for the COS and the ESX Server.

How to Access the COS

For the Console Operating System to be of any value there has to be one or more methods to access it. The first and foremost starting place to access the COS is at the physical console of the ESX host server. In the paradigms of good security, as well as by default, this is the only location the primary administrator account (root) can directly access the COS. At first glance, there doesn't appear to be a way to login to the VMware ESX host console. Instead of providing a login screen, the console provides information about the ESX host. Figure 7.3 shows a typical ESX informational screen. To actually login to the console, a virtual terminal must be opened. By pressing the ALT key and one of the Function keys (F1-F6), a login prompt is presented.

NOTE

To return to the ESX information screen, press ALT-F11. To show a non-interactive VMkernel log on the screen, press ALT-F12.

```
        VMware ESX Server version 3.5.0

        esxtest1.jasemccarty.com (192.168.1.101)

  To manage this ESX Server, use any browser to open the URL:

  http://192.168.1.101/

  To open the ESX Server console, press Alt-F1.
  To return to this screen, press Alt-F11.
```

Figure 7.3   VMware ESX Informational COS Screen.

```
 root@esxtest1/
[root@esxtest1 /]#
```

Figure 7.4   SSH Session Via PuTTY Console Screen.

The COS is also available remotely using various tools and protocols. In the early days of Linux systems, a popular protocol called TELNET (TELecommunication NETwork) was used to connect to the console remotely. Unfortunately, the TELNET protocol is not secure and passes communication traffic in a clear text, unencrypted fashion. As a result of this vulnerability, the Secure Shell (SSH) protocol was created. Using the SSH protocol with a SSH client (PuTTY is shown in Figure 7.4) will provide a similar experience to TELNET, but securely. This is because the SSH client and the SSH server (or daemon) connect to each other using a secure channel. One security configuration of the SSH daemon allows or disallows remote connections by the administrator account. This provides an additional layer of security should the SSH traffic be compromised, and it also provides better control and auditing of elevated access. The "su" (substitute user) command will allow a user to change the ownership of the interactive session they are logged in with to the root user. As stated before, this allows for better network security. But how does it control auditing? Anytime a user logs in, through any protocol method, the login session is captured and logged. That being said, if Joe logs in to a host and then issues the "su" command and makes changes, the audit logs will show that Joe logged in, then "became" root, and so on.

If configured to do so, the COS can allow many different types of connections. Connections to the COS can be made through several different protocols and clients. Because VMware ESX has an SSH daemon running, not only is SSH available, so is Secure Copy (SCP). Secure Copy is a network file copy utility that allows for a connection that is similar to a SSH connection, but is used for the purpose of file transfer rather than a terminal session. SCP can be used to copy configurations from or to the COS, as well as copy various 3rd-party agents or applications, or various other data including things like CD/DVD ROM image files (ISOs) of your favorite operating systems.

Many OEMs provide management agents that are certified to run on VMware ESX. They in fact do not run "on" VMware ESX, but rather in the Service Console. These agents communicate with the Service Console to perform various duties such as system monitoring, system management, backup and the like. One such agent is the HP Enterprise Discovery agent. This agent is installed in the Service Console and provides inventory and performance metrics to an HP Enterprise Discovery server.

The Service Console is also an excellent place to start proactive VMware ESX monitoring, or a great place to start troubleshooting a failed ESX host server. Because communication between the ESX host and the VirtualCenter server are coordinated through the Service Console, there are several log files that can be reviewed to see if there are any looming problems before a crash, or to spot any issues after a crash. Some of the places that can be looked at are:

■ VMkernel Related logging
/var/log/vmkernel—Keeps information about the host and guests
/var/log/vmkwarning—Collects VMkernel warning messages
/var/log/vmksummary—Collects statistics for uptime information
■ Host Agent logging
/var/log/vmware/hostd.log—Information on the agent and configuration of an ESX host
■ Service Console logging
/var/log/messages—Contain general log messages for troubleshooting. This also keeps track of any users that have logged into the Service Console, and their actions.
■ Web Access logging
/var/log/vmware/webAccess—Web access logging for VMware ESX

- Authentication logging
  var/log/secure—Records all authentication requests
- VirtualCenter agent logging
  /var/log/vmware/vpx—Logs for the VirtualCenter Agent
- Virtual Machine logging—Look for a file named vmware.log in the directory of the configuration files of a virtual machine.

Commands

Other than acting as a bootstrap for the loading of the VMkernel, the Service Console really shines as a management interface for VMware ESX. There are a wide variety of commands available to configure VMware ESX from the command-line.

Service Console Configuration and Troubleshooting Commands

- **esxcfg-advcfg**—VMware ESX Server Advanced Configuration Option Tool
  Provides an interface to view and change advanced options of the VMkernel.
- **esxcfg-boot**—VMware ESX Server Boot Configuration Tool
  Provides an interface to view and change boot options, including updating initrd and GRUB options.
- **esxcfg-configcheck**—VMware ESX Server Config Check Tool
  Checks the configuration file for format updates.
- **esxcfg-info**—VMware ESX Server Info Tool
  Used primarily for debugging, this command provides a view into the state of the VMkernel and Service Console components.
- **esxcfg-module**—VMware ESX Server Advanced Configuration Option Tool
  This command provides an interface to see which driver modules are loaded when the system boots, as well as the ability to disable or add additional modules.
- **esxcfg-pciid**—VMware ESX Server PCI ID Tool
  This utility rescans the PCI ID list (/etc/vmware/pci.xml), and loads PCI identifiers for hardware so the Service Console can recognize devices.
- **esxcfg-resgrp**—VMware ESX Server Resource Group Manipulation Utility
  Using this command, it is possible to create, delete, view, and modify resource group parameters and configurations.
- **esxupdate**—VMware ESX Server Software Maintenance Tool
  This command it used to query the patch status, as well as apply patches to an ESX host. Only the root user can invoke this command.
- **vdf**—VMware ESX Disk Free Command
  As df works in Linux, vdf works in the Service Console. The df command will work in the Service Console, but will not show free disk space on VMFS volumes.

NOTE

Using vdf –h will show the file sizes with M for megabytes and G for gigabytes, rather than in a raw byte format.

- **vmkchdev**—VMware ESX Change Device Allocation Tool
  This tool can assign devices to either the Service Console or VMkernel, as well as list whether a device is assigned to the SC or VMkernel. This replaced the vmkpcidivy command found in previous versions of VMware ESX.
- **vmkdump**—VMkernel Dumper
  This command manages the VMkernel dump partition. It is primarily used to copy the contents of the VMkernel dump partition to a usable file for troubleshooting.
- **vmkerrcode**—VMkernel Status Return Code Display Utility
  This command will decipher VMkernel error codes along with their descriptions.
- **vmkfstools**—VMware ESX Server File System Management Tool
  This utility is used to create and manipulate VMFS file systems, physical storage devices on an ESX host, logical volumes, and virtual disk files.
- **vmkiscsi-device**—VMware ESX iSCSI Device Tool
  Used to query information about iSCSI devices.
- **vmkload_mod**—Vmkernel Module Loader
  This application is used to load, unload, or list, device drivers and network shaper modules into the VMkernel.
- **vmkloader**—VMkernel Loader
  This command loads or unloads the VMkernel.
- **vmkpcidivy**—VMware ESX Server Device Allocation Utility
  This utility in previous versions of VMware ESX, allowed for the allocation of devices to either the Service Console, or the VMkernel. In VMware ESX 3.0, this utility is deprecated, and should only be used to query the host bus adapter allocations using the following: **vmkpcidivy -q vmhba_devs**
- **vmkuptime.pl**—Availability Report Generator
  This PERL script creates HTML that displays uptime statistics and downtime statistics for a VMware ESX host.
- **vmware-hostd**—VMware ESX Server Host Agent
  The vmware-hostd script acts as an agent for an ESX host and its virtual machines.
- **vmware-hostd-support**—VMware ESX Server Host Agent Crash Information Collector
  This script collects information to help determine the state of the ESX host after a hostd crash.

Networking and Storage Commands

- **esxcfg-firewall**—VMware ESX Server Firewall Configuration Tool
  Provides an interface to view and change the settings of Service Console firewall.

- **esxcfg-hwiscsi**—VMware ESX Server Hardware iSCSI Configuration Tool
  Provides an interface to allow or deny ARP redirection on a hardware iSCSI adapter, as well as enable or disable jumbo frames support.

- **esxcfg-linuxnet**—No specific name
  This command is only used when troubleshooting VMware ESX. It allows the settings of the vswif0 (virtual NIC for the Service Console under normal operation), to be passed to the eth0 interface when booting without loading the VMkernel. Without the VMkernel loading, the vswif0 interface is not available.

- **esxcfg-mpath**—VMware ESX Server multipathing information
  This command allows for the configuration of multipath settings for Fibre Channel and iSCSI LUNs.

- **esxcfg-nas**—VMware ESX Server NAS configuration tool
  This command is an interface to manipulate NAS files systems that VMware ESX sees.

- **esxcfg-nics**—VMware ESX Server Physical NIC Information
  This command shows information about the Physical NICs that the VMkernel is using.

- **esxcfg-rescan**—VMware ESX Server HBA Scanning Utility
  This command initiates a scan of a specific host bus adapter device.

- **esxcfg-route**—VMware ESX Server VMkernel IP Stack Default Route Management Tool
  This can set the default route for a VMkernel virtual network adapter (vmknic).

- **esxcfg-swiscsi**—VMware ESX Server Software iSCSI Configuration Tool
  The command line interface for configuring software based iSCSI connections.

- **esxcfg-vmhbadevs**—VMware ESX Server SCSI HBA Tool
  Utility to view LUN information for SCSI host bus adapters configured in VMware ESX.

- **esxcfg-vmknic**—VMware ESX Server VMkernel NIC Configuration Tool
  Configuration utility for managing the VMkernel virtual network adapter (vmknic).

- **esxcfg-vswif**—VMware ESX Server Service Console NIC Configuration Tool
  Configuration utility for managing the Service Console virtual network adapter (vswif).

- **esxcfg-vswitch**—VMware ESX Server Virtual Switch Configuration Tool
  Configuration utility for managing virtual switches and settings.

■ **esxnet-support**—VMware ESX Server Network Support Script.
This script is used to perform a diagnostic analysis of the Service Console and VMkernel's network connections and settings.

NOTE

This script originated in VMware ESX 3.0, but has become broken in ESX 3.5 Update 1 due to some changes in the esxcfg-vswitch –l and esxcfg-vmknic –l commands. A VMTN Community member (ThalesSMS) has some instructions on how to correct this in ESX 3.5. The post is located here: http://communities.vmware.com/message/885344

■ **vmkping**—Vmkernel Ping
Used to ping the VMkernel virtual adapter (vmknic)
■ **vmkiscsi-ls**—VMware ESX iSCSI Target List Tool
This command shows all iSCSI Targets that the iSCSI subsystem knows about, including Target name, Target ID, session status, host number, bus number, and more.
■ **vmkiscsi-tool**—VMware ESX iSCSI Tool
This command will show the properties of iSCSI initiators.
■ **vmkiscsi-util**—VMware ESX iSCSI Utility
This command will display LUN Mapping, Target Mapping, and Target Details.

VMware Consolidated Backup Commands

■ **vcbMounter**—VMware Consolidated Backup—Virtual Machine Mount Utility
This utility is used to mount a virtual machine's virtual disk file for the purpose of backing up its contents.
■ **vcbResAll**—VMware Consolidated Backup—Virtual Machine Restore Utility
This utility is used to restore multiple virtual machines' virtual disk files.
■ **vcbRestore**—VMware Consolidated Backup—Virtual Machine Restore Utility
This utility is used to restore a single virtual machine's virtual disk files
■ **vcbSnapAll**—VMware Consolidated Backup—Virtual Machine Mount Utility
This utility is used to backup one or more virtual machines' virtual disk files.
■ **vcbSnapshot**—VMware Consolidated Backup—Snapshot Utility
This utility is used to backup a virtual machine's virtual disk files.

- **vcbUtil**—VMware Consolidated Backup—Resource Browser and Server Ping
  This utility provides different information, depending on argument. The ping argument attempts to log into the VirtualCenter Server. The resource pools argument lists all resource pools, and the vmfolders argument lists folders that contain virtual machines.
- **vcbVmName**—VMware Consolidated Backup—VM Locator Utility
  This utility performs a search of virtual machines for VCB scripting. It can list individual VM's, all VM's that meet a certain criteria, or VM's on a specific ESX host.
- **vmres.pl**—Virtual Machine Restore Utility
  This PERL script is depreciated, and vcbRestore should be used instead.
- **vmsnap.pl**—Virtual Machine Mount Utility
  This PERL script is depreciated, and vcbMounter should be used instead.
- **vmsnap_all**—Virtual Machine Mount Utility
  This script is depreciated, and vcbSnapAll should be used instead.

Summary

The Service Console, or Console Operating System, plays a very important role in the initial boot up process and continues with the operation and management of a VMware ESX host. With ties to Red Hat Enterprise Linux, administrators that have experience in a Linux environment will find themselves at home using and navigating through the Service Console. As a specially compiled operating system for VMware ESX, the Service Console can be used for advanced configuration and troubleshooting that in some cases cannot be done through a graphical user interface. As a result, VMware administrators should take it upon themselves to become familiar with it.

Chapter 8

Networking

Just as CPU, memory, and disk are essential, networking plays a vital role in the capabilities and flexibility of VMware ESX. In VMware ESX, networking is a highly flexible piece of the resource puzzle.

Networking Architecture

VMware ESX provides for true enterprise network capabilities. These capabilities are implemented in VMware ESX and configured and managed with VirtualCenter. The capabilities of VMware ESX networking offer flexible configurations that work well with both small and large networks. This networking can be designed to work in many ways, giving the best fit for production, test, and development environments. Using virtual networking, VMware ESX can easily accommodate networks that are simple, complex, or completely isolated.

Virtual networking behaves in a very similar way to physical networking, without requiring additional network hardware. Virtual switches allow guests on the same VMware ESX host the ability to communicate with each other using the same protocols used on physical switches. From a networking perspective, virtual NICs behave the same as physical NICs, and they are also assigned a MAC address and an IP address just like physical NICs.

Virtual Network Interface Cards

Virtual NICs provide connectivity for guests, the Service Console and the VMkernel. There are a total of five types of virtual NICs, three of which are reserved for virtual machines, one for the Service Console and one for the VMkernel.

vswif

In VMware ESX 3.x, the Service Console uses a virtual NIC to communicate with the rest of the network, and most importantly with VirtualCenter for VMware ESX management. This is a departure from the way that VMware ESX 2.x allowed the Service Console to talk to the network and VirtualCenter. In VMware ESX 2.x, the Service Console, by default, used the first physical adapter recognized during the VMware ESX installation. This NIC was configured as eth0, much the same as that of a physical NIC in a Linux installation. Because this was a dedicated NIC automatically configured at installation and without additional configuration, it was a single (non-redundant) connection to the network. Adding redundancy to this configuration meant taking away another NIC from the VMkernel and as a result from the guests on the host. The new vswif virtual adapter gives VMware ESX 3.x the ability to bind the Service Console's connectivity to one or more physical adapters through a virtual switch, resulting in redundancy and the ability to operate in conjunction with other virtual NICs on one or more virtual switches.

vmknic

This virtual adapter is used by the VMkernel to facilitate various network functions like remote console communication, VMotion, NFS and software based iSCSI clients.

Prior to VMware ESX 3.x, the only remote storage available was that of Fibre Channel based storage. VMware ESX 3.x added the capability to attach Network File System (NFS) exports and software based Internet Small Computer Systems Interface (iSCSI) presented Logical Unit Number (LUNs) without any additional hardware. The ability to add remote storage, without requiring the use of an expensive Storage Area Network (SAN), has added to the appeal and flexibility of VMware ESX 3.x.

With VMware ESX 2.x, in order to utilize VMotion, a separate virtual switch was required. Often times, this meant yet another dedicated physical adapter. In addition to this added virtual switch, one port of any switch that a VMotioned guest was on would also be utilized. With VMware ESX 3.x, VMotion has been moved to the virtual switch that the VMkernel utilizes, and it no longer allocates a port on the virtual switches that guests are attached to.

vlance

This virtual device emulates an AMD Lance PCNet32 Ethernet adapter, which can be recognized easily by most 32-bit operating systems. When a guest is configured with a "flexible" network adapter, this virtual device is used until the VMware Tools are installed in the guest operating system.

vmxnet

This is a paravirtualized device that is only made available to a guest once VMware Tools is installed in the guest operating system. The vmxnet virtual adapter is a high performance adapter that is aware it is operating in a virtualized environment.

e1000

Like the vlance adapter, the e1000 virtual adapter emulates a specific type of physical adapter, in this case, an Intel e1000 Ethernet adapter. This device can be used in 32-bit guests, but is the default virtual adapter type in 64-bit virtual machines.

Each of these adapter types is a Layer 2 Ethernet adapter device, and each have their own MAC address and unicast, multicast and broadcast filters.

These virtual adapters do not have to worry about speed or duplex settings like physical adapters. As an example, in VMware ESX 2.x, the vlance and vmxnet adapters reported speeds of 10Mbps and 1Gbps respectively to their guest operating system, when in fact they operated at the same speeds, albeit, the vmxnet device was more efficient. The reason that virtual adapters do not need to worry about speed and duplex is simply because the virtual network data communications take place in the VMware ESX host's RAM. Because of this, collisions and other errors are not possible due to the immediate transfer of data.

Virtual Switches

The other main networking component in VMware ESX is the virtual switch. The virtual switch implementation in VMware ESX can behave very much like a physical switch and in many cases unlike a physical switch. VMware uses the term "built to order" to describe how virtual switches are created at run time. Virtual switches are modular in that they only load the appropriate components when they are created. The modular components of a virtual switch include:

■ A core Layer 2 forwarding engine—Disregarding the types of physical and virtual adapters connected to it for speed and precision, the forwarding engine only processes Layer 2 Ethernet headers.
■ VLAN tagging, stripping and filtering components
■ Layer 2 segmentation offload, checksum and security components

Because VMware chose a modular approach, vendors will have the ability to design components that can be added to a VMware ESX installation, thereby providing for additional capabilities.

Virtual switches are similar to physical switches in that they:

- Keep an up-to-date lookup table for MAC addresses and ports
- Support assigning a VLAN to a single port—called virtual switch tagging
- Support assigning multiple VLANs, behaving like a trunk port—called virtual guest tagging
- Can use a virtual switch's promiscuous mode to allow for the copying of packets to a mirror port, making it possible to utilize network monitoring applications

Virtual switches are different than physical switches in that:

- It is not necessary to "learn" unicast addresses or use IGMP snooping to learn multicast information.
- There is no need for the spanning tree protocol because virtual switches cannot be connected to each other—providing isolation of virtual switches and mitigating the risk of network loops.
- Have a maximum of 1016 virtual ports, similar to physical ports, that are directly aware of the configuration of virtual adapters connected to them, and do not have to learn any addresses for the forwarding table.
- Have port groups, which capture the settings for a switch port, similar to a Cisco SmartPort feature in some switches. Port groups give virtual switches the ability to provide VLAN capabilities to guests when the guests are connected to the port group rather than to the virtual switch directly.

NOTE

In VMware ESX 2.x, virtual switches had a limitation of 32 ports with the necessity of having one port available for VMotion if that feature was going to be utilized. This presented a significant bottleneck when the number of virtual NICs on a host was greater than or by a factor of 32. With VMware ESX 2.x, in order to present more than 32 ports to the virtual NICs, it was necessary to have additional virtual switches and associated physical adapters. This added to the complexity of an installation, especially when it was desired to have redundancy on each virtual switch.

Virtual switches act as "good citizens" in that there are some things that they could do, but do not. It would be very easy for VMware to allow within the networking of a single host the ability for a guest connected to a virtual switch in one VLAN to talk to a guest connected to the same virtual switch in another VLAN. This would allow for the same expedient communication as two guests on the same virtual switch in the same VLAN. However, a good example of an exploit that this could introduce would be if a guest were in a demilitarized zone (DMZ) VLAN, and another guest on the same virtual switch was on an internal VLAN, it would be easy to cross over and exploit the internal guest. To ensure that data is contained in the appropriate VLAN, private copies of frame data are used to handle forwarding or filtering decisions.

Figure 8.1 displays a virtual switch with virtual adapters for guests and the Service Console. The grouping displayed in the figure shows that virtual machine adapters are attached to the switch using a port group, while the Service Console is connected to the Service Console Port and the VMkernel is connected to a VMkernel port. The Service Console and VMkernel cannot be connected to port groups. The Service Console and VMkernel ports, like port groups, can be assigned a VLAN ID should it be necessary.

As shown, virtual switches have many characteristics of physical switches, combined with characteristics that enhance the capabilities of networking within a VMware ESX host. With the flexibility of virtual switch tagging, virtual guest tagging, mirror port capability and a lookup table, they are very much like a physical switch. Adding to the feature set of physical switches, they do not have the overhead of learning unicast or multicast addresses, have no need for spanning tree protocol, have a significantly greater number of ports that are virtual NIC aware and have port groups.

Physical Network Adapter Teaming and Link Aggregation (IEEE 802.3ad)

The IEEE 802.3ad standard addresses the ability to link multiple network adapters together to form a network adapter team which is called a bond in the VMware ESX environment. Benefits of using physical network adapter teaming and link

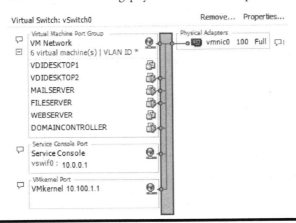

Figure 8.1   VMware Virtual Switch.

aggregation play an important part in the redundancy and performance of a VMware ESX host.

Load Balancing

The first benefit of the 802.3ad standard, often called NIC Teaming, is load balancing. By teaming or bonding two network adapters to a virtual switch, overall network throughput is increased by the speed of the second. In a two adapter, 1Gbps configuration, the total available bandwidth is doubled to 2Gbps. In a two adapter configuration where there is a 1Gbps adapter and a 100Mbps adapter, the total available bandwidth is 1.1Gbps.

A basic load balancing configuration can be seen in Figure 8.2. There are two virtual machines connected to a single virtual switch that is configured to use two physical adapters in a teamed NIC configuration. At any point, traffic can flow from Virtual Machine 1 to either Physical NIC 1 (pNIC1) or Physical NIC 2 (pNIC2), as well as from Virtual Machine 2 through either pNIC1 or pNIC2.

Because VMware ESX has no control over which physical adapter traffic enters, inbound load balancing is not truly even across adapters. Load balancing at the incoming level would require a properly configured physical switch to evenly balance data. However, as network traffic is flowing outward, VMware ESX balances the data evenly across the two or more physical NICs, based on the destination address. Data, however, is not sent out through both NICs simultaneously. Two 1Gbps physical adapters in a NIC team could support up to 2Gbps of outgoing data while only supporting up to 1Gbps for any particular data stream.

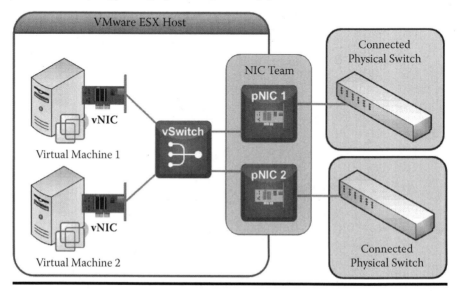

Figure 8.2   Virtual Switch Load Balancing.

Fault Tolerance

The second benefit of the 802.3ad standard provides for fault tolerance. By teaming two or more physical adapters, if there is a physical or link failure on one of the physical adapters, traffic is no longer routed to that physical adapter.

The illustration in Figure 8.3 displays a configuration where a team of two physical adapters are connected to the network via two separate physical switches. Should the connection to one of the physical switches fail, connectivity is not lost, as all traffic is routed through the remaining physical adapter. In physical systems, it is common to use NIC teaming to provide redundancy in a similar configuration. NIC teaming is not necessary in virtual machines when the virtual switch is configured with teamed physical adapters. This is an added benefit for virtual machines because each guest does not have to have teaming installed in the guest operating system; it can instead be done at the VMware ESX host level. Microsoft versions up to Windows Server 2003 do not support NIC teaming natively, but require specialized drivers from the network adapter vendor.

VLAN Tagging (IEEE 802.1Q)

When designing a network, it is often a requirement to isolate a small number or large number of devices in a Virtual Local Area Network, or VLAN. VLANs provide the ability to segment a network virtually, instead of physically. In a small environment using a basic unmanaged switch, all physical devices connected to that switch would be in the same physical Local Area Network, or LAN. If one of

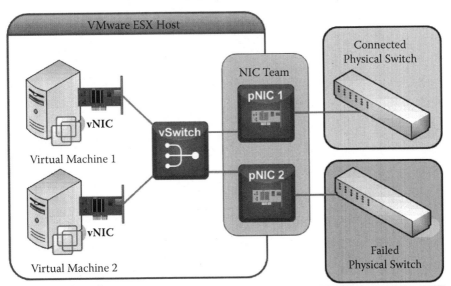

Figure 8.3   Virtual Switch Failover.

those devices were moved to another switch on a different segment of the network, it would at that point become part of a separate LAN segment.

VLANs provide network administrators the ability to organize network connections virtually. In the above mentioned single physical switch configuration, all devices would receive the same broadcast traffic. Devices on the second switch mentioned would not receive the same broadcast traffic because those devices are on a different physical segment. Using managed switches, VLANs come into play. Using VLANs, a device could be moved from one switch to another switch in a different location and still be on the same VLAN, depending on the switch configuration.

Often times, VLANs are associated with IP segments, and as a result, can be confused as being the same. It is possible for a VLAN to only include a portion of an IP subnet range, or even span across multiple IP subnet ranges. IP subnets are based on Layer 3, or the Network Layer of the TCP/IP model. VLANs are based on Layer 2, or the Data Link Layer of the TCP/IP model. In the physical world, VLANs can be dynamic or static. Dynamic VLANs operate in the sense that when a device is connected to a network port, through the use of network management software, the MAC address is queried upon connection and the VLAN assigned to the port corresponds to the appropriately assigned VLAN for the device's MAC address. VMware ESX operates in the same fashion of a static VLAN. In a physical environment, when a device is connected to a port, that device is then attached to the VLAN assigned to that port.

Virtual switches can utilize VLAN configurations in several ways. Depending on the types of guests, as well as the requirements of the guest and its use will determine which configuration is best.

External Switch Tagging

External switch tagging, or EST, can be described as when a VMware ESX host is connected to one or more network connections which have a VLAN assigned at the physical switch to which the host is connected to. Out of the box, VMware ESX natively supports EST. Depending on the size of the network and its topology, EST may be the extent of VLAN support needed for VMware ESX.

Figure 8.4 displays a typical EST configuration. In this illustration, the virtual switch is connected to a port on a physical switch that is configured for VLAN 100. Using EST, the virtual machines connected to this virtual switch will automatically be connected to VLAN 100. Using EST, port groups are not required to pass along VLAN configuration settings.

EST does have some drawbacks. If it is required to have guests on several different VLANs, a separate physical connection is required for each virtual switch that will access that VLAN. Depending on the number of VLANs that are needed, this configuration could require many physical adapters. Add redundancy to this setup and even more physical adapters and physical switch ports will be required.

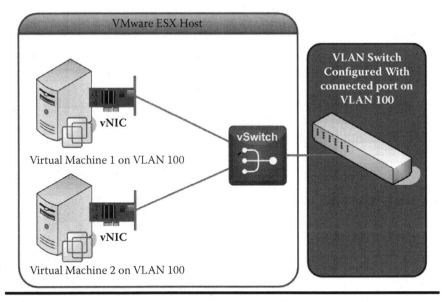

Figure 8.4   A Typical External Switch Tagging Configuration.

Virtual Guest Tagging

When a physical adapter is connected to a physical switch that is said to be "trunked", Virtual Guest Tagging, or VGT, can pass the trunked connection to the guest. Trunking is the act of configuring a port to present multiple VLANs. Through the use of guest operating system based drivers and software, the guest can be configured to access any of the VLANs that the trunked port has configured. This can be very beneficial when it comes to virtual switch flexibility, as the guest takes the role of configuring VLAN access. To enable this configuration, a port group on a virtual switch must be set to have a VLAN ID of 4095.

Figure 8.5 shows a typical VGT configuration. The virtual switch is connected to a trunked port on a physical switch. Because the port group is configured for VLAN ID 4095, the guest operating system in the virtual machine can be configured for the required VLAN it is desired to be connected to.

This configuration does have some disadvantages, however. Not all guest operating systems have efficient drivers to allow for VLAN tagging at the guest level. Additionally, when configured in this fashion, additional CPU cycles are used to add the VLAN tag and remove the VLAN tag to outgoing and incoming data respectively.

Virtual Switch Tagging

Virtual Switch Tagging, or VST, gives virtual switches the role of adding VLAN tags to communications as they come and go. This alleviates the CPU resources

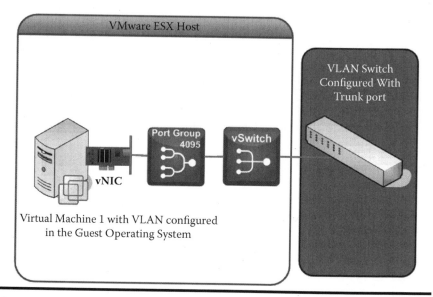

Figure 8.5   A Typical Virtual Guest Tagging Configuration.

in the virtual machines that are desired to be connected to a specific VLAN. Additionally, no guest drivers or special software are required to take advantage of this configuration.

Figure 8.6 shows a typical VST configuration. The virtual switch is connected to a trunked port on a physical switch. Virtual Switch Tagging requires a port group for each VLAN that is to be presented to guests. In the illustration, there is a port group for VLANs 100 and 200, and the guests are in the appropriate VLAN for the port group they are connected to. Keep in mind, because they are using different port groups, to talk to each other, unlike guests on the same port group (and the same vswitch), they must send data external to the VMware ESX host, out to the rest of the network to properly return to the other guest.

As in Virtual Guest Tagging, the physical adapter or adapters the virtual switch is bound to must be connected to a trunked physical port on the physical switch it is connected to. In contrast to VGT where only a single port group is required on the virtual switch, VST requires a separate port group for each VLAN that the virtual switch provides access to. In an environment of many VLANs, this could result in many port groups on a virtual switch. As in VGT, VST requires a VLAN ID number which corresponds to the VLAN number it is to allow access to.

Summary

Through the use of different types of virtual network adapters, the use of multiple virtual switch configuration types and appropriate physical networking settings,

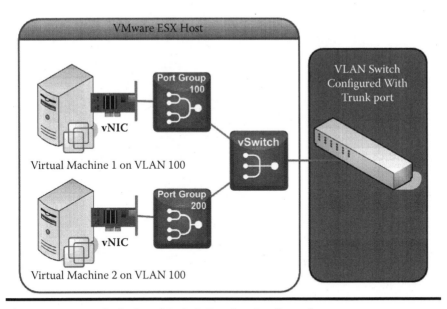

Figure 8.6   A Typical Virtual Switch Tagging Configuration.

VMware ESX can provide a very flexible virtual network environment. Using External Switch Tagging, Virtual Guest Tagging or Virtual Switch Tagging, virtual switches can be easily configured for multiple capabilities. And NIC Teaming can add to the overall redundancy of a virtual network.

With multiple, highly configurable settings and methods of implementation, VMware ESX virtual networking, including virtual adapters and virtual switches, and physical networking, including physical adapters and external switches, can integrate easily into a wide variety of enterprise networks.

Chapter 9

Storage

When designing a Virtual Infrastructure environment, one of the single most important things to consider and plan for is the storage backend. There are several options available that range from local storage, Fibre Channel and iSCSI. The first thing to think about is where you store and run your virtual machines. VMware's VMFS file system is specially designed for the purpose of storing and running virtual machines.

Virtual Machine File System

VMware developed its own high performance cluster file system called VMware Virtual Machine File System or VMFS. VMFS provides a file system which has been optimized for storage virtualization for virtual machines through the use of distributed locking. A virtual machine stored on a VMFS partition always appears to the virtual machine as a mounted SCSI disk. The virtual disk or *.vmdk file hides the physical storage layer from the virtual machine's operating system. VMFS versions 1 and 2 were flat file systems, and typically only housed .vmdk files. The VMFS 3 file system now allows for a directory structure. As a result, VMFS 3 file systems can contain all of the configuration and disk files for a given virtual machine. The VMFS file system is one of the things that set VMware so far ahead of its competitors. Conventional file systems will allow one server to have a read/write access or lock to a given file at any given time. VMware's VMFS is a file system which will allow multiple nodes or multiple VMware ESX servers to read and write to the same LUN or VMFS partition concurrently.

Now that we know about VMFS, let's take a look at the different storage options that are made available.

Direct Attached Storage

Direct-attached storage (DAS) is storage that is, as the name implies, directly attached to a computer or server. DAS is usually the first step taken when working with storage. A good example would be a company with two VMware ESX Servers directly attached to a disk array. This configuration is a good starting point, but it typically doesn't scale very well.

Network Attached Storage

Network-attached storage (NAS) is a type of storage that is shared over the network at a filesystem level. This option is considered an entry-level or low cost option with a moderate performance rating. VMware ESX will connect over the network to a specialized storage device. This device can be in the form of an appliance or a computer that uses Network File System (NFS).

The VMkernel is used to connect to a NAS device via the VMkernel port and supports NFS Version 3 carried over TCP/IP only. From the standpoint of the VMware ESX servers, the NFS volumes are treated the same way VMware ESX would treat iSCSI or Fibre Channel storage. You are able to VMotion guests from one host to the next, create virtual machines, boot virtual machines as well as mount ISO images as CD-ROMs when presented to the virtual machines.

When configuring access to standard Unix/Linux based NFS devices, some configuration changes will need to be defined. The directory /etc/exports will define the systems that are allowed to access the shared directory. And there are a few options in this file that you should be aware of.

1. Name the directory to be shared.
2. Define the subnets that will be allowed access to the share.
3. Allow both "read" and "write" permissions to the volume.
4. no_root_squash—The root user (UID = 0) by default is given the least amount of access to the volume. This option will turn off this behavior, giving the VMkernel the access it needs to connect as UID 0.
5. sync—All file writes MUST be committed to the disk before the client write request is actually completed.

Windows Server 2003 R2 also natively provides NFS sharing when the Windows Services for Unix (SFU) service is installed and configured. Out of the box, Windows Server 2003 R2 has this ability, but it can also be run on Windows Server 2003 (non-R2), and Windows 2000 Server after downloading SFU from Microsoft's Website.

1. After storage has been allocated, the folders are presented similarly as NFS targets.

2. Because there is no common authentication method between VMware ESX and a Microsoft Windows server, the /etc/passwd file must be copied to the Windows server, and mappings must be made to tie an account on the ESX server to a Windows account with appropriate access rights.

Fibre Channel SAN

When using Fibre Channel to connect to the backend storage, VMware ESX requires the use of a Fibre Channel switch. Using more than one allows for redundancy. The Fibre Channel switch will form the "fabric" in the Fibre Channel network by connecting multiple nodes together. Disk arrays in Storage Area Networks (SAN) are one of the main things you will see connected in a Fibre Channel Network along with servers and/or tape drives. Storage Processors aggregate physical hard disks into logical volumes, otherwise called LUNs, each with its own LUN number identifier. World Wide Names (WWNs) are attached by the manufacturer to the Host Bus Adapters (HBA). This is a similar concept as used by MAC addresses within network interface cards (NICs). All Zoning and Pathing is the method the Fibre Channel Switches and SAN Service Processor (SP) use for controlling host access to the LUNs. The SP use soft zoning to control LUN visibility per WWN. The Fibre Channel Switch uses hard zoning, which controls SP visibility on a per switch basis as well as LUN masking. LUN Masking controls LUN visibility on a per host basis.

The VMkernel will address the LUN using the following example syntax:

```
Vmhba(adapter#):target#:LUN#:partition# or Vmhba1:0:0:1
```

So how does a Fibre Channel SAN work anyway? Let's take a look at how the SAN components will interact with each other. This is a very general overview of how the process works.

1. When a host wants to access the disks or storage device on the SAN, the first thing that must happen is that an access request for the storage device must take place. The host sends out a block-based access request to the storage devices.
2. The request is then accepted by the HBA for the host. At the same time, it is first converted from its binary data form to optical form which is what is required for transmission in the fiber optical cable. Then the request is "packaged" based on the rules of the Fibre Channel protocol.
3. The HBA then transmits the request to the SAN.
4. One of the SAN switches receives the request and checks to see which storage device wants to access from the host's perspective; this will appear as a specific disk, but will really be a logical device that will correspond to some physical device on the SAN.

5. The Fibre Channel switch will determine which physical devices have been made available to the host for its targeted logical device.
6. Once the Fibre Channel switch determines the correct physical device, it will pass along the request to that physical device.
7. When a host wants to access the disks or storage device on the SAN, the fist thing that must happen is an access request for the storage device. The host sends out a block-based access request to the storage devices.
8. The request is then accepted by the HBA for the host. At the same time, it is first converted from its binary data form to optical form which is what is required for transmission in the fiber optical cable. Then the request is "packaged" based on the rules of the Fibre Channel protocol.
9. The HBA then transmits the request to the SAN.
10. One of the SAN switches receives the request and checks to see which storage device wants to access from the host's perspective; this will appear as a specific disk but will really be a logical device that will correspond to some physical device on the SAN.
11. The Fibre Channel switch will determine which physical devices have been made available to the host for its targeted logical device.
12. Once the Fibre Channel switch determines the correct physical device it will pass along the request to that physical device.

Internet Small Computer System Interface

Internet Small Computer System Interface or iSCSI is a different approach than that of Fibre Channel SANs. iSCSI is a SCSI transport protocol which enables access to a storage device via standard TCP/IP networking. This process works by mapping SCSI block-oriented storage over TCP/IP. This process is similar to mapping SCSI over Fibre Channel. Initiators like the VMware ESX iSCSI HBA send SCSI commands to "targets" located in the iSCSI storage systems.

iSCSI has some distinct advantages over Fibre Channel, primarily with cost. You can use the existing NICs and Ethernet switches that are already in your environment. This brings down the initial cost needed to get started. When looking to grow the environment, Ethernet switches are less expensive then Fibre Channel switches.

iSCSI has the ability to do long distance data transfers. And iSCSI can use the Internet for data transport. You can have two separate data centers that are geographically apart from each other and still be able to do iSCSI between them. Fibre Channel must use a gateway to tunnel through, or convert to IP.

Performance with iSCSI is increasing at an accelerated pace. As Ethernet speeds continue to increase (10Gig Ethernet is now available), iSCSI speeds increase as well. With the way iSCSI SANs are architected, iSCSI environments continue to increase in speed the more they are scaled out. iSCSI does this by using parallel connections from the Service Processor to the disks arrays.

iSCSI is simpler and less expensive than Fibre Channel. Now that 10Gig Ethernet is available, the adoption of iSCSI into the enterprise looks very promising.

It is important to really know the limitations and/or maximum configurations that you can use when working with VMware ESX and the storage system on the backend. Let's take a look at the one's that are most important.

1. 256 is the maximum number of LUNs per system that you can use and the maximum during install is 128.
2. There is a 16 port total maximum in the HBAs per system.
3. 4 is the maximum number of virtual HBAs per virtual machine.
4. 15 is the maximum number of targets per virtual machine.
5. 60 is the maximum number of virtual disks per Windows and Linux virtual machine.
6. 256 is the maximum number of VMFS file systems per VMware ESX server.
7. 2TB is the maximum size of a VMFS partition.
8. The maximum file size for a VMFS-3 file is based on the block size of the partition. A 1MB block size will allow up to a 256GB file size and a block size of 8MB will allow 2TB.
9. The maximum number of files per VMFS-3 partition is 30,000.
10. 32 is the maximum number of paths per LUN.
11. 1024 is the maximum number of total paths.
12. 15 is the maximum number of targets per HBA.
13. 1.1GB is the smallest VMFS-3 partition you can create.

So, there you have it, the 13 VMware ESX rules of storage. The setting of the block file size on a partition is the rule you will visit the most. A general best practice is to create LUN sizes between 250GB and 500GB. Proper initial configuration for the long term is essential. An example would be, if you wanted to P2V a server that has 300GB total disk space, and you did not plan appropriately, you would have an issue. Unless you planned ahead when you created the LUN and used a 2MB block size, you would be stuck. Here is the breakdown:

1. 1MB block size = 256GB max file size
2. 2MB block size = 512GB max file size
3. 4MB block size = 1024GB max file size
4. 8MB block size = 2048GB max file size.

Spanning up to 32 physical storage extents (block size = 8MB = 2TB) which equals the maximum volume size of 64TB.

NOTE

Now would be a very good time to share a proverb that has served me well over my career. "Just because you can do something, does not mean you should." Nothing could be truer than this statement. There really is no justification for creating volumes that are 64TB or anything remotely close to that. As a best practice, I start thinking about using Raw Device Mappings (otherwise known as RDMs) when I need anything over 1TB. I actually have 1TB to 2TB in my range, but if the SAN tools are available to snap a LUN and then send it to Fibre tape, that is a much faster way to back things up. This is definitely something to consider when deciding whether to use VMFS or RDM.

System Administrators today do not always have the luxury of doing things the best way they should be done. Money and management ultimately make the decisions, and we are then forced to make due with what we have. In a perfect world, we would design tier-level storage for different applications and virtual machines running in the environment, possibly comprised of RAID 5 LUNS and RAID 0+1 LUNS. Always remember the golden rule—"Spindles equal Speed."

As an example, Microsoft is very specific when it comes to best practices with Exchange and the number of spindles you need on the backend to get the performance that you expect for the scale of the deployment. Different applications are going to have different needs, so depending on the application that you are deploying, the disk configuration can make or break the performance of your deployment.

Summary

So we learned that the number of spindles directly affects the speed of the disks. And we also learned the 13 VMware ESX rules for storage and what we needed to know about VMFS. Additionally, we touched on the different storage device options that have been made available to us. Those choices include DAS, iSCSI and Fibre Channel SAN. We also presented a very general overview on how a Fibre Channel SAN works.

Knowing one of the biggest gotchas is the block size of VMFS partitions and LUNs, and then combining that knowledge with the different storage options made available, you can now make the best possible decisions when architecting the storage piece of your Virtual Infrastructure environment. Proper planning up front is crucial to making sure that you do not have to later overcome hurdles pertaining to storage performance, availability, and cost.

Chapter 10

Advanced Features

In this chapter we are going to review the essentials about the advanced options available when using VMware Virtual Infrastructure. There is some very cool stuff that can be done that you cannot find in any of the other virtualization platforms. So let's get started by taking a look at our first advanced feature, VMotion.

VMotion

VMware VMotion enables the live or hot migration of running virtual machines from one physical server to another with zero downtime. VMotion is the gateway technology for creating a dynamic, automated and self optimizing data center. The keys to VMotion are VMware's VMFS file system, allowing multiple installations of VMware ESX to all access the same virtual machine files concurrently, and the ability of VMware ESX to transfer the virtual machine's active memory from one host to another. A virtual machine itself is encapsulated by a set of files that are stored on shared storage that is using the VMFS file system. This shared storage could be Fibre Channel, iSCSI, or NAS.

During the VMotion process, the active memory and precise execution state of the virtual machines is transferred from the source host server to the destination host server over a high speed dedicated VMkernel network port. The last part of the transfer is getting networking started again. Since the networks used by the virtual machines are so virtualized by the host server, the virtual machine's network connection and identity are preserved through the migration. VirtualCenter manages the virtual machine MAC address as part of the process. Once the virtual machine gets to its destination, VMotion pings the network router to let it know of the new physical location of the virtual machine MAC address. This results in a live migration with zero downtime and no disruptions for the end user.

VMotion is an administrator's technological dream come true. Before VMotion, it was almost unheard of for an administrator to be able to perform maintenance on a server during business hours. VMotion makes that dream a reality, and VMware keeps adding more functionality to keep making our administrative lives easier. Imagine that when it came time to perform an update or patch on a VMware ESX host server that is running thirty virtual machines—what if you could simply click a button and have all the virtual machines migrate to another host automatically? Wouldn't that be cool and extremely useful? Well this is no longer just a dream, it is a reality and much, much more. The new technology called VMware Distributed Resource Scheduler adds the automation to VMotion. So let's take a closer look at the VMware Distributed Resource Scheduler and see what is under the hood.

Distributed Resource Scheduler

VMware Distributed Resource Scheduler (DRS) will dynamically allocate and intelligently balance the virtual machines resources across the physical hosts. VMware DRS will achieve this intelligent balance by applying a complex set of rules, user-defined resource pools and VMotion technology to place virtual machines in their optimal location. VMware will never publish the algorithms or metrics they use for DRS but we can share what we do know.

VMware DRS will take into account processor affinity, which includes both the affinity and anti-affinity rules.

1. **Affinity Rules**—Run virtual machines on the same host. Rules are defined based on performance benefits.
2. **Anti-affinity Rules**—Run virtual machines on different hosts. Rules are defined based on high availability.

The dynamic balancing component of DRS is adjusted based on the resource requirement of the virtual machines. This component performs a re-evaluation of the resource pools, every few minutes, based on millisecond performance evaluation over a period of time. A balancing re-evaluation is also done when resource pool settings have changed, which also includes resource entitlement or virtual machine assignments. If there is a big imbalance in the resource pool, then the balancing component will be more aggressive in the balancing process then it would have if the imbalance was low.

It is also suggested that the rules for the virtual machines will be allocated fairly and evenly across VMware ESX hosts, based on the virtual machine and pool resource settings. VMotion would be evaluated based on the final effect of the migration on the destination host as well as the migration cost.

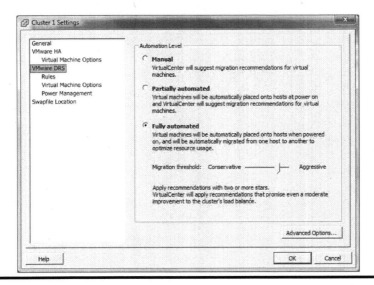

Figure 10.1   VMware DRS Settings.

VMware DRS has three levels of automation to choose from, with five steps or stars of migration thresholds, which range from conservative to aggressive. A conservative threshold will apply only five star recommendations. What this means is VirtualCenter will only apply recommendations that must be taken to satisfy cluster constraints like affinity rules and host maintenance. On the other hand, an aggressive migration threshold will apply all recommendations. This means VirtualCenter will apply recommendations that promise even a slight improvement in the cluster's load balance. (See Figure 10.1)

NOTE

For DRS to automatically VMotion all virtual machines to another host when placed in Maintenance mode, the automation level must be set to fully automated.

VMware DRS has the ability to add custom rules to be able to group virtual machines together on the same hosts or to separate virtual machines and keep them apart on separate hosts. DRS also gives us the option to define the automation level on a per machine basis.

VMware has added additional capabilities with the release of VMware Distributed Power Management (DPM). VMware DPM reduces power consumption by intelligently balancing a datacenter's workload. VMware DPM will automatically power off VMware ESX servers whose resources are not immediately required and powers these servers back on when the demand for compute resources increases again.

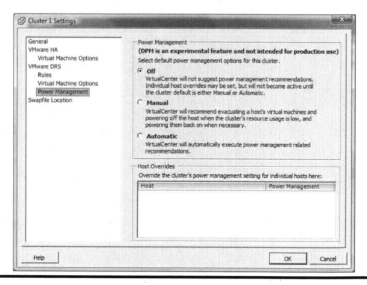

Figure 10.2   VMware DRS Power Management.

VMware DPM was released with VirtualCenter 2.5 and currently, at the time of this writing, is an experimental feature and is not intended for production use. (See Figure 10.2)

Resource automation is a great addition to the virtual infrastructure feature set, but it doesn't have to end there. To augment resource automation, wouldn't high availability automation be a great feature to have? VMware had the same thought, and as a result, came out with the VMware High Availability feature which can restart virtual machines in case of a host failure. Let's take a closer look at the HA module.

VMware High Availability

VMware High Availability (HA) will continuously monitor all virtual machines running in a resource pool on a VMware ESX server cluster, looking for a physical host failure. All VMware ESX servers in HA mode have an agent on the host machine that maintains communication with the other hosts. This communication is called the "heartbeat". A loss of this "heartbeat" initiates the restart of all affected virtual machines on the other servers in the cluster. VMware HA will also monitor the available resources in the resource pools to guarantee it has the resources available to recover all virtual machines in the event of a host failure. Actually, VMware HA can be configured to recover from up to four host failures in a cluster if the resources are available. (See Figure 10.3)

This gives you the ability to provide near-zero clustering for any operating system and application with no special configuration. I have seen VMware HA do

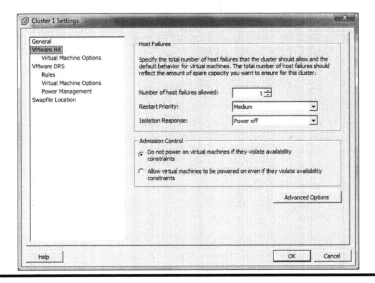

Figure 10.3 VMware HA Settings.

its magic and watched the failed virtual machines recover in less then five minutes. In theory, depending on how your enterprise monitoring is set up, a failed virtual machine could recover before alerts ever go off. On the same token, similar high availability configurations, with similar or longer recovery times, can cost significantly more and require more complex configurations.

There is a special kind of host failure which is called host isolation and/or split brain. This happens when a VMware ESX server loses contact to the default gateway, therefore losing communication with the other hosts. The host is still running its virtual machines and is therefore still functioning. By default, the virtual machines would be terminated on the isolated host and restarted on another host in the cluster. This is a dramatic event that could cause disk corruption. It is therefore a best practice to leave the virtual machines running in a host isolation event.

Virtual Machine Failure Monitoring

Virtual Machine Failure Monitoring (VMFM), which is new to VirtualCenter 2.5, is an extension of VMware HA. This HA feature can be configured to monitor the virtual machines themselves as well as the host. At the time of this writing, this feature is still experimental and is currently not supported for production use, however it indicates the directions things are going and the added functionality that keeps on coming with each and every release.

VMware VMFM uses the VMware Tools installed in the virtual machine to send a heartbeat signal out every second. VMFM will check for a heartbeat every twenty seconds. When no heartbeat has been received within a specific user configured amount of time, the virtual machine is declared failed and is then restarted.

Virtual Machine Failure Monitoring has the ability and logic behind it to know the difference between a virtual machine that has been powered on but has stopped sending heartbeats and a virtual machine that is powered-off, suspended and or migrated. VMFM works by ensuring an absolute arrival rate of heartbeats in the specified time. This gives VMFM the logic to distinguish between a virtual machine that is heavily loaded, resulting in fewer heartbeats, and a virtual machine that has stopped sending any heartbeats out all together.

Virtual Machine Failure Monitoring is not enabled by default and to enable it there are a few hoops we need to jump through. VMFM can only be configured after the cluster has been created and VMware HA has been enabled. To enable VMFM you must edit the global cluster settings.

1. Log in to the VMware VI Client and right click the cluster in the inventory panel.
2. Choose "Edit Settings".
3. Choose "VMware HA" in the left panel and click the advanced options on the right.
4. Enter the following options in to the dialog box and then click OK.

- **das.vmFailoverEnabled**—True or False with the default being False or Disabled.
  This option is used to enable or disable Virtual Machine Failure Monitoring for the entire cluster.
- **das.FailureInterval**—Integer value (number of second) with the default being 30.
  This option is to set how long to wait to declare the virtual machine failed when no heartbeats are received.
- **das.minUptime**—Integer value (number of seconds) with the default being 120.
  After a virtual machine has been powered on, its heartbeats are allowed to stabilize for a specific number of seconds which should also include the guest operating system boot-up time.
- **das.maxFailures**—Integer value (number of seconds) with the default being 3.
  This is the maximum number of failures and automated resets allowed for the time that das.maxFailureWindow specifies. If das.maxFailureWindow is −1 (no window) das.maxFailures represents the absolute number of failures after which the automated response is stopped and further investigative review is needed. If a virtual machine exceeds this threshold, you will have bigger problems to deal with.
- **das.maxFailureWindow**—Integer value (number of seconds) with the default being -1 (no failure window).

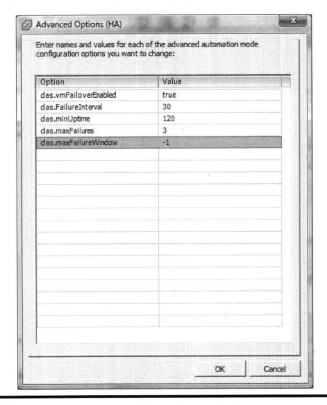

Figure 10.4   VMware HA Advanced Options Configuration.

If das.maxFailures is set to a number, and that many automated resets have occurred within that specified failure window, automated response will stop and further investigative review will be needed. (See Figure 10.4)

If you do not set a value for a field, then the default value is used. That means VMFM will remain disabled unless the value das.vmFailoverEnabled is specified with a value of True.

Storage VMotion

Storage VMotion is new to VirtualCenter in version 2.5. VMware provided a sneak peak at this technology when doing migrations from VMware's ESX 2.x to ESX 3.x, but the ability was one way and only worked for moving virtual machines from a VMware ESX 2 to ESX 3 environment. This function allows you to do live migrations of virtual machines while moving all the disk files to another datastore with no downtime. This process has worked very well for me during the upgrade and migrations that I have done when migrating from VMware ESX 2.x to ESX 3.x.

Unfortunately, they added this feature back in the form of command-line only using the Remote Command Line Interface or Remote CLI. The process looks something like this:

```
vicfg:~# svmotion --url=https://vc.yourdomain.com/sdk --
username=someuser \
--password=password --datacenter='SomeDatacenter' \
--vm="[source-datastore] vm1/vm1.vmx:
destination-datastore"
```

Dominic Rivera has written and posted on his website (http://www.vmprofessional.com) a small wrapper script for the Remote CLI which simplifies the use of Storage VMotion. I highly encourage using this script. The manual way is a little rough, and I am not sure why the functionality was not added to VirtualCenter. The script makes the feature a bit more user-friendly, just edit the script to include your VC URL, username, password, cluster and Datacenter, and then you will be prompted with a list of VMs to choose from, and a list of target datastores to choose from. Output will look similar to the following:

```
vicfg:~# ./vmpmotion.pl
cluster: dominic
[0] vm1 : [dominic-lun01] vm1/vm1.vmx
[1] vm2 : [dominic-lun02] vm2/vm2.vmx
Enter selection: 0
You selected vm1
[0] dominic-lun01
[1] dominic-lun02
Enter target : 1
You selected dominic-lun02
Performing Storage VMotion of vm1 to dominic-lun02
```

Additionally, the sVMotion plug-in for VirtualCenter takes the command-line work out of the equation, giving administrators who aren't as comfortable with the command-line the ability to perform the same operation through the VirtualCenter client.

As with any script, process, or plug-in, always test in your development area first before using on your production systems.

VMware Consolidated Backup

Another area VMware is working to improve is the ability to back up the virtual machines. The goal is to do so without adding an extra performance load on the host server, which could ultimately impact the performance of other virtual machines. A typical back up design would put backup agents on each of the virtual machines. This increases the load on the VMware ESX host server during backups and should be avoided whenever possible.

When VMware released ESX Server 3.0, it also introduced VMware Consolidated Backup (VCB). VMware VCB is a proxy server with the agent of the backup software you use in your environment. An integration module, which runs over the dot net framework, provides the link between the backup software and VCB.

NOTE

You must use diskpart on the Consolidated Backup Server to disable automatic mounting of new volumes BEFORE you attach to the fabric and scan for the LUNS, otherwise you risk corrupting the VMFS file system when Windows tries to write a signature to the volume.

So how does this really work? Consolidated Backup takes a snapshot of a virtual machine and mounts that snapshot to the backup proxy VCB server directly from the SAN. As part of this process, the virtual machine file system is quiesced (the process used to guarantee a consistent and usable backup), or to ensure that the entire state of the virtual machine is captured at the point in time the snapshot is created. The backup agent then backs up the contents of the virtual machine as a virtual disk or as a set of files and directories depending on the operating system of the virtual machine. VMware VCB can only currently do file level backups to Microsoft Windows operating systems but can do image level backups of any operating system that can run on VMware ESX. The last step that VCB will do is to tear down the mount and then remove the snapshot. When ESX 3.0 was released, VCB would only work in a SAN environment on a physical system that has connectivity to the VMFS volumes via a Fibre Channel connection. VCB 1.1 now allows access to iSCSI and NFS storage through IP based connectivity. This addition allows for a VCB proxy to be run in a virtual machine, if it is only used to backup and restore iSCSI and NFS based storage.

Although VCB is pretty much a straightforward process, it has no graphical interface to use so you must learn how to manipulate the options and switches with the command-line utilities. There are five executable commands when working with VMware VCB. These files are located by default in C:\Program Files\VMware\ VMware Consolidated Backup Framework. Let's take a look at these commands and find out what they can do. The first three utilities are the one's used the most.

1. **mountvm.exe**—This utility does what the name implies, it mounts the VMware virtual disk files so that you can browse and copy files from the virtual disk.

2. **VCBMounter.exe**—This is the VCB work horse and the most used utility in VCB. It performs the core operations of VCB. And it can either do image level or file level backups of the virtual machines. This is also the utility that will quiesce the file system on the virtual machine's operating system. An example of the syntax would be something like this:

```
vcbMounter -h virtualcentersrv.domain.com -u AdminAccount
-p ThePassword -a name:VMBackup -r c:\mount\VMBackup
-t fullvm -m san
```

Once finished, you will need to unmount of the export just created.

```
vcbMounter -h virtualcentersrv.domain.com -u AdminAccount
-p ThePassword -U c:\mount\VMBackup-fullVM
```

3. **vcbVmName.exe**—This utility will report the VMware URL, VMware UUID, system name, IP address, and much more. An example of the syntax would be:

```
Vcbvmname-h virtualcentersrv.domain.com -u AdminAccount
-p ThePassword -s Any:
```

4. **vcbSnapshot**—This utility is for working with snapshots. Some of the options that are available are to create, find, list, delete and more.
5. **vcbSanDbg**—This utility is a Windows program that collects the SAN information as seen from the proxy server. This is a good starting point to see whether your storage is configured properly.

I have written an application that will read a file and get a list of server names, and it will then do a full image backup of those virtual machines. The application creates a script based on the server list and then backs up the files to TSM.

```
Imports System
Imports System.IO
Imports System.Collections
Imports System.Runtime
Imports Scripting
Module Module1
Sub Main()
     Dim objReader As New StreamReader("c:\scripts\
vmlist.ini")
```

```
    Dim objWriter As New StreamWriter("C:\Scripts\
vcbscript.cmd")
    'objWriter = New StreamWriter("C:\Scripts\
vcbscript.cmd")
    Dim sLine As String = ""
    Dim arrText As New ArrayList()
    Dim oshell
    Dim AppToRun As String
    Dim fs As FileSystemObject
    fs = New FileSystemObject
    oshell = CreateObject("Wscript.Shell")
    AppToRun = "C:\Scripts\vcbscript.cmd "
    Do
       sLine = objReader.ReadLine()
       If Not sLine Is Nothing Then
          arrText.Add(sLine)
       End If
    Loop Until sLine Is Nothing
    objReader.Close()
    For Each sLine In arrText
       Console.WriteLine(sLine)
       objWriter.WriteLine("REM " & sLine & "***********")
       objWriter.WriteLine("""C:\Program Files\VMware\
VMware Consolidated Backup Framework\vcbMounter.exe"" -h
VCserver.domain.com -u vcbadmin -p password -a name:" &
sLine & " -r e:\mnt\" & sLine & "-FullVM -t fullvm -m
san""")
       objWriter.WriteLine("cd \")
       objWriter.WriteLine("cd ""Program Files\Tivoli\
TSM\baclient""")
       objWriter.WriteLine("dsmc incremental e:\mnt\"
& sLine & "-FullVM\*")
       objWriter.WriteLine("""C:\Program Files\VMware\
VMware Consolidated Backup Framework\vcbMounter.exe"" -h
VCserver.domain.com -u vcbadmin -p password -U e:\mnt\" &
sLine & "-FullVM""")
       objWriter.WriteLine("REM *********************")
       objWriter.WriteLine(" ")
    Next
    'Console.ReadLine()
    objWriter.Close()
    oshell.Run("C:\Scripts\vcbscript.cmd")
  End Sub
End Module
```

Virtual Desktop Infrastructure

Virtual Desktop Infrastructure or VDI is more of a technology than a product, and VMware VDI integrates Virtual Infrastructure 3 and VMware Desktop Manager 2 to create VMware's desktop virtualization. VMware Virtual Desktop Manager or VDM is a desktop management server, as the name suggests, as well as the desktop connection broker. VMware VDM securely connects the users to the virtual desktop located in the data center. You have the option of setting up the connection to the virtual desktop either through the VDM or directly to the virtual machine.

So what do we gain with desktop virtualization? VDI provides users with desktop continuity, high availability as well as disaster recovery. Basically all the same bells and whistles you get from running your virtual servers in a VMware virtual environment plus a little more.

VMware VDM has the capability to do some really cool stuff. The VMware VDM uses web pages for administrative tasks as well as the client connection. VDM will create virtual machines on demand as needed from a pre-configured template and has the ability to shutdown or even delete the virtual desktop machines when the demand has dropped. VDM gives you the control to set up a minimum amount of virtual desktops that would be running at all times as well as a limit on the total number of machines that can be created and/or running. Because the virtual desktop machines are created from a template, the process can be time consuming, so proper planning is a must. Otherwise, you will end up having a client sitting at a web page, wondering what's happening while waiting for the process to finish.

There are a few benefits that you can achieve with VDI environments that are worth mentioning.

- VMware VDI and the VMware Virtual Desktop Manager give you the ability to provide a unique virtual environment for each and every user.
- You are able to create multiple environments that each has the ability to be customized with different settings and applications with no effect on the end users.
- The end users can be granted more control of their own desktop to be able to install and configure application when needed.

As the technology matures, virtual machine deployment will be a much faster process. Different storage technologies can mitigate some of the wait through storage virtualization techniques. NetApp has a technology known as Flex-Clone that will allow you to clone a virtual machine in a very short period of time. There is a video demonstration on YouTube where a NetApp employee clones a virtual machine 100 times, and presents the deployed virtual machines to users in around 10 minutes. Until the time that the deployment speeds are increased using traditional storage, proper consideration must be taken for the maximum load in a farm in a given amount of time. Let's use 15 minutes as a reference point. So if you could accept 10 new logons in 15 minutes, then the minimum number of Virtual Desktops you would need to make available at any given time is 10. When one virtual desktop is used by a user logging in, another would then be deployed.

This method works and if you take advantage of the fact that VMware Virtual Desktop Manager can start and stop virtual machines, you should be able to maintain a pretty consistent and available solution.

Summary

The features and advanced abilities that are getting built and incorporated into VMware Virtual Infrastructure are moving along at great speeds. The future is looking very bright for virtualization in the data center and our jobs as administrators are getting better and easier at the same time. I don't know about you, but I do like having the ability to work on hosts and servers while having no down time of the applications. Less downtime, easier management, and more capabilities are wonderful things. It makes you wonder. What can they possibly think of next?

Actually, VMware gives hints and clues in the different products. VMware will get a feature working in the VMware Workstation product first, and then develop it along until it has matured enough for the server class systems. The next step would be to add the feature into VMware Server and then finally into VMware ESX. This can help give some kind of clue as to what might be coming next. VMware also likes to get suggestions from customers, as well as deliver technologies that are similar to those provided by their competitors so that they can be the best virtualization platform vendor around.

Chapter 11

Resource Management

Resource management is the ability to control how resources are handled in VMware ESX 3.x. There are four main resources that we really look at when working in the virtual environment:

1. Processor
2. Memory
3. Disk
4. Network

Processor

Processor resource management for the virtual machine can be configured in three ways:

1. Limits—This is a hard limit of the use of computer processor time in the virtual machine which is measured in MHz.
2. Reservations—A reservation will take a configured amount of processor cycles and reserve that amount for a specific virtual machine. This is also measured in MHz. A virtual machine will only start if the reservations can be guaranteed.
3. Shares—When there is a true contention for processor cycles on a VMware ESX server, the number of shares will determine which virtual machine will have priority.

Processor scheduling for a virtual machine must be scheduled simultaneously. What I mean by that is if a virtual machine is using more than one processor, those processors must be scheduled at the same time. This is all or nothing. If a virtual machine has two processors, the physical processors / cores must be available at the same time.

VMware Virtual SMP

Symmetric multiprocessing, otherwise called SMP, is a multiprocessor computer architecture which will allow a computer the ability to utilize multiple processors connected to a single shared memory. VMware has developed this ability to be used in the virtual machine and has called this VMware Virtual SMP. Currently, a virtual machine has the ability to utilize up to four processors.

Some things to consider before utilizing this feature would be to make sure the running applications are multi-threaded or implemented to use multiple processors. Not all applications are designed to be multi-threaded, and unless they are, it will be a waste of resources and can slow things down in the long run. The reason behind this is the CPU scheduler for the virtual machine. The virtual processors from the same virtual machine are co-scheduled if the physical processors are available for instructions. Multiple processor virtual machines will send instructions to all processors at the same time. This is an all or nothing task. Having unused virtual CPUs will cause CPU scheduling constraints on the virtual CPU being used. If there are not enough physical CPUs available to match the number of virtual processors, then the task will wait until there are enough available processors to service the request. Even the unused virtual CPU will still consume timer interrupts and execute the guest CPU idle loops. From the point of view of VMware ESX, this is still CPU consumption. And this boils down to performance that can be degraded.

When implementing VMware Virtual SMP, proper consideration needs to be planned out and this should not be attempted unless you have double the amount of processors and/or processor cores in the physical host. With that said, the best practice to follow is to use as few virtual CPUs as possible. Do not use virtual SMP if your application is single threaded and does not benefit from the extra CPUs, as one example.

Memory

Memory resource management for a virtual machine can be configured in three ways:

1. Limit—This is a hard limit on the consumption of memory by a virtual machine and is measured in megabytes (MB).
2. Reservation—It is a configured amount of memory that is reserved for a virtual machine and is also measured in MB. A virtual machine will only start if its reservation can be guaranteed.

3. Shares—When there is true contention or competition for resources, the virtual machine with the most shares assigned to it will be the first to get the memory that it needs.

In past releases, VMware ESX used a specific VMFS partition that held one swap file for all the virtual machines to swap to when needed. With the release of VMware ESX 3.x, a virtual machine specific swap file is now created and stored with the virtual machine. The VMkernel allocates the virtual machine swap file to cover the range between limit and reservation.

Virtual machines use a proportional-share system for relative resource management. Competition only happens during resource contention which will help to have predictable resources sharing and prevents virtual machines from monopolizing any resources and/or taking over all of the host resources.

Trying to set up resource management on a per virtual machine basis would be a daunting task. But thanks to something called "Resource Pools", we do not have to. A VMware ESX resource pool is a defined group of compute resources placed in a virtual pool that can then be allocated to various workloads based on demand. This effectively eliminates the need for manual intervention. Resource pools can either be used on a stand-alone host or on a group of hosts that have formed a cluster. Resource pool permissions can be configured much in the same way that permissions are applied to virtual machines.

Resource Pools have several configurable settings to choose from for both memory and CPU:

1. Shares—Low, Normal, High and Custom
2. Reservations—in MHz and MB
3. Limits—in MHz and MB with the option of no limit or unlimited
4. Expandable Reservation
   a. YES—Virtual machines and any sub resource pools may draw from the parent resource pool
   b. NO—Virtual machines and any sub resource pools may only draw from the current pool even if the parent resource pools have free available resources.

There are a couple of resource management best practices that you can follow. If you are expecting frequent changes to the total available resources, use "Shares" and not "Reservations". Using "Shares" will help allocate resources evenly across virtual machines. When configuring "Reservations" to specify the minimum amount of CPU or memory, make sure you are setting the minimal acceptable amount, rather than the optimally desired amount. The host will assign resources based on the limits and number of shares.

Another note about shares and reservations, the number of shares will change as you add or remove virtual machines. To give you an example, if you have a resource pool with 2000 shares available and four virtual machines in this resource pool, each virtual machine would be given 500 shares each. If you were to add four more virtual machines to this resource pool, for a total of eight virtual machines, each virtual machine would then have 250 shares each when all things are equal. Shares are a dynamic setting, and reservations will not change when there is a change in the environment, such as when you add or remove virtual machines. Once you set a reservation, you guarantee the virtual machine will be granted the value set at all times. If you add too many virtual machines with a reservation, the host will prevent the virtual machine from starting.

Page sharing, ballooning and *swapping* are the three memory management tools VMware ESX servers use to expand or contract the amount of dynamically allocated virtual machine memory.

1. **Page sharing**—VMware ESX hosts will use the VMware propriety transparent memory page sharing. This will eliminate redundant or duplicate copies of memory between the virtual machines. This is the most preferred and least intrusive memory method between the three.

2. **Ballooning**—The VMware ESX server works with the vmmenctl module to reclaim memory pages that are considered the least valuable by the guest operating system. The vmmenctl driver is installed as part of VMware Tools. The virtual machine must be configured with enough swap space for ballooning to work.

3. **Swapping**—VMware ESX will use swapping to forcibly reclaim memory from a virtual machine. This is the last resort process and the most intrusive. When both page sharing and ballooning fail to reclaim the memory needed, the VMware ESX server will swap out the memory to the system swap file. When using this swapping method, inactive pages that are swapped out to disk won't affect performance, but if the working set is large enough that active memory pages are swapped in and out, performance can greatly suffer.

TIP

Memory Ballooning—As previously mentioned, the vmmenctl module or ballooning will use the swap file configured with a virtual machine to reclaim the memory. Be sure to store all the virtual machine virtual swap files on the fastest available disks or create a special VMFS partition just for the swap files. By default the virtual machine's swap file is created and stored in the same location that the virtual machine is located. This setting can be changed by setting the sched.swap.dir option (in the VI client, *Edit Settings ‡ Options ‡ Advanced ‡ Configuration Parameters*) to another location.

Disks

Disk resource management provides dynamic control over the relative amount of disk bandwidth that is allocated to each virtual machine. The disk shares are configured per virtual machine in the virtual machine setting under the "Resource" tab. When working with disk shares, it is important to remember that a disk share is a guarantee of access to the disk, not a restriction.

This is about the only setting per virtual machine to configure in regards to the disk. The rest of the disk management would be configured and set up on the SAN or storage back end. Since workload, vendor, RAID level, cache sizes, strip sizes and so on can all play a big part in the disk performance of the virtual machine, several considerations should be made when setting up the sub systems and realize there is no magic "one size fits all."

Network

VMware ESX shapes network outbound traffic by establishing parameters for three characteristics: average bandwidth, burst size and peak bandwidth. All of these settings are configured through the VI client which will establish a traffic shaping policy for each uplink adapter.

NOTE

Traffic shaping is outbound only. No shaping is done on inbound traffic.

1. Average Bandwidth—Establishes the number of bits per second to allow across the virtual switch (vSwitch), and is averaged over time to get the allowed average load.
2. Burst Size—Establishes the number of bytes to allow in a burst. If the burst size is exceeded, then the excess packets are queued for a later transmission. If the queue is full, then the packets are dropped.
3. Peak Bandwidth—This is the maximum bandwidth the vSwitch can take without dropping any packets. If traffic exceeds the peak bandwidth, then the excess is queued for later transmission and if the queue is full the packets are then dropped.

Summary

There is a lot more "tweaking" that can be done with processors and memory than is available with disk and network. CPU and memory are the main resources that have the biggest potential and need to be controlled. We have taken a look at Resource Pools, as well as the difference between shares, reservations and limits. We made a special mental note that disk shares have to do with guarantees and the network resource management lets you control maximum sustained rate of transmission as well as peak transmission rates and bursting.

Chapter 12

Performance Optimization

VMware ESX is and has been one of the highest performing server virtualization platforms on the market for some time now. So what that means is VMware typically does a really good job of providing high performance out of the box; however, that doesn't mean that performance tuning and tweaks aren't necessary. In fact, there are still plenty of opportunities for you to get your hands dirty by doing a little bit of work to help further optimize the performance of your virtual infrastructure's environment.

You might be one of those users of VMware ESX that is happy with the performance of your virtualization platform or the performance of your individual or collective virtual machines. But what happens tomorrow if something in the environment changes and it negatively affects your performance? What happens if you need to achieve a 12:1 server consolidation ratio on an existing VMware ESX that today only hosts eight virtual machines? At that point, it may become extremely important to fine tune the environment in order to squeeze out every ounce of performance that your environment can offer.

While this chapter won't go into any great detail on any one single area of performance, it will cover a number of different options that apply to most implementations or discuss other practices that might cause performance problems.

In order to achieve performance optimization, we will focus on three main target areas where improvements can be made. The first target area covered is the VMware ESX host server machine. The configuration of the host server should be carefully examined at both the physical hardware layer and the virtualization platform layer. Decisions made here will ultimately affect the overall performance of every virtual machine contained on the host server. The second target area is the virtual machine layer. Configuration options are one such factor that can affect the performance of the virtual machines. And finally, the third target area that can be optimized is the configuration of the guest operating systems themselves that operates within each virtual machine. Tuning the guest operating system is often times overlooked simply because it operates within a virtual machine. If you normally optimize the operating system installed on a physical server, why wouldn't you try to perform similar tuning techniques to your virtual machines?

Configuration of the Host Server

Virtualizing your infrastructure or even a small number of your physical servers can offer enormous benefits to your organization. But it is important to realize that virtualization can also negatively affect the performance of your server, operating system and/or the applications if not properly setup, configured or planned. Therefore, you should understand the trade-offs that occur at the hardware layer with virtualization and to make sure to properly configure the host server on a component-by-component basis. In this section, we will focus our optimization efforts on the physical host server including the virtualization platform chosen, its processor, memory, storage and its network.

TIP

Make sure you check all the installed hardware items in your host server against the most recent supported hardware compatibility list (HCL) from VMware for whatever version of ESX you are installing. Adding unsupported hardware components can cause performance problems, or worse.

Upgrade your Version of VMware ESX

If your environment is still operating with some earlier version of VMware ESX Server 2.x, now might be the time to start thinking about upgrading, or better yet migrating it to the latest version. In case your VMware sales representative hasn't told you yet, there are significant performance improvements that can be made by simply running the latest version of VMware ESX. By upgrading your environment to VI3 3.5, you not only gain out-of-the-box performance improvements, but you also get significant improvements in scalability, usability, hardware compatibility and a host of new features and benefits described throughout this book.

VMware has optimized several of the component areas in VMware VI3. Doing so allows organizations to see an increase in overall performance, and it also offers the ability to now virtualize high demanding and intensive workloads that might have been previously difficult to do.

With the latest version of VMware ESX, virtual machines can enjoy an increase in the number of virtual CPUs that can be assigned to them. Early versions of VMware ESX restricted virtual machines to a single-processor environment. Since then, VMware has created Virtual SMP technology to give virtual machines the ability to operate with multiple processors. With the latest version of VI3, virtual machines can now enjoy the freedom of using up to four virtual processors. ESX 3.5 now makes use of 32 logical processors on a single host, with experimental support of as many as 64 logical processors. And it can also take advantage of ACPI power saving mode to better handle the wasted cycles consumed by idle virtual machines. Virtual memory limitations have also been increased. Virtual machines can now enable Physical Address Extensions (PAE) to access up to 64GB of memory where the early limitations had been set at 3.6GB of memory for quite a number of years. The memory limit for VMware ESX host servers has also been increased to 256GB. ESX 3.5 has also improved its Non-uniform Memory Access (NUMA) scheduling algorithms which should greatly benefit the virtual machines running on NUMA platforms.

Virtual networking has also gone through a significant overhaul and refresh with the latest version of VI3. Improvements have been made with both the virtual network adapter and the virtual switch. Virtual adapters are capable of GigE speeds, the number of virtual switches has increased as did the number of ports available, and an additional load balancing method called port ID is also now offered. A new version of the VMXNET virtual device called Enhanced VMXNET is available, and it includes several new networking I/O enhancements such as support for TCP/IP Segmentation Offload (TSO) and jumbo frames. ESX 3.5 hosts now fully support 10 GigE NICs which offer huge performance improvements compared to traditional 100 Mb Ethernet cards. Experimental support for Intel I/O Acceleration Technology (I/OATv1) has also been added. If your system's chipset has this feature, you should be able to see improvements in your networking performance.

A number of architectural improvements were made to the ESX 3.5 storage subsystem. VI3 now supports Infiniband-based Host Channel Adapters (HCA). Instead of using NICs and Fibre Channel adapters, you can install Infiniband HCA adapters which would look like Fibre Channel adapters and Ethernet NICs to the virtual machines. VMFS-3 is a new version of the VMFS family of clustered file systems that offers enhanced performance and scalability over previous versions. Virtual machines are less dependent upon the Service Console and their user-level virtualization components can now run on any available processor core which gives the ability to scale up to 50% more virtual machines per host server.

Other features available in VI3 that enhance performance and scalability include VMware Distributed Resource Scheduler (DRS), Resource Pools, High Availability (HA), VMotion, Storage VMotion and VMware Consolidated Backup

(VCB) to name but a few. These and other VI3 enhancements are discussed in more detail throughout this book.

Host Server Processor Performance

The physical hardware of your host server greatly affects the performance of all of the virtual machines that reside upon it. And the processor is considered one of the most vital resources contained within your host server.

As cliché as this may sound, a general rule of thumb to follow is the more physical processors in your server—the better. Likewise, most new servers are now shipping with multiple cores to increase the processing power found in the box. Packing in multiple core processors can help achieve higher densities per server while at the same time increasing the performance of existing virtual machines because of reduced CPU contention. And the newer versions of VMware ESX have official support for multi-core processors.

You should also be aware that although VMware ESX is compatible with a broad range of server hardware, including older server equipment, it doesn't necessarily pay to virtualize those aging servers. Without getting into a cost game here, let's just stay focused on performance. Yesterday's servers have single-core processors that are significantly slower in GHz speed and have slower or less cache. You can greatly improve the performance of your guest environments by simply upgrading your servers and improving the CPU used. If the performance of the virtual environment calls for it, use the highest performing processors you can afford.

In addition to being faster, these newer and more modern processors are also more efficient. Be aware, virtualization environments are typically making more efficient use of the server by fully utilizing the processor, in many cases, reaching and sustaining between 60-80% utilization. That's fine, except if you are dealing with older processor technology that is less efficient with heat and power consumption. Many processors automatically step down their performance when a certain thermal threshold is reached. Remember, these older processors were designed with the notion that they would probably only reach 80% utilization for a small period of time during a spike in usage; once they reach the thermal threshold, they step down and downgrade their performance, which will negatively affect every virtual machine hosted on that server.

It is also important to optimize the ratio between the number of active virtual machines hosted on a server and the number of physical processors or cores available on the host. Usually, the more cores the higher the density. But watch out, operating too many virtual machines per processor core can adversely affect the overall performance of the server and its virtual machines. There is no magic formula that gets the ratio mix right every time and for each scenario. For years, virtualization administrators have been trying to come up with this formula but to no avail. Instead, VMware created DRS and resource pools to try and take much of the guess work out of the equation. While it may not be perfect, it certainly helps keep the performance of the environment at a certain level and without the need for constant human attention.

TIP

Avoid running programs in the service console that consume large amounts of the processor. By allowing a third-party service console application to excessively consume CPU resources, the virtual machines and the host server performance will be adversely affected. Use esxtop to monitor service console CPU usage.

Host Server Memory Performance

Much like the processor in a VMware ESX host server, the memory of the host server is also considered a significant bottleneck. And just like the processor scenario, it is important to add as much memory to your VMware ESX host server as possible. Having a sufficient amount of memory for all of your virtual machines is important to achieving good performance. A sufficient amount of memory is roughly equivalent to the amount of memory you would have assigned to each virtual machine if they were physical. As an example, to effectively run a Windows XP Professional virtual machine you might allocate 512MB of memory to it.

It is important to note here that system memory has quickly become one of the most expensive components found in today's modern server; so you need to make sure that you properly match up the amount of memory in the system to the virtual machine density that can be achieved with the amount of processing power available. In other words, if you have enough processor resources in your host server to support ten virtual machines, don't overpopulate your host server with expensive additional memory beyond what that density is capable of consuming if you cannot achieve a higher consolidation ratio due to processor limitations.

VMware ESX server hosts are required to have a minimum of 1GB of memory. In reality, 4GB is probably more of a normal minimum requirement. Today's modern virtualization host servers are more typical with 8 or 16GB of memory, and larger environments are seeing host servers with 32 or even 64GB. ESX server hosts require more RAM than a typical application server. It must be equipped with enough memory to concurrently power and operate a number of virtual machines plus its service console and any third-party tools that may be installed.

When raw virtual machine performance is the most important metric, avoid over committing memory. Make sure the host server has more memory than the total amount of memory needed by ESX plus the sum of the memory sizes assigned to each virtual machine. Although ESX can handle over committing memory, that doesn't mean you should do it. Doing so creates a swap file per virtual machine that is located on disk in the same location where the virtual machine is located. Make sure you have enough disk space available for the swap. And remember, disk is much slower than RAM, so for performance reasons, it is best to avoid swapping to disk.

TIP

If swapping cannot be avoided, make sure you at least assign the swap file to a location on a high speed storage system.

Host Server Storage Performance

When searching for a performance bottleneck in your virtualization system, the CPU and the RAM are usually the first two suspects. But by increasing the density and usage of a physical machine with numerous virtual machines, the amount of disk I/O activity greatly increases across that server's disk subsystem. And certain workloads are also very sensitive to the latency of I/O operations. Because of that, the host server's storage system becomes the third bottleneck that needs to be addressed in a virtual world.

Storage performance issues are usually the result of a configuration problem. With ESX, you have the choice of using either local or remote storage. Either selection comes with its own set of configuration choices to be made that can affect performance. And there are also a number of other dependencies such as workload, RAID level, cache size, stripe size, drive speed and more.

Without sounding too obvious, using the fastest and highest performing disks and controllers will greatly improve the performance of your virtual environment. If you have decided to go the route of local or direct-attached disk storage in your environment, you should go with 15K RPM disks to improve the I/O performance across all of your virtual machines on that host server.

In addition to the speed of the disk drive, you should also consider the type of disk drive. While SATA drives are now possible to use with the latest version of ESX, you are better off for performance reasons spending the money and selecting either Ultra320 SCSI drives, or even better if your system supports it, SAS disks.

Many disk controllers can support multiple channels on the card, and by splitting your disks across multiple channels, you can achieve a performance improvement. For example, if you have six SCSI disks and a two-channel controller, your hardware might allow you to place three disks on each channel and configure them in a six-disk RAID-5 array. This would allow you to effectively split your I/O across two channels.

You might also be able to install multiple disk controllers and additional disks within your host server. This would allow you to split up your file system and strategically place your virtual machines according to I/O needs. In other words, if you have ten virtual machines on a host server and two of those virtual machines are running disk I/O intensive applications, you have a choice on how to configure your environment for the best possible performance. You can either locate the eight low intensive virtual machines on one controller with the two high intensive virtual machines on the other controller, or you can configure five virtual machines on each controller where only one disk I/O intensive virtual machine is allocated to each file system.

If your organization is lucky enough to afford one, it is recommended to use SAN storage rather than using locally attached disks so that you can achieve much better performance. SAN storage technology allows VMware ESX to shine with its added capabilities. Using a SAN will offload I/O operations from the ESX host server which leaves more resources available to the virtual machines. To further optimize performance, spread the I/O loads across multiple 4Gbps Fibre Channel SAN HBAs where possible. And make sure that heavily used virtual machines aren't accessing the same VMFS volume at the same time. Spread them across multiple VMFS volumes so that disk performance won't suffer.

TIP

Make sure I/O traffic isn't queuing up in the VMkernel. To verify, monitor the number of queued commands with esxtop over a period of time.

VI3 has added new options for you to take advantage of in your remote storage. In addition to Fibre Channel SAN, you can now use iSCSI and NFS to take advantage of cheaper storage solutions using your existing IP networking technology. For iSCSI and NFS, it is important to make sure that your configuration and design does not result in an oversubscribed Ethernet link. The TCP session control will ensure that there is recovery from packet loss, but frequently recovering from dropped network packets will result in huge performance problems. Virtual machines with intensive I/O applications should not share Ethernet links to a storage device. And they will perform even better if they have multiple connection paths to its storage.

When your virtual machines share access to the ESX host server's I/O subsystem, use the I/O share allocation for each virtual machine to adjust the amount of I/O resources that the virtual machine is given. For virtual machines running applications that aren't very I/O intensive, you can set their resource shares to something low, like 500. And for the more resource intensive virtual machines that require more priority to I/O resources, set their shares to something higher, like 2000.

Host Server Network Performance

Network utilization can also present bottleneck issues in your environment much like CPU, memory and storage. But in most virtualized environments, you will find that the network is probably the least likely culprit of performance problems. However with that said, the host server still needs to be supplied with the appropriate amount of network bandwidth and network resources so that the virtual machines don't add any significant amount of network latency into the equation.

If you haven't already done so, upgrade your network environment with Gigabit Ethernet. With 10GigE waiting to take over, Gigabit Ethernet network adapters and switches should be affordable. Using Gigabit network adapters allows more virtual machines to share each physical network adapter and it greatly improves the amount of network bandwidth made available to network intensive virtual machines.

When configuring your physical network adapters, the speed and duplex settings on each card must match the speed and duplex setting used on the switch port to which it is connected. The VMkernel network device drivers start with a default speed and duplex setting of auto-negotiate. The auto-negotiate setting is fine and should work correctly with network switches that are set to auto-negotiate. This is the default and preferred setting for gigabit connections. When using 100Mbit Fast Ethernet adapters, you should set the network adapter and the switch port speed and duplex settings to match at 100/Full. If you have conflicting settings between the network adapter and the switch, it can not only cause a performance problem but in some cases a connectivity issue as well.

TIP

If you encounter bandwidth issues, check to make sure the NIC auto-negotiated properly. If not, change the speed and duplex settings manually by hard coding them to match. Do so at the switch or the VMkernel networking device using the VI Client.

You can also increase the available network bandwidth and increase network fault tolerance by teaming multiple Gigabit network adapters into a bond. This will also simplify the number of virtual switches being mapped to physical network adapters as well. You can also use separate physical network adapter and vSwitches to avoid network contention between the service console, the VMkernel and the virtual machines. It can also be used to segment network I/O intensive virtual machines from one another.

You might want to leverage the new VMware ESX 3.5 networking enhancements that have been integrated into its networking code. Jumbo Frames are now supported. Supporting Ethernet frames up to 9000 bytes (as opposed to standard Ethernet frames supporting a Maximum Transfer Unit of 1500 bytes) allows guest operating systems using Jumbo Frames to require fewer packets to transfer large amounts of data. Not only can they achieve a higher throughput, but they also use less CPU than a standard Ethernet frame.

Another new feature in 3.5 is the support for TCP Segmentation Offload (TSO). TSO is widely used and supported by today's network cards. It allows for the expensive task of segmenting large TCP packets of up to 64KB to be offloaded from the CPU to the NIC hardware. ESX 3.5 utilizes this concept to provide virtual NICs with TSO support even when the underlying hardware doesn't have the special TSO capabilities. Because the guest operating system can now send packets that are larger than the MTU to the ESX server, processing overheads on the transmit path are reduced. TSO improves performance for TCP data coming from a virtual machine and for network traffic that is sent out from the server.

Configuration of the Virtual Machine

When you create virtual machines for your environment, accepting default responses aren't necessarily the right choice. Will it work? Sure. Will it be optimized for performance? Perhaps not. There are things that you should be aware of and things that you can do with the configuration of your virtual machines to squeeze out additional performance.

Remove Unneeded Virtual Hardware

One of the nice things about working with a virtual machine is the ease with which you can add or remove hardware components. You don't need any tools, and you don't need to open the hood of the server. A quick and easy way to gain a small amount of performance back in your guest environment is to disconnect or remove any unused or unnecessary devices. If your virtual machine doesn't need a CD-ROM drive, Floppy drive, Network Adapter or COM and LPT ports, get rid of them. When you do need them, it is extremely easy to either enable them or add them back. This can free up IRQ resources and it eliminates IRQ sharing conflicts.

Power off Idle Virtual Machines

Because virtual machines can so quickly and easily be created, a common problem called virtual machine sprawl has erupted. If it isn't managed properly with processes and controls, unmanaged and forgotten virtual machines can spring up and consume datacenter resources. It is important to identify virtual machines that are no longer necessary or no longer being used, because these virtual machines should be powered off or suspended to keep them from wasting valuable resources. Even if a virtual machine is idle, it still uses memory and CPU that other virtual machines could be leveraging for their own performance.

Virtual Machine Processors

When a virtual machine's performance seems sluggish, many people automatically assume that it just needs more processing power. And since VMware has upped the ante on the number of virtual processors that can be assigned to any given virtual machine, why not just add more virtual CPUs to the virtual machine to increase performance? Unfortunately, that doesn't always work. In fact, in many cases, doing so may adversely affect the entire environment and further degrade performance.

Adding additional processors to a virtual machine by using VMware's Virtual SMP is not always going to solve the performance problem. Why? First off, your performance problem may not even be caused by a lack of processing power. Your bottleneck could be memory, disk I/O or network I/O. If the guest operating system or applications aren't being starved for CPU resources, adding more CPUs may only negatively affect the rest of the environment on that host server.

And second, not all operating systems and applications are able to take advantage of having multiple CPUs. If your application is single threaded and will not benefit from the additional VCPUs, you shouldn't use Virtual SMP. In this case, adding Virtual SMP may consume valuable physical processor resources without actually offering the virtual machine any added performance benefits, and as a result, take away resources from other virtual machines on the same physical host server. Virtual SMP should therefore be used sparingly and only after determining whether or not an application is indeed multi-threaded. Running a virtual machine with a single virtual CPU, in many cases, will outperform the same virtual machine with Virtual SMP turned on. This determination should be treated on a case by case scenario, and you should test each virtual machine environment to see if Virtual SMP will help or not.

Make sure to configure your virtual machines with the correct HAL or kernel. Single processor virtual machines should be configured with a UP HAL or kernel while a multi-processor virtual machine should be configured with an SMP HAL or kernel. SMP versions are required in order to fully utilize multiprocessor systems but can also be used on single-processor systems. Because of their synchronization code, SMP operating systems used on single-processor systems will operate slower than a UP operating system.

Another way to affect virtual machine performance is by altering the virtual machine's minimum and maximum CPU resource allocation percentages. If you want to avoid CPU starvation for a virtual machine, set its minimum percentage to something other than zero. Conversely, to keep low priority virtual machines from consuming too many CPU cycles, you can set its maximum percentage to something lower, like 50%, thereby effectively throttling down that virtual machine and allowing other more pertinent virtual machines to make use of those valuable CPU cycles.

In addition to setting thresholds with MIN and MAX settings, you also have the ability to control which physical processor or processors that each virtual machine can use. This control is called processor affinity. The default setting is to use no affinity, and this is usually the best choice for most situations. You should really only set a virtual machine's CPU affinity when absolutely necessary. As an example, if you have a very resource intensive virtual machine running on a host server, you might want to set its CPU affinity to isolate that virtual machine and to protect its performance. Doing so will also protect the performance of all other virtual machines running on that same host server by changing each of their affinity settings to a different processor from that of the resource intensive virtual machine.

Virtual Machine Memory

If you are trying to optimize the performance of your virtual machine and find that the performance degradation isn't being caused by the processor, examine the virtual machine's use of memory. If the guest operating system is paging or swapping memory too much, performance will suffer since writing to disk is much slower than writing to memory. To identify if your virtual machine is paging, use vmstat from the command line on Linux or the Performance tool found under Administrative Tools on Windows to check the value for pages/second. If the number is high, such as 1000 pages/second, increase the amount of memory assigned to the virtual machine to eliminate excessive paging.

Only allocate as much memory to the virtual machine that is needed to allow enough memory to hold the working set of applications being asked to operate in the guest environment. Some amount of testing is needed here since giving a virtual machine too much memory will reach diminishing returns and simply be wasteful. The wasted memory could have been used as an additional resource elsewhere on the host server.

If possible, configure Linux virtual machines to use less than 896MB of memory. Linux uses different techniques to map memory in the kernel if the amount of physical memory is greater than 896MB. Every physical page of memory up to 896MB is mapped directly into the kernel space. This memory section is faster and more efficient and can keep your guests running optimally. Any amount of memory over that is no longer permanently mapped but is instead temporarily mapped. These techniques add additional overhead on the virtual machine monitor and can lower performance.

NOTE

It usually depends on whether you are talking to the VMware ESX administrator or the virtual machine end–user as to what the "proper" configuration amount of memory is for each virtual machine. The amount of memory a virtual machine actually needs and the amount of memory the end-user wants normally doesn't match up. Finding a proper balance is the key to a successful infrastructure implementation.

Virtual Machine Networking

If you are trying to create a networking connection between virtual machines that live on the same host server, connect the virtual machines to the same vSwitch. While it isn't mandatory that these virtual machines be connected to the same vSwitch, doing so will keep the networking traffic from going out and across the wire. At the same time, it also keeps CPU and network overhead down and increases the performance of the network communications that take place between those virtual machines.

When you create a new virtual machine, the default network adapter that is emulated on a 32-bit guest is the AMD PCnet32 device and it is configured with VMware's vlance driver. For performance reasons, in a GigE environment, you should change the emulated network adapter to use either VMware's vmxnet driver or e1000. The vmxnet driver passes through network traffic from the virtual machine to the physical network adapter with minimal overhead. And the latest version of VMware ESX provides a new version of the vmxnet virtual device called Enhanced VMXNET. It includes several new networking I/O performance improvements such as support for TCP/IP Segmentation Offload (TSO) and Jumbo Frames. It also includes 64-bit guest operating system support. The vmxnet driver comes with the VMware Tools.

Configuration of the Guest Operating System

As mentioned earlier in this chapter, if you are trying to increase the performance of your virtualization environment, why wouldn't you attempt to tune your guest operating system? Just because this is a virtual environment, don't think that many of your normal operating system tweaks used in your physical servers isn't applicable here. They very well could be the case.

There are numerous books, Web sites and other informational sources available to you that help with common operating system tweaks. This section of the chapter cannot possibly cover them all. Instead, it will discuss some of the tuning options available that are specific to a virtual machine environment.

TIP

Make sure to use supported guest operating systems. VMware Tools may not be available for an unsupported guest.

Updating VMware Tools

As simple as this may seem, it is important to remember to keep your VMware Tools up-to-date inside your guest operating system.

You should always install the latest version of the tools in your virtual machine, and you should ensure that it gets updated after each VMware ESX upgrade or patch. There are times when update patches include fixes for components of VMware Tools, which would make these updates very important to your virtual machines. If you migrate or convert virtual machines from an earlier version of ESX or from another VMware virtualization platform, make sure to remove the old VMware Tools and then install the latest version for your platform. There are differences in the editions of VMware Tools from one VMware platform to the next. If you migrate or convert a virtual machine from another vendor's virtualization platform, make sure to remove that vendor's tools and replace them with VMware's.

By installing the VMware Tools in your guest operating system, you also get these performance enhancement capabilities:

- VMXNET driver—As discussed earlier, VMware Tools provides a new updated and enhanced high speed networking driver to help improve networking performance.
- Improved video graphics driver—VMware Tools installs an improved graphics driver which gives you better mouse, keyboard and screen performance. In a Windows virtual machine, enable the hardware acceleration feature under the advanced graphics display settings on the Troubleshooting tab. This will help smooth out the mouse when remoting into the virtual machine.
- BusLogic driver—Installing VMware Tools updates the BusLogic SCSI driver within the guest operating system to the VMware supplied driver. This VMware version of the driver has certain optimizations that the guest operating system supplied driver does not.
- Memory balloon driver—The balloon driver is part of VMware Tools and is used for memory reclamation on ESX. It helps to minimize ESX swapping by better managing guest memory. Memory ballooning will not work without Tools installed.
- Idler program—An idler program is added for Netware guests to help de-schedule these guests when they go idle.

- Timer sponge—An experimental timer sponge has been added to give a correct accounting of time within the guests.
- Time sync—When VMware Tools are installed, a time synchronization feature is added to improve the time keeping function within the guests.

TIP

The time synchronization feature is not turned on automatically. Be sure to enable time sync between the ESX host server and the virtual machine from within VMware Tools. When using VMware Tools to do the time synchronization, you should not use another form of time sync within the guest operating system. Do not enable VMware Tools time sync for Windows virtual machines that are members of an Active Directory because they should time sync with a domain controller instead.

Microsoft Windows® Guest Operating System Performance

Many normal tweaks and tuning techniques used to increase the performance of a Microsoft Windows environment on a physical server can translate over to a virtual machine. And just like a physical server, not every virtual machine is alike—so the tuning method used on one machine may not work the same on another.

The latest version of VMware ESX now supports 64-bit Windows guest operating systems as well as 64-bit applications. These 64-bit versions will typically have better performance than their corresponding 32-bit counterparts.

Defragmenting the contents of a virtual machine's hard disk can have a positive effect on its disk I/O performance. Using a third-party tool like Diskeeper can keep your disk structure well organized. Be sure not to schedule the defrag task during critical or normal business hours or else you might cause more performance problems than you fix.

You can free up resources within a virtual machine by stopping and disabling unnecessary services and background tasks. Make sure however that you don't disable a service that is needed by one of your applications. The following list contains a subset of common Windows services that can usually be stopped and disabled in a Windows virtual machine. This list should only be used as a suggestion until you know if a particular service is needed or not.

- Alerter
- Clip Book
- Computer Browser
- DHCP Client (Unless using DHCP IP addresses)
- Fast User Switching Compatibility (Windows XP)
- IMAPI CD-Burning COM Service (Windows XP)

- Indexing Service (Unless needed)
- Internet Connection Firewall (ICF) / Internet Connection Sharing
- IPSEC Services
- Messenger
- Network DDE
- Network DDE DSDM
- Network Location Awareness (NLA)
- Print Spooler (May be needed in some cases)
- Remote Desktop Help Session Manager
- Remote Registry (May be needed)
- Routing and Remote Access (May be needed)
- Smart Card
- SSDP Discovery Service
- System Restore Service (Windows XP)
- Telnet (May be needed)
- Themes
- Uninterruptible Power Supply
- Windows Audio (Windows XP)
- Windows Image Acquisition (WIA)
- Windows Time (May be needed)
- Wireless Zero Configuration

If your guest operating system is Windows XP, you may want to disable the System Restore feature. Doing so will free up system resources like CPU, disk space and I/O. Instead, use the more powerful VMware snapshot feature.

Keep your Windows virtual machine as lean as possible. Uninstall any of the Windows components that aren't going to be used. Doing so will reduce the amount of memory and CPU consumed within the operating system, and will offer more resources to the applications installed in the guest. Power features such as hibernation and hardware power management (turning off hard drives, monitors, etc) really don't have much meaning in a virtual machine or add any value. Likewise, screen savers, visual effects and animations consume additional CPU resources unnecessarily and should be disabled. In most cases, you probably don't need desktop wallpaper on your virtual machine either. One exception to that might be to use something like Microsoft's Sysinternal BgInfo tool which can be very useful by offering system metrics and information as the desktop wallpaper.

Linux Guest Operating Systems Performance

Many normal tweaks and tuning techniques that are used to increase the performance of a Linux environment on a physical server can translate over to a virtual machine. And just like a physical server, not every virtual machine is alike—so the tuning method used on one machine may not work the same on another.

The latest version of VMware ESX now supports 64-bit guest operating systems as well as 64-bit applications. These 64-bit versions will typically have better performance than their corresponding 32-bit counterparts.

The guest operating system timer rate found in the Linux kernel can impact the performance of a Linux virtual machine. Linux operating systems keep time by counting its timer interrupts. Unpatched 2.4 and earlier Linux kernels request clock interrupts at 100Hz or 100 interrupts per second. By default, some 2.6 Linux kernels request interrupts at 1000Hz while others do so at 250Hz. The overhead involved with delivering so many virtual clock interrupts can unnecessarily stress the virtual hardware and negatively impact performance. The only way to change the behavior is to reduce the number of ticks per second and then recompile the kernel. Where possible, it is best to try and use a Linux kernel that uses lower timer rates to avoid this problem.

If your virtual machine is running a server-class Linux guest operating system and X server is not required for the environment, disable it. Unnecessarily running X server and screen savers in your guest environment will consume extra resources that can negatively affect performance of the virtual machine or its host server. When you do need a graphical desktop, make sure you select a light-weight window manager.

When optimizing your Linux virtual machines, make sure that you disable or remove any unnecessary daemons, services and background tasks. At the same time, be sure to remove any unneeded packages as well. This will free up processor and memory resources that can be redirected to your applications.

Backups and Anti-Virus Configuration

Backup and anti-virus configurations will probably vary based on the use of your virtual environment. In other words, how you configure backups and anti-virus to improve performance in your environment will depend on if your virtual infrastructure is a production environment or a non-production environment such as test and development. A non-production environment may not need to have anti-virus software installed (unless you are testing the anti-virus solution or the effects of anti-virus solutions). However, if this is a production environment running a Windows guest operating system, you will probably be required to have an anti-virus package installed. In that case, it should be configured in the most optimal way in order to help maximize the performance of the virtual machine.

One of the first things you can do is to setup scheduled virus scans to take place during off-peak hours so that the applications in the virtual machine do not compete for resources with the anti-virus solution. Unless your organization specifies otherwise, in most cases, a single, daily virus scan should be adequate. Additionally, most servers typically do not need real-time virus scanning turned on since this can greatly impact server performance. Disable the real-time virus scanning features when possible for production virtual machines, especially those used as database or web servers. Also, most anti-virus solutions have the ability to exclude certain files, file types, and directories from being scanned. Some application file types, such as database data files, do not need to be scanned, and in fact doing so could destroy performance. You should also configure the anti-virus solution to exclude mission critical application files that are not high risk for virus infection. Swap files are also good candidates for exclusion.

If you are running a backup agent in your virtual machines, you should also schedule the backups to take place during off-peak hours, and equally important, not during a scheduled virus scan. Again, just as with anti-virus software, scheduling backups to take place during off-peak hours will help alleviate performance degradation from applications competing for resources with the backup solution. If your organization is using VMware VI3, it's also a really good idea to make use of VMware's Consolidated Backup feature or use a third-party application that leverages the technology. Doing so will help eliminate a lot of performance overhead within the virtual machines and on your network because the technology will offload much of the overhead onto your SAN and off of your host server.

Summary

If you decide that you don't want to perform any other optimization or tuning suggestion found in this chapter, at least consider upgrading your environment to the latest version of VMware ESX. Doing so will offer you immediate environmental optimization and give you additional tools with which to better operate and control your virtual infrastructure. Upgrading can make it even easier for organizations to virtualize their most resource intensive and demanding applications. Otherwise, each of these best practice performance enhancements can be viewed on a case by case basis as needed.

Chapter 13

Automating and Extensibility

When software providers create applications and services, often times, there are things that could have been implemented but were left out of the release for one reason or another. Users of such an application or service frequently ask why a feature would be left out. The fact is, there are many reasons that come into play as to why a software company would leave out features, or functions or some component of a software product. Some reasons to limit functionality could include explanations that the provider:

- Did not know there would be a want or need for a particular feature, whether it be by the market, or by a particular segment of the market
- Did not believe that a feature was important enough to delay the release of a product so they could ensure that a particular feature would be 100% tested and complete
- Did not fully comprehend the capabilities of their software, and that by adding a feature, they could extend the usefulness or management of their product
- Chose not to provide native integration with other applications or services

Those are all valid points in the business world. Those of you that work for software companies know first hand that getting a product "to market" is sometimes more important than just having the best product. As a result, the end users of these products sometimes have to wait a while before desired features are made available. With any product or set of products, as the technology proliferates and attains different levels of maturity, additional features become available and more capable.

VMware has provided several different venues for software developers and systems administrators to automate and extend the capabilities of the Virtual Infrastructure 3 platform through the use of different Software Development Kits (SDKs) and through VI Client extensions. These tools create an environment where automating and extensibility come into play.

Software Development Kits and Toolkits

Software Development Kits (SDKs) allow for development of applications that can communicate with VMware ESX and ESXi, VMware VirtualCenter, and virtual machines residing on VMware ESX and ESXi. In addition to SDKs, Toolkits provided by VMware give developers the ability to write code to interact with VMware products. By allowing developers the ability to create environment specific applications, the capabilities of VMware's VI3 products can be significantly automated, customized, and as a result, become very extensible. A good starting point for information on the SDKs and toolkits can be found at **http://www.vmware.com/sdk/**.

VI SDK

The Virtual Infrastructure SDK communicates with the Virtual Infrastructure Application Programming Interface (VI API). The VI API is made available to applications using a Web service embedded in the Web interfaces of VirtualCenter and the VMware ESX 3.x Web service. This model allows for applications to "call" the VI API on a VirtualCenter or VMware ESX Web interface. Applications can send instructions to the VI API and then respond accordingly to those instructions. The instructions sent or calls made to the VI API can tell the VI API to have VirtualCenter or ESX behave in a particular fashion, execute instructions, or simply return data. To allow for this communication, the VI SDK is comprised of the following components:

- Web Services Description Language (WSDL)—files for making client side proxy code, sometimes called stubs
- Pre-compiled Java client libraries
- Documentation that references the API, detailing different instructional and property information including operations, data structures, and object properties
- Some sample code to give developers a starting point for developing applications

In an effort to maintain backward compatibility, the VI SDK 2.5, includes the VIM25 and VIM2 WSDL files. With both of these still available, code that is written for VMware ESX 3.0 and VirtualCenter 2.0 is still usable with the newer ESX 3.5 and VC 2.5 releases.

NOTE

The VI API is compliant with the Web Services Interoperability Organization Basic Profile 1.0 or WS-I Basic Profile 1.0, including XML Schema 1.0, SOAP 1.1, and WSDL 1.1.

On VMware ESX and VirtualCenter, the Web service acts as a communications focal point for VI API based communications. The Web service is presented in the same fashion on the VirtualCenter server as it is on the ESX host. Both instances of the VI API can recognize the same instructions, but Virtual Infrastructure features that only VirtualCenter can act upon will be disregarded by an ESX host accepting the same instructions.

Client applications communicate with the Web service using secure, or if desired non-secure, POSTs and GETs to the Uniform Resource Locator (URL) where the WSDL file is located. POSTs are data submissions from one application to another, or service. In the obverse, GETs are data requests. Telling another person to close the door could be compared to POSTing, while asking a person how their day is going could be compared to a GET. Applications post Simple Object Access Protocol (SOAP) based Extensible Markup Language (XML) messages to the Web service to instruct VirtualCenter or VMware ESX to perform actions or respond with information. SOAP is language and platform independent, coupled with being simple and extensible, which makes it a good fit for a common starting point for application programming for different platforms and languages.

Provided as part of the VI SDK, sample applications give developers a head start on writing their own managed code. Some of the sample applications include instructions to clone or migrate guests, change the power state of guests, show performance metrics, view and modify the list of tasks scheduled, a simple client, and manage snapshots of guests. By examining the sample applications along with the reference guide, creating third-party applications that can effectively integrate with VMware ESX and VirtualCenter can be developed quickly and easily.

The VI API, now at version 2.5 with the release of VirtualCenter 2.5 and VMware ESX 3.5, removes the requirements of particular types of code being run against the VI API. The VI API uses interfaces that are not specific to any particular programming language.

VI PERL Toolkit

The Virtual Infrastructure PERL Toolkit is yet another vessel used to communicate with VMware ESX and VirtualCenter. It is an easy interface to use, and often times, the interface of choice for developers that are very familiar with using the Practical Extraction and Report Language (PERL). Unlike the VI SDK, the VI

PERL Toolkit has different distributions for use by developers, depending on their platform of choice for custom coded applications. There are packages available for multiple Linux platforms, Microsoft Windows systems, as well as a Linux Virtual Appliance for the development of scripts to use with the VI PERL Toolkit. This toolkit includes many commands that automate routine commands and configuration settings. The toolkit includes the VI PERL Toolkit Runtime, VI PERL Toolkit Utility Applications, and some Sample Scripts. The utility applications, as well as sample scripts, leverage four primary subroutines to accomplish tasks. They are:

- Connect and disconnect to a VMware ESX host or VirtualCenter server
- Find server side objects on the ESX host or VirtualCenter server
- Display or change server side objects' settings on the ESX host or Virtual-Center server
- Manage Sessions

The utility applications include prewritten scripts that can display information about a host or guest, view or modify configuration settings for a host or guest, view host diagnostic information, view host performance data, manage whether a host is in maintenance mode or not, modify the power state of a guest, create or clone a guest, and much more. The code samples provide a much more in depth view of how each of the included utility applications can be used in conjunction with each other in addition to custom written code. With the success of the PERL programming language coupled with the significant number of developers familiar with it, the VI PERL Toolkit can be leveraged as a very flexible and powerful interface to VMware ESX and VirtualCenter.

VMware VI Toolkit (for Windows)

Many developers familiar with Linux platforms will choose to utilize the VI PERL Toolkit. For developers, and often times Windows administrators, PERL is not necessarily a viable language for developing scripts for the management of VMware ESX and VirtualCenter.

Windows administrators have had much more success using Visual Basic Scripting and batch files for years to manage Windows systems. In 2006, Microsoft released the PowerShell command line interface and scripting language to help administrators easily write scripts to manage and automate tasks. VMware, in an effort to give Windows administrators better scripting capabilities, has listened and is working hard on the additional new interface.

The VMware VI Toolkit is a VMware extension to Microsoft's PowerShell. To use the VMware VI Toolkit, Microsoft's Powershell 1.0 is required. With 102 VMware commands, or cmdlets, this toolkit allows for the use of Microsoft PowerShell type scripting to monitor, manage, and automate Virtual Infrastructure components with the same ease as writing Windows management and configuration scripts. Windows administrators can have a "native" platform to write VMware scripts against.

VMware CIM APIs

The CIM is a common standard information model for the management of systems, networks, applications, and services. VMware ESX supports access via the Common Information Model (CIM) using the CIM SDK.

Initially the CIM SDK was released in 2006 as a 1.0 release, supporting VMware ESX 3.0.x. This release of the CIM SDK primarily provided support for storage management of an ESX host, and a virtual machine's storage components, with a limited set of instructions for other operations. This SDK allows developers the ability to leverage the CIM SDK in vendor specific and industry standard applications that utilize the CIM.

With so many OEMs adding VMware ESXi embedded as an option for their systems, in 2008, the CIM SDK updated version was released, version 2.0, to support VMware ESXi 3.5 Update 1. With support for the CIM Server Management API, or CIM SMASH API, developers can better control an installed or embedded VMware ESXi installation.

The CIM SDK includes the following components:

- **VMware CIM SDK Reference**—a set of HTML documents describing the objects and associations the VMware CIM schema uses
- **VMware CIM SDK Programming Guide**—a book that describes how VMware applies the CIM object model to ESX host and virtual machine storage resources
- **Code Samples**—sample code allowing developers a starting point including c++, java, and python code types.
- **Data Diagrams**—diagrams that show some typical storage configurations for ESX hosts and virtual machines
- **Managed Object Format files**—MOF files that specify the CIM SDK schema

With the release of the CIM SDKs (1.0 and 2.0), VMware has again provided another interface for the integration of management and data collection functions for various VMware products.

VMware VDDK

As the CIM SDK 1.0 is primarily geared toward storage, the VMware Virtual Disk Development Kit is geared for the creation, manipulation, and the accessing of virtual disk files. The VDDK includes the Virtual Disk Library, C++ code samples, the Virtual Disk Manager utility, the DiskMount utility, and associated documentation. The Virtual Disk Library is made of a set of C function calls that define how to manipulate virtual disk files. The Virtual Disk Manager is a precompiled application that can create, clone, move, rename, extend or shrink, or defragment offline virtual disk files. The DiskMount utility allows an offline virtual disk to be attached, or mounted to a current Windows or Linux system, as a drive or mount point respectively. These tools, along with sample code, give developers more flexibility when not only viewing, but manipulating virtual disks.

VMware Guest SDK

All of the Software Development Kits and Toolkits mentioned thus far have worked from outside of the VMware environment, looking in. The VMware Guest SDK is an SDK specifically designed to run within a guest virtual machine. Another aspect of the VMware Guest SDK is that it only has access to read information through API calls. This SDK has no ability to make any changes to the guest. From the capabilities of the previously mentioned SDKs, this could seem to be less than useful. The VMware Guest SDK was designed with the idea in mind that it could be used to collect information from the guest for use by other applications, such as management agents or services running in the guest operating system. Some of the statistics that the VMware Guest SDK can collect are resource statistics and limits (including CPU and memory), amount of time since the guest was reset, or powered on. Unfortunately, during operations like VMotion, the collection abilities of code developed with the Guest SDK will be unavailable. To be able to use Guest SDK code, the only requirement for a virtual machine is that the guest operating system is supported and the VMware Tools be installed in the guest operating system (and of course the Guest SDK is enabled).

VI Client Extensions

When VirtualCenter 1.0 was released, many administrators hailed the new ability to manage multiple VMware ESX hosts simultaneously through a single interface. The Web based MUI, along with the VMware Remote Console, up until that point were the only two graphical interfaces available, and they only managed individual VMware ESX hosts. VirtualCenter 1.x was a great new interface for management and control of a VMware environment. VMware ESX hosts were no longer stand-alone virtualization platforms, but rather a Datacenter, or Farm, of VMware resources. With this newfound interface of centralized management, managing VMware ESX hosts became significantly less complicated. Even though there were some features not available for management at the VirtualCenter level, through the ease of management, along with additional capabilities it provided like VMotion, VirtualCenter has become the central management interface for VI3.

When VMware ESX 3.0 was released, the Web based MUI was replaced with a less capable interface, and more features and settings were added to the Virtual Infrastructure Client. The VI Client could manage individual VMware ESX hosts and VirtualCenter alike. More capabilities were now present in the application.

Initially, the VI SDK gave developers and systems administrators the ability to write custom applications to manage, configure, and operate an ESX host, without any ability to integrate into the VirtualCenter interface. Using these custom developed applications provided relief to some of the limitations the VI Client had. As a result, management took a step forward in functionality, but a step backwards in centralized management.With the release of VMware ESX 3.5, VirtualCenter 2.5, and the VI Client 2.5, VMware has added the ability to integrate custom developed code into the VI Client interface. The first VI Client plug-ins available addressed integrating the VMware Converter application and a new application, the VMware Update Manager. These plug-ins added the ability to convert and import physical and virtual machines into a VI3 environment, as well as manage security patches for VMware ESX hosts and virtual machine guest operating systems.

It wasn't long before several developers reverse engineered the process of how the plug-ins worked, as well as how they were installed. After that, several plug-ins were almost immediately made available. Some of these plug-ins included:

- **Storage VMotion Plug-in**—A Graphical interface for Storage VMotion
- **Add Port Groups Plug-in**—An interface to add port groups to many VMware ESX hosts simultaneously
- **Juxtaposition RDP Plug-in**—Gives the ability to launch Microsoft Remote Desktop Protocol from the VI Client to a guest machine
- **Console Plug-in**—An embedded console for VMware ESX hosts, integrated into the VI Client
- **Invoke Plug-in**—A generic script launcher that could call scripts specific to datacenters, hosts, clusters, resource pools, and guest by right clicking on the object type.

Storage VMotion Plug-in

The Storage VMotion Plug-in adds an important piece to the guest machine migration capabilities of VirtualCenter. Before this plug-in was released, command-line based instructions were required to migrate a guest's virtual disk file(s) from one datastore to another. The plug-in is initiated by right clicking on a virtual machine, and selecting "Migrate Storage." Shown in Figure 13.1, available datastores are

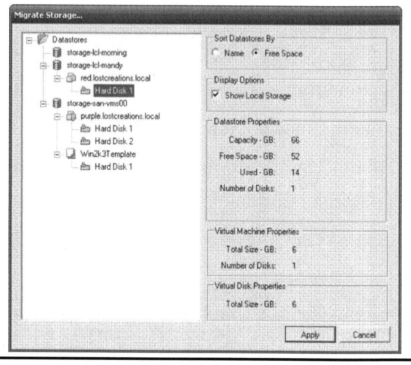

Figure 13.1 Migrate Storage with the SVMotion Plug-In.

displayed with virtual machines and their disk(s) in a tree type fashion. Without ever having to touch a command-line, an administrator may click and drag a virtual machine or their disk file(s) from one datastore to another.

> **NOTE**
>
> Clicking and dragging virtual disk files, will only migrate the virtual disks themselves, and not the guest's configuration files. To keep the configuration files and disks together, the virtual machine must be moved from one datastore to another.

Add Port Groups Plug-in

For VMware administrators that have only a few hosts, it is relatively easy to make configuration changes or additions to their environment. When managing a significant number of hosts, it can be very challenging to push out changes or additions to many hosts in a short amount of time. This is where the Add Port Groups Plug-in

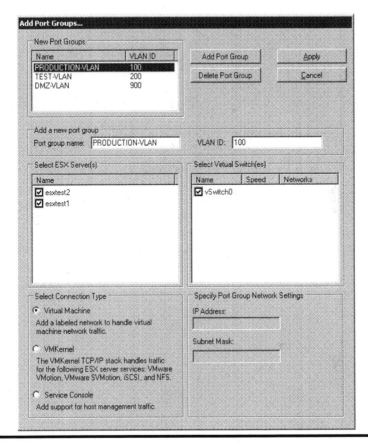

Figure 13.2   Add Port Groups Plug-In.

comes into play. With this plug-in, shown in Figure 13.2, an administrator can add or delete port groups to one or many VMware ESX hosts simultaneously.

Juxtaposition RDP Plug-in

Given the fact that virtual machines are not really ever connected to a physical monitor, the primary way to access a guest's console is either through the VI Client or through the embedded remote console. When working in a virtual machine, it is necessary to maintain a connection to that machine while performing various tasks. With that being said, there may or may not be a requirement to keep the VI Client open. Unfortunately to be connected to the guest, the VI Client is required to be kept open. There are many ways to connect to a Windows guest and using Microsoft's Remote Desktop Protocol is one of those very popular choices.

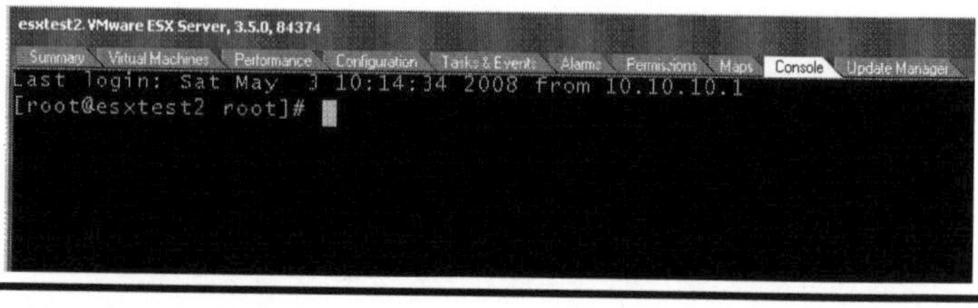

Figure 13.3   Console Plug-In.

To use Microsoft's RDP client, the name or IP address of the target machine must be known after the client has been launched. This plug-in takes the opening of the RDP client and connects it to the target guest and makes it very easy. This could be somewhat trivial, but it only shows how plug-ins coupled with the SDK's can add to the overall ease and use of VirtualCenter.

Console Plug-in

Just as the Juxtaposition RDP plug-in adds remote console capabilities to the VI Client for Windows systems, the Console plug-in does for connections to the console of VMware ESX hosts. This plug-in adds the ability to work on the console of an ESX host while still having the console available in the same place. The RDP plug-in definitely adds value for working with the guests, but the Console plug-in could almost be determined to be just as significant. Just as the VI Client natively provides a console for guest systems, shown in Figure 13.3, the Console plug-in provides a console for ESX hosts. Many functions in the VI Client are for the configuration and management of VirtualCenter and VMware ESX hosts. In previous versions of VMware ESX, many functions and configurations were only available at the console of the host. This plug-in gives administrators the flexibility to work in the console of the managed ESX hosts, while still in VirtualCenter.

Invoke Plug-in

The Invoke plug-in could be one of the most significant plug-ins published to date. This is because it gives administrators the ability to use previously written scripts from within VirtualCenter. A good example of the flexibility of the Invoke plug-in can be seen in Figure 13.4. There are two scripts labeled "Change to Windows Vista Guest Type" and "Change to Windows 2008 Guest Type" shown in the illustration. These scripts use information passed from VirtualCenter to invoke a PowerShell script that changes the guest operating system type in a guest's configuration. These scripts were written to overcome the fact that VirtualCenter 2.5 cannot upon deployment customize a Windows 2008 guest. However, if the guest type is

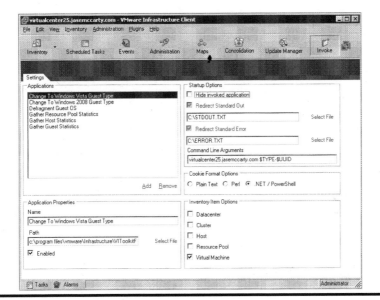

Figure 13.4   Execute Scripts with the Invoke Plug-In.

Windows Vista, it can be customized. Using the Invoke plug-in can, through a few simple clicks, change the guest type to overcome this limitation. Now a guest that is running Windows Server 2008 can easily be customized. Without the SDK, the toolkits, and VI Client Extensions, automation like this would not be possible.

Summary

With any software platform, there are always going to be features that users and administrators want but aren't present. In an effort to make the Virtual Infrastructure 3 platform easy to manage and integrate, VMware has provided several Software Development Kits and toolkits. The release of these SDKs and toolkits has made a profound impact on the integration of VMware's products into other enterprise management products, as well as the ability to create environment specific custom applications. Often times, custom applications or scripts give VMware more insight into what we, the end users, want from their products. As long as there are users and developers with imaginations and needs for more capabilities, use of the SDKs and toolkits will proliferate.

Chapter 14

Additional Useful Resources

So now that you've read most of this book, does the information flow have to stop there? The answer is no. It would be extremely difficult to capture the entire VMware universe in a single book, so we've made additional information resources available to you so that you can continue your virtualization journey beyond the pages of this book.

In addition to the information described throughout this book, there are also additional third-party products and services available to you that can help address niche areas of server virtualization to further extend and enhance your VMware ESX implementation. In this chapter, we'll provide a brief look at some of the resources provided by a few of these vendors along with a look at other valuable resources that are being offered via the Internet that provide a wealth of information on the subject.

Product Vendor Resources

VMware offers a number of resources and informational sites to help get you down the path.

VMware Web Site

The VMware Web site (http://www.vmware.com) provides a tremendous amount of resources relating to the various product offerings made by VMware. They offer

Figure 14.1   VMware Community Web site

news and events that customers of their products will more than likely be interested in hearing about. The Web site also provides you with the latest updates and security patches for all of their products in a download section. Other information provided includes links to documentation, frequently asked questions (FAQs), technical resources in the form of guides and white papers, as well as developer resources in the form of code and SDK packages.

But perhaps the most important area on VMware's Web site is the Communities page (http://www.vmware.com/communities/content/). The Communities page shows that VMware is also a big proponent of information sharing (see Figure 14.1). This section of the Web site provides for a searchable knowledge base as well as a discussion forum where users are able to post questions and receive answers from other users as well as from VMware employees. This resource is probably the most likely place you will find answers to VMware specific product questions. Unfortunately, as with any open forum such as this, there is also erroneous information that must be waded through in order to find the correct answer to the question.

VMware User Group

The VMware User Group (VMUG) program (http://www.vmware.com/communities/content/vmug/) is designed to encourage and support communities of VMware users who want to hold regular meetings in their local area. The purpose of these gatherings is to provide a forum in which VMware users can share best practices and expertise, and VMware can in turn obtain feedback from the user community.

VMware User Groups are made up of independent communities of VMware users who get together to exchange ideas and information. There are many benefits to participating in a VMware User Group:

- Learn best practices and optimal use of VMware products
- Get answers, advice, tips, and suggestions from experts
- Discover new ideas and gain insight about Virtual Infrastructure
- Receive special information about new VMware products
- Network with other technical professionals in your area
- Be part of the leading edge of VMware users

VMUG has its own set of Web pages on the VMware Communities section on the company's Web site. Here, you can find a list of upcoming VMUG events, a forum for user group members to discuss important topics, you can find a local group in your community to join and participate in, and if one doesn't exist, you can find out more information about starting your own group in your community.

VMware Appliance Marketplace

If you aren't familiar with what a virtual appliance is, you should be. Virtual appliances are simply pre-built, pre-configured, ready-to-run enterprise applications packaged with an operating system inside a virtual machine. It offers a paradigm shift in the way software is developed, delivered and then consumed. Rather than creating complex software installation requirements and procedures, software customers can now easily install and deploy these pre-integrated solution stacks into their environment, and greatly speed up time to value.

The Appliance Marketplace (http://www.vmware.com/appliances/) currently has somewhere in the neighborhood of 400 virtual appliances being made available for download and consumption. The solution categories are very diverse, covering software products in a number of categories such as: Administration, App/Web Server, Communications, Database, Networking, Operating Systems, Security and more. The marketplace makes it easy to find what you are looking for, by breaking things down into categories, offering a search component, and showing the most recently added appliances or the most popular or most downloaded.

VMTN Blogs

The VMware Technology Network (http://blogs.vmware.com/vmtn/) has a great news and information section that provides content from VMware as well as the community of virtualization users. The VMTN Blog section is also broken out further into Planet V12n (a conglomeration of community blog sites covering virtualization topics) and Planet VMware (a great listing of VMware employee blogs). The growing list of blogs on this site is a testament to the growing awareness, understanding and proliferation of virtualization in the industry. This is a great place to go to find out what VMware and the community at large are talking about. And because this is a community of virtualization blogs, VMware isn't necessarily limiting blog posts to its own technology. You will find blog discussions about VMware competitors as well as other virtualization technologies, third-party software and hardware related discussions.

VMworld Conference

In 2004, VMware created its first annual user conference, VMworld (http://vmworld.com), which was the first and only industry conference dedicated solely to the virtual infrastructure. The inaugural event welcomed nearly 1,600 attendees to the conference and somewhere in the neighborhood of 30 show sponsors. Only three years later, VMworld 2007 attendance grew to almost 11,000 IT professionals and executives and had an impressive 147 sponsors and exhibitors. And even though the conference is hosted by VMware, it has grown to become the largest virtualization event in the world. In addition to the large showing of virtualization exhibitors, VMworld also has hundreds of unique sessions and panel discussions as well as more than 100 hands-on-labs in order to learn about any number of topics and applications. The event is also a great place to interact and network with VMware executives and engineers or with your virtualization peers. In 2008, VMware took the show on the road and crossed the ocean, bringing a similar experience to European users with VMworld Europe in Cannes, France. The VMworld Web site contains more information about the conference, and it also contains a well established online community around the event.

Third-Party Vendor Resources

VMware owes much of its success to its global partner ecosystem. To help further validate and extend VMware's ESX technology, third-party vendors have stepped up to the plate to try and fill in the gaps left by VMware.

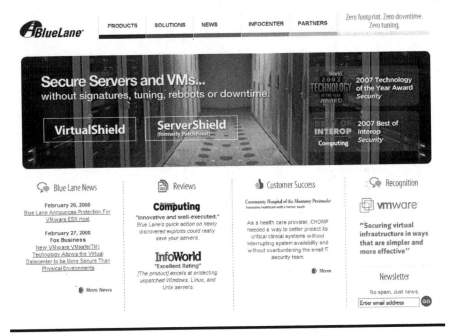

Figure 14.2   Blue Lane Technology—Virtualization Security

Blue Lane Technologies

As virtualization technologies began to move from development and test into enterprise production environments, security issues started to surface when talking about the readiness of server virtualization. Blue Lane Technologies (http://www.bluelane.com) took the charge and started providing solutions that would secure virtual and physical data centers with zero footprint, zero downtime and zero tuning (See Figure 14.2). Blue Lane's solution reduces the vulnerability of unpatched servers and virtual machines by applying application logic in the network and correcting traffic aimed at known software vulnerabilities. It checks for the same conditions in enterprise servers and virtual machines, and then it applies the same corrective action as the software vendor security patch so that it can fix application-specific vulnerabilities at the root cause.

Catbird

Catbird (http://www.catbird.com) provides a fully-hosted managed security platform for virtual and physical networks, enabling its global partners to deliver enterprise-grade hacker protection that is cost-effective for businesses of all sizes. Founded in 2000 by Internet pioneer Ron Lachman, the company's in-the-cloud architecture protects thousands of customer systems and networks who rely on Catbird and its partners to protect their valuable IT assets from external and internal threats. Catbird delivers completely non-invasive Web Security and Network Admission Control (NAC) through its unique Security-as-a-Service™ model. The Catbird V-Agent offers VMware Infrastructure customers a comprehensive suite of security capabilities never before available. In addition, the seamless integration to the Catbird Security Services allows each VMware customer to manage their security from a highly secure web portal, allowing global access by IT staff.

Gear6

Gear6 (http://www.gear6.com) solutions enhance VMware deployments in several ways: Large scale virtual server deployments often place heavy stress on I/O and storage subsystems, particularly when server utilization increases 3-4x. Gear6 products remove I/O bottlenecks and accelerate data access. VM provisioning and migration with VMotion can be accelerated by caching VMs and VM state in Gear6 appliances. CACHEfx appliances deliver high I/O operations per second and extremely low latency to accelerate the performance of data intensive applications. The appliances scale to multiple terabytes of capacity and attach to the network, complementing both traditional Network Attached Storage (NAS) deployments and clustered file systems. Serving requests from high speed memory provides applications a massive throughput increase and real time access to data. Large files, data sets, and entire databases are reliably cached to accelerate I/O performance between 10 and 50 times.

PlateSpin

PlateSpin (http://www.platespin.com) currently has several virtualization solutions on the market that attempt to bring optimization to the IT industry and help enterprises adopt, manage and extend their use of server virtualization in the data center (See Figure 14.3). They also have a rich virtualization history as one of the early pioneer third-party software companies in the virtualization community. One of their early products is a physical to virtual (P2V) solution called PlateSpin PowerCovert. The software product is a powerful workload portability solution that provided one of the first offerings to remotely decouple workloads from the underlying server hardware and then offer the ability to stream them to and from any physical or virtual host with a simple drag and drop. The product was designed to take over from VMware's P2V Assistant. The company's PowerRecon product addresses two key areas of virtual infrastructure management: chargeback and virtual machine growth reporting. And the latest offering from PlateSpin is a product called PlateSpin Forge which helps provide business continuance and disaster recovery via a hardware appliance. PlateSpin was recently acquired by Novell—which further validates the need for these types of tools.

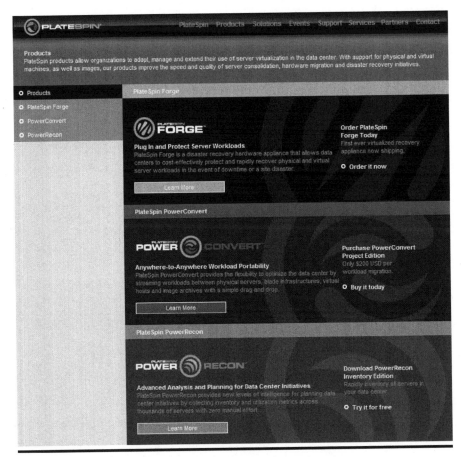

Figure 14.3   PlateSpin—P2V and Disaster Recovery Solutions

rPath

For application providers that want to accelerate license growth, expand into new markets, and reduce support and development costs, rPath's (http://www.rpath.com) platform transforms applications into virtual appliances. Virtual appliances eliminate the hassles of installing, configuring and maintaining complex application environments. rPath's technology produces appliances in multiple virtual machine formats which simplifies application distribution, and lowers the customer service costs of maintenance and management. The company's product, rBuilder, enables an ISV to combine their application with the operating system to create a software appliance that readily installs on industry standard servers or via a virtual machine. The rPath Appliance Platform provides the perfect complement to rBuilder by enabling a seamless management experience for the customer throughout the application lifecycle. All configuration and maintenance is handled from a simple browser interface, and you control the release of all updates.

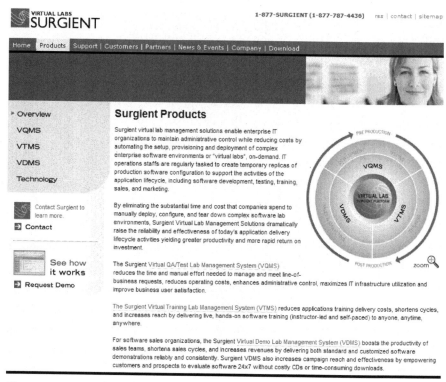

Figure 14.4   Surgient—Software Demo, Training and Testing

Surgient

As an early adopter of server virtualization, Surgient (http://www.surgient.com/) was a pioneering company becoming one of, if not, the first companies to leverage virtualization as an API platform for a software solution (See Figure 14.4). Surgient provides on-demand applications that enable companies to increase the effectiveness of their direct sales, online marketing, technical training, and QA/Verification processes. The company has created its own virtualization vendor agnostic management interface that not only provides a comprehensive management solution, but when packaged with its application offerings, it enables the use of distributed enterprise application environments by any user, on-demand, from anywhere at anytime. It eliminates the complexities of hardware configuration and software environment provisioning. Surgient is able to offer its products to its customers in the form of a hosted solution as well as a licensed package.

Veeam

Veeam Software (http://www.veeam.com) helps IT professionals better manage their VMware environment (See Figure 14.5). The company is perhaps best known

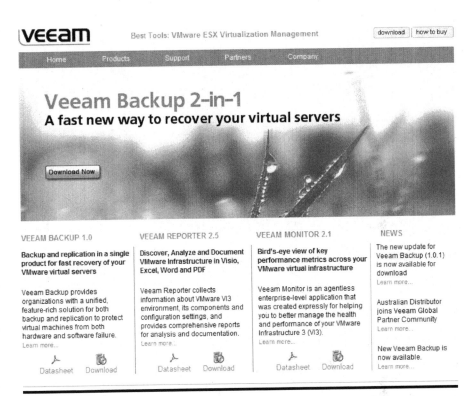

Figure 14.5 **Veeam—Providing Backup, Reporting and Monitoring Tools**

for its FastSCP product, a fast, secure and easy-to-use tool to perform file management in VMware ESX environments. Since the launch of the free FastSCP product, the company has created other VMware solutions such as: Veeam Reporter, an automated way to discover and document VMware environments; Veeam Monitor, an enterprise level application designed to better manage the health and performance of VMware Infrastructure 3; and Veeam Configurator, providing GUI-based centralized control over VMware ESX settings and subsystems.

Vizioncore

Vizioncore Inc. (http://www.vizioncore.com) provides software that helps organizations safeguard and optimize their virtualized environments. Vizioncore's software products support essential IT strategies, including business continuity, high availability and disaster recovery. Vizioncore has been building the company around its flagship product, vRanger Pro, which has quickly become one of the leading standards for hot image backup in a virtual environment (See Figure 14.6). vRanger Pro is a backup solution that was built with virtual environments in mind, but it can also perform file-level recovery as well. Today, it is one of the most recognized and

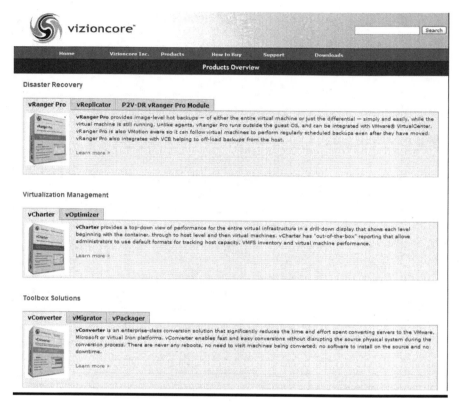

Figure 14.6 Vizioncore—Offering a Suite of Virtualization Management Tools

widely used backup solutions in the VMware community. Vizioncore also offers a number of other solutions such as vCharter, vMigrator, vRepicator, vConverter, vOptimizer and vPackager to form a more comprehensive suite of applications to enhance VMware ESX.

VKernel

VKernel (http://www.vkernel.com) recognized the need for virtual appliances that could answer problems with point solutions such as monitoring and tracking resources on VMware ESX hosts (See Figure 14.7). To help with performance problems, the company created the Capacity Bottleneck Analyzer virtual appliance which identifies capacity bottlenecks on hosts, clusters and resource pools. And the company also offered help to organizations trying to answer the question "How do I charge departments for virtual machine usage?" VKernel's Chargeback Virtual Appliance helps organizations charge users for the resources consumed in the virtual environment (CPU, memory, storage and network).

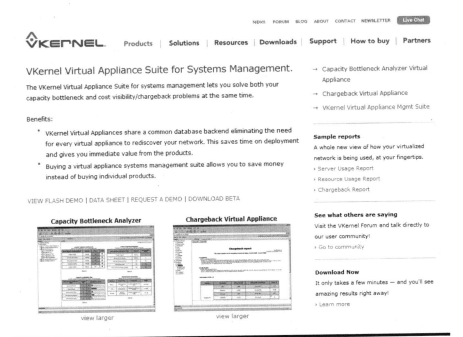

Figure 14.7   VKernel—Virtual Appliances for Chargeback and Capacity

VMLogix

VMLogix (http://www.vmlogix.com) provides groundbreaking software solutions that help software companies and IT organizations leverage virtualization to consolidate lab infrastructure and automate build and test processes so that software can be delivered more quickly, cost-effectively and reliably (See Figure 14.8). With its LabManager product suite offering, VMLogix can assist the way software development teams around the globe manage their automated software lifecycle and quality assurance processes. By offering agile, self-service virtualization tools, VMLogix enables these teams to deliver more reliable products at lower costs, more quickly than ever before.

Information Resources and Web Links

VMBlog.com

Full disclosure, one of the authors of this book, David Marshall, owns and operates VMBlog.com (http://vmblog.com). David has been involved in the virtualization industry since 1999, and has been accumulating and sharing this type of information with friends and co-workers for many years. Within this virtualization news

VMLogix LabManager

Software development & QA teams are mandated to deliver feature-packed, high quality products with small teams, tight budgets and compressed timelines. Development of enterprise software requires the setup of varied and complex environments, which is a tedious, time consuming and often unreliable process.

Yet, enterprises are faced with the challenge of ensuring fast, repeatable and consistent dev & test environment setups while also trying to improve resource utilization and employee productivity. LabManager is a revolutionary software product that automates this entire process.

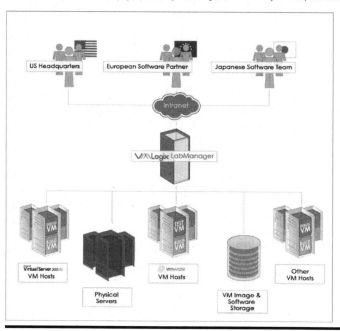

Figure 14.8   VMLogix—Virtual Lab Automation Solution

site, he makes it a point to cover all the latest trends, technologies and news that relates to virtualization (See Figure 14.9). This particular Web site was launched in 2005, and it was created and designed to keep track of everything that was happening within the IT industry—specifically within the context of virtualization. Rather than solely focusing on one vendor or one type of virtualization, the Web site covers all the latest information across a broad spectrum of server, desktop, application, storage and network virtualization from software to hardware. The site also offers numerous links to other informational Web sites, vendors and projects.

InfoWorld Virtualization Report

More full disclosure, InfoWorld's Virtualization Report is also operated by one of the authors of this book, again, David Marshall. The InfoWorld Virtualization Report (http://weblog.infoworld.com/virtualization) covers a wide range of news and information that relates to all of the various virtualization technologies in the industry. In addition to covering the latest news, the Virtualization Report also

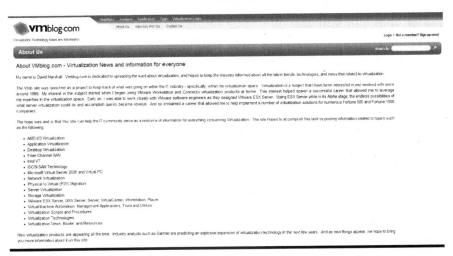

Figure 14.9   VMBlog.com—Virtualization Technology News and Information

offers key insight into virtualization technology through interview Q&A sessions with many of today's virtualization executives, analysts and industry experts from the field. And if you can't get enough reading about virtualization, the site also offers two Virtualization Report Podcasts each week for your listening pleasure.

Virtual Strategy Magazine

Occupying a unique niche among magazines, Virtual Strategy Magazine (http://www.virtual-strategy.com) is an online-only technical magazine that is solely focused on virtualization. The magazine provides its readers with news and technical information in a single, easy to read source (See Figure 14.10). Information is also supplemented with technical tips and real-world experiences from virtualization users, and it also offers audio recorded Podcast interviews with many key individuals in the virtualization field. Members of the magazine can also take part in free teleconferences and Web seminars as they are offered. And to keep you further informed, the site also lists several virtualization whitepapers, webinars and events, and also provides its members with a free newsletter.

RTFM Education

If you've ever been told to RTFM, you probably already know that someone wants you to "read the manual". And so attempting to help educate the masses within the virtualization community, RTFM's owner, Mike Laverick, has been providing free educational content in the form of RTFM Guides and whitepapers (http://www.rtfm-ed.co.uk). Offered in PDF format, these guides cover the various VMware enterprise products (ESX, VirtualCenter, P2V, etc) and they have been a big hit within the community. And if you are interested in taking the VMware

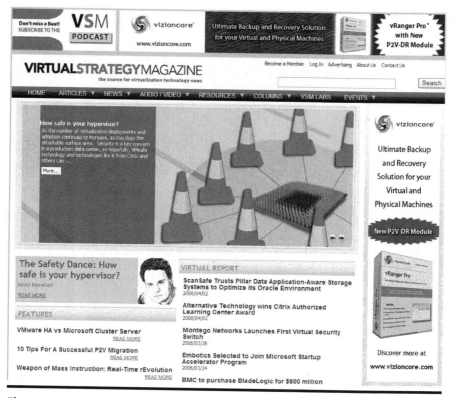

Figure 14.10 Virtual Strategy Magazine—Online Magazine Dedicated to Virtualization

administrator certification exam (VCP), you might want to check out the RTFM VCP Guides. And finally, if you are thinking about performing a P2V conversion in your environment and don't know where to start, you should look at the Ultimate P2V page on the Web site. It offers an informational and free tool to help you perform a physical to virtual migration—dubbed, Ultimate P2V.

Virtualization.Info

One of the oldest dedicated virtualization news sites on the Internet, Virtualization. info (http://virtualization.info) was established in 2003 by its founder Alessandro Perilli. This site is another good place to get aggregated news and analysis on the virtualization industry (See Figure 14.11). In addition to the news and insight that it offers readers, the site also provides unique tools such as the Virtualization Industry Challenges Report, the Virtualization Industry Radar, the Virtualization Industry Roadmap and the Virtualization Industry Predictions. Teaming up with a company called Kybernetika, the site is able to offer something called "Rent-A-Lab",

VIRTUALIZATION.INFO

Home   About   Advertise   Contact   Subscribe   Get Together >   Community   Virtualization Congress

What is Virtualization?   Industry Analysis Tools >   Challenges   Radar   Roadmap   Predictions   TechTalk   Services >   Bookstore

About virtualization.info

Established 2003, virtualization.info is the most popular news site about virtualization industry.

Several points differentiate it from any other online media in the space:

- **News digest**
  virtualization.info daily tracks tents of news sources, verifying informations published in every major news magazines, corporate and personal blogs, web forum and newsgroups.
  From over 500 articles per day we publish **no more than 10 major news per day**, cutting away all the marketing hype, to avoid waste of time and informations overload.

- **The big picture**
  Most news are enriched with references to the companies' market position, including past and upcoming product releases, declared and implicit alliances, expected evolutions and more.
  So each article contributes to **detail the overall industry status**, to give readers always the big picture.

- **Strategical insights**
  Along with daily news, virtualization.info publishes periodic insights about different aspects of the market, covering competition, emerging trends, customers and partners relationships.
  Where connections between vendors and their strategies are unclear, our **analysis helps connecting the dots**.

- **Unique tools**
  On top of filtered news and strategical insights virtualization.info also offers unique tools with simplifies the understanding of virtualization industry for newest customers.
  The Virtualization Industry Challenges report details implementation problems that every virtualization adopter has to face.
  The Virtualization Industry Radar provides rating and critical informations about all market players.
  The Virtualization Industry Roadmap highlights past and future product releases for each vendor.
  The Virtualization Industry Predictions keeps track of all forecasts issued by major industry analysis firms in the world.

Figure 14.11   Virtualization.info—Virtualization Information Web Site

which gives people the ability to rent a server, network switch and SAN to perform various functions in a rented virtual environment.

TechTarget

TechTarget is one of the Web's most comprehensive sources of information for IT professionals. The site offers two sources of virtualization information. The older of the two, SearchServerVirtualization (http://searchservervirtualization.techtarget. com), offers a much broader look at virtualization, covering more than just the technologies offered by VMware. The newer Web site, SearchVMware (http://searchvmware. techtarget.com), is more focused on VMware environments. Both Web sites however have dedicated editors, resident experts and news writers that are focused on providing readers with access to the latest news, tips, expert advice, whitepapers and webcasts on all areas of server virtualization, such as virtualization platforms, server hardware, managing virtual environments, virtualization architectures and strategies, application issues and more.

Virtualization Events

With the success of both VMworld and the virtualization technology itself, there has been a sudden rise in the number of events that cater to this technology. While there still aren't many dedicated virtualization conferences, most IT events have been adding virtualization tracks to their list of sessions. Some of the more popular events include the Virtualization Conference & Expo (http://www.virtualizationconference.com), InfoWorld's Virtualization Executive Forum (http://www.infoworld.com/event/virtualization/index.html), IDC Virtualization Forum (http://www.idc.com/events/eventshome.jsp), Interop (http://www.interop.com), TechTarget Virtualization Seminars (http://searchvmware.techtarget.com/events), and LinuxWorld Conference & Expo (http://www.linuxworldexpo.com).

Summary

Server virtualization as a platform is starting to take hold and spread throughout the IT community. Its popularity and usefulness is evidenced by the numerous third-party software packages that are being developed, sold, and downloaded in addition to all of the news and information Web sites that are starting to appear across the Internet. The resources discussed in this chapter are but a brief look at the many informational Web sites, events and commercial products being offered to help fully utilize and understand server virtualization. It is important to keep in mind; these are merely a select few of the server virtualization resources that are currently available. A complete list of Web sites and products would not be possible, however, links to more vendors, products, projects and news and information web sites can be found on VMBlog.com.

Appendix I

Useful Log Files

For the most part, trying to diagnose a problem with a virtual machine or a virtualization host server is not that different than trying to diagnose a problem with an application or a physical server. Just as physical servers and applications exhibit strange behavior that lead to problems needing to be researched, virtualization hosts and virtual machines also have problems that need to be identified as quickly as possible to correct some adverse situation. One of the best places to start looking for answers is the virtualization log files. This chapter provides a quick reference to commonly used log files as well as their locations as shown in Figure I.1.

If problems are encountered while running VMware ESX, VMware requests that they are reported to the VMware support team. In order to report the problem and have VMware support help diagnose the situation, the company provides a support script to conveniently collect and package all relevant ESX log files as well as system and configuration information needed for troubleshooting. This section will describe how to run the support script as well as identify most of the important ESX log files.

ESX Support Script

On an ESX host machine, use the following steps:

1. Open a service console window.
2. Log in as the root user.
3. For ESX Server versions 2.1.x and earlier, the latest vm-support script should be downloaded from VMware's Web site. Archive the original vm-support script and then replace it with the newer version. For ESX Server 2.x and VI3

Platform*	Log	Location
ESX	ESX Support Script	/usr/bin/vm-support
ESX	Virtual Machine Log	Located in the same directory as the virtual machine's configuration file and named vmware.log.
ESX	VMKernel Warnings	/var/log/vmkwarning
ESX	VMKernel Messages	/var/log/vmkernel
ESX	Service Console Messages	/var/log/messages
ESX Server 2.x	Service Log	/var/log/vmware/vmware-serverd.log
ESX 3.x		/var/log/vmware/hostd.log
ESX	Virtual Machine Kernel Core	/root/vmkernel-core.<date> and /root/vmkernel-log.<date>
ESX3.x	VI Client Agent Log	/var/log/vmware/vpx/vpxa.log
ESX 3.x	VI Client Installation Log	Located in the temp directory on the client machine. (ex. C:\Documents and Settings\<user name>\Local Settings\Temp\vmmsi.log
ESX 3.x	VI Client Service Log	Located in the \vpx directory in the temp directory of the client machine. (ex. C:\Documents and Settings\<user name>\Local Settings\Temp\vpx\viclient-x.log, where x=0, 1, ... 9)
ESX	VMKernel Log	/proc/vmware/log

Figure I.1   Log Files At-A-Glance A001x001.

versions through 3.5, the script is located in /usr/bin. For ESX Server 1.5.x, the script is located in /usr/lib/vmware.

4. Execute the following script: /usr/bin/vm-support (For ESX 1.5.x, run /usr/lib/vmware/vm-support).

5. The script will collect and package all relevant ESX system and configuration information and ESX log files. This information could prove quite valuable when trying to analyze problems that you might encounter with the host environment.

6. The resulting file will be saved as a compressed .tgz file called esx-<date>-<unique-xnumber>.tgz. The script will display the output filename and the file location.

7. The output file should be included with support requests made to VMware. It can also be uncompressed to help with internal troubleshooting as the log files are now conveniently located in one place.

Log Files

The following log files are created by ESX and are among the log files collected by the support scripts described above. Log files such as VMkernal Warnings, VMkernal Logs, and Service Console Logs can be viewed through the GUI VMware Management Interface by logging in as root and choosing Options followed by System Logs. These and other log files can also be viewed directly by accessing the service console. If the VMkernel fails, an error screen normally appears for a short period of time and then the virtual machine reboots. Additionally, when configuring the virtual machine, a VMware core dump partition should be specified. By doing so, the VMkernel may also generate a core dump file and an error log.

Virtual Machine Log File

If a virtual machine crashes or ends abnormally, this file should be saved off immediately for the affected virtual machine. It is important to save off this file before the virtual machine is powered back on. The log file is located in the same directory as the affected virtual machine's configuration file and is named vmware.log.

VMkernal Warnings

The VMkernel warnings log file is a good resource when experiencing problems with the ESX server or the virtual machines. From the console, the data is logged at /var/log/vmkwarning. The log should be checked periodically for any alerts that may get recorded.

VMkernel Messages

The VMkernel messages log file is a good resource when experiencing problems with the ESX server or the virtual machines. From the console, the data is logged at /var/log/vmkernel. The log should be checked periodically for any alerts that may get recorded.

Service Console Messages

The service console messages log file is a good resource when experiencing problems with the ESX server or the virtual machines. From the console, the data is logged at /var/log/messages. The log should be checked periodically for any alerts that may get recorded.

ESX Service Log

If a problem is encountered while connecting to virtual machines or using the management interface, this log file may help in diagnosing the problem. In a VMware ESX Server 2.x environment, the log file is identified as vmware-serverd. log and is located in /var/log/vmware. In a VMware ESX 3.x environment, the log file is identified as hostd.log and is also located in /var/log/vmware.

Virtual Machine Kernel Core File

The virtual machine kernel core files are present after you reboot your machine. The files are logged as /root/vmkernel-core.<date> and /root/vmkernel-log.<date>.

VI Client Agent Log

The VI client agent log file is logged at /var/log/vmware/vpx/vpxa.log.

VI Client System Logs

The VI Client machine also contains a list of important log files.

VI Client Installation Log

The installation log file is a good resource to validate installation issues with the VI Client. The log files are by default located in the Temp directory on the VI Client machine. As an example, the log file would be located in C:\Documents and Settings\<user name>\Local Settings\Temp\vmmsi.log.

VI Client Service Log

The log file is located in the \vpx directory in the temp directory on the VI Client machine. As an example, the log files would be located in C:\Documents and Settings\<user name>\Local Settings\Temp\vpx\viclient-x.log, where x(=0, 1, ... 9).

Appendix II

Useful TCP and UDP Ports

VMware virtualization and its related technologies commonly use TCP/IP network protocols to provide specific features such as management of the virtualization host server or they can be used to provide remote access to the virtual machine. This appendix consolidates the most commonly used TCP and UDP ports that are used and additionally will provide the necessary information on what features will use the port as shown in Figure II.1. If the host server is behind a firewall, the firewall may need to be reconfigured to allow access to the appropriate ports.

VMware Ports

- 8222 TCP (HTTP)
  Used to connect to an older version of VMware ESX host machine by using the VMware Management Interface (if SSL is disabled). For backward compatibility, ESX handles this port as an HTTP redirect to TCP port 80.
- 8333 TCP (HTTPS)
  Used to connect to an older version of VMware ESX host machine by using the VMware Management Interface (uses SSL). For backward compatibility, ESX handles this port as an HTTPS redirect to TCP port 443.
- 21 TCP (FTP)
  Used for transferring files between machines. Often used in a low to medium security environment.

Port	TCP/UDP	Protocol	Description	Security
21	TCP	FTP	File Transfers	Low to medium
22	TCP	SSH	Remote Access	Medium to high
23	TCP	Telnet	Remote Access	Low
80	TCP	HTTP	Old Web Management Interface or to Connect VI Client to VirtualCenter	Low
111	TCP	Portmap	Portmap - NFS	Low to medium
427	TCP	-	Used for the CIM Client	
443	TCP	HTTPS	Web Management interface and Connects VI Client to VirtualCenter	Medium to high
902	TCP/UDP	-	VMware Remote Console, Authentication Traffic for VI3, VI3 Migration and Provisioning	Low to high
903	TCP	-	VI Client Access and VI Web Access Client to Virtual Machine Consoles	Low to high
2049	TCP	-	NFS Storage Devices	Low
2050 - 2250	TCP/UDP	-	Traffic Between VI3 Hosts for HA and EMC Autostart Manager	Low to high
3260	TCP	-	iSCSI Storage Devices	Low
3389	TCP	RDP	Connection to a Microsoft Windows VM	Low to high
5900 - 5906	TCP	RFB	Used by VNC Management Tools	Low to high
5988	TCP	-	Used for CIM XML over HTTPS	Medium to high
5989	TCP	-	Used for CIM XML over HTTP	Low to high
8000	TCP	-	Incoming Requests for VMotion	Medium to high
8042 - 8045	TCP/UDP	-	Traffic Between VI3 Hosts for HA and EMC Autostart Manager	Low to high

Figure II.1   TCP/IP Ports At-A-Glance.

■ 22 TCP (SSH)
Used to establish a secure shell connection to the ESX service console or a Linux virtual machine. Often used in a medium to high security environment because it is more secure than connecting with a simple Telnet connection.

■ 23 TCP (Telnet)
Used to establish a non-secure shell connection to the ESX service console or a Linux virtual machine in a low to medium security environment.

■ 111 TCP (portmap)
Used by the NFS client when mounting a drive on a remote machine in a low to medium security environment.

- 3389 TCP (RDP)
  Used to connect to a Microsoft Windows virtual machine.

- 80 TCP (HTTP)
  Used to connect to an older version of VMware ESX host machine by using the VMware Management Interface in a low security environment. Used to insecurely connect the VI Client to VirtualCenter. Port 80 redirects traffic to an HTTPS landing page (port 443) from which you launch the virtual machine console. Use port 80 for connection to VI Web Access from the Web.

- 427 TCP
  The CIM client uses the Service Location Protocol, version 2 (SLPv2) to find CIM servers.

- 443 TCP (HTTPS)
  Used to connect to an older version of VMware ESX host machine by using the VMware Management Interface in a medium to high security environment. And it is used to connect the VI Client to VirtualCenter, the Web Access Client to VirtualCenter and VirtualCenter to the ESX host. It is also used for WS-Management, VMware Update Manager and VMware Converter.

- 902 TCP, UDP (vmware-authd)
  Used when connecting to virtual machines by using the VMware Virtual Machine Console. Used for authentication traffic for the ESX 3. The VMware ESX host will use this port to communicate with VirtualCenter and for ESX 3 host access to other ESX Server 3 hosts for migration and provisioning.

- 903 TCP
  Used for Remote console traffic to virtual machines generated on a specific ESX 3 host server. Used for VI Client access to virtual machine consoles and for VI Web Access Client access to virtual machine consoles.

- 2049 TCP (NFS storage devices)
  This port is used on the VMkernel interface rather than the service console interface.

- 2050-2250 TCP, UDP
  Traffic between ESX 3 hosts for VMware High Availability (HA) and EMC Autostart Manager. These ports are managed by the VMkernel interface.

- 3260 TCP (iSCSI storage devices)
  This port is used on the VMkernel interface and the service console interface.

- 5900-5906 TCP
  RFB protocol which is used by management tools such as VNC.

- 5988 TCP
  This port is used for CIM XML transactions over HTTPS.

- 5989 TCP
  This port is used for CIM XML transactions over HTTP.

- 8000 TCP (VMotion)

  This port is used on the VMkernel interface rather than the service console interface. Used for incoming requests from VMotion.

- 8042-8045 TCP, UDP

  These ports are used for traffic between ESX 3 hosts for HA and EMC Autostart Manager.

- 27000 and 27010 TCP

  These ports are used for communication between VirtualCenter and the VMware License Server.

Appendix III

Useful VMware COS Commands for Windows Users

As a Microsoft Windows user first diving into a VMware ESX environment, you will more than likely be exposed to a fair amount of new terminology or commands that don't look very familiar to you. Some of these commands, more than others, may be called upon numerous times to successfully navigate throughout the VMware environment. This section will hopefully lessen some of the confusion a new VMware ESX user may face. The information being offered here is not meant to provide you with an in-depth tutorial on Linux commands. However, the goal of this appendix is to attempt to provide a Windows user who is a first time VMware ESX user with a general explanation of some of the more commonly used VMware COS commands. Figure III.1 will attempt to draw a comparison between the DOS/Windows commands and their VMware COS counterparts. Other useful commands that you might use to help navigate VMware ESX effectively and efficiently can be found in Figure III.2.

DOS Command	Linux Command	Action
..\	../	Parent directory
.\	./	Current directory
\	/	Directory path delimeter
CD	cd	Used to change directory
CHDIR	pwd	Displays current directory location
CLS	clear	Clears the screen
COPY	cp	Used to copy a file
DATE or TIME	date	Shows the server's date and time
DEL	rm	Used to delete or remove a file
DIR	ls or ls -l	Used to provide a directory listing
EDIT	vi	Editor program used to edit a file
EXIT	exit	Exits a shell
FDISK	fdisk	Used to partition a hard drive
FORMAT	mke2fs	Used to format a partition for ext2 or ext3 file system
HELP or /?	man	Provides an online manual or explanation of a command
HOSTNAME	hostname	Used to print the host name of the server
IPCONFIG	ifconfig	Used to display the network interface configuration
MEM	free	Shows the free memory on the server
MKDIR	mkdir	Used to create a new directory
MORE	more	Pipes the output of a file a single page at a time
PING	ping	Used to send ICMP packets to a server
PKZIP	tar, zip, gzip and gunzip	Used to compress and uncompress files and directories
RENAME or MOVE	mv	Used to rename or move a file
RMDIR	rmdir	Used to remove a directory
RMDIR /S or DELTREE	rm -R	Removes all directories and files recursively below a specified directory
ROUTE PRINT	route -n	Used to print the routing table
TRACERT	traceroute	Used to show routes and hops to a given network address
TYPE	cat	Dumps the contents of a file to the screen
VER	uname -a	List the operating system version
WIN	startx	Command to start the GUI window application
XCOPY	cp -R	Used to copy all files in directory recursively

Figure III.1   DOS and VMware COS Equivalent Commands.

Command	Actions	Example Use
chgrp	Change ownership of each file to group	chgrp newgroup newDisk.vmx
chmod	Change permissions on files using numeric values to represent rwx	chmod 755 newFile.htm
chown	Change ownership of a file	chown newuser newDisk.vxm
dd	Can copy raw data and disk images to and from devices	dd if=/dev/cdrom of=/isoimages/linux.iso
fdformat	Does a floppy disk format	fdformat /dev/fd0
find	Finds files under a specified directory that match conditions you specify	find / -name myfile*
grep	Search for a specified text pattern in a specified directory or list of files and display the lines in which the text pattern is found	grep "file info" *
groupadd	Adds a new group	groupadd newgroup (Adds a new group named newgroup to the system)
halt	Performs a halt on the server - Does "force power off" for the VMs	
head	Displays the first 10 lines of a file unless otherwise stated	head -15 myfile.txt (would list the first 15 lines of myfile.txt)
kill	Kills a specified process	kill 194 (kills the process with PID 194) kill -9 is a sure way to kill a process - use as a last resort
kudzu	A tool used to detect and configure new hardware	When in doubt, select "do nothing" - kudzu may remove hardware dedicated soley to the VMs
ln	Creates a link from one file or directory to another file or directory	ln -s /root/vmware/program runme (creates a symbolic link between the program in /root/vmware and runme
lsmod	List all loaded modules	
lspci	List PCI devices available to the service console	lspci -v (list all in verbose mode)

Figure III.2   Other Useful VMware ESX Server Commands.

Command	Actions	Example Use
md5sum	Check the integrity of a file	md5sum /vmfs/vmhba0:0:0:1/newDisk.vmdk
mount and umount	The command manually mounts and unmounts CD-ROMs, floppies, local partitions and remote directories to a selected directory	mount /dev/cdrom umount /dev/cdrom mount /mnt/floppy
ntpdate	Takes an NTP server as a parameter and synchronises the clock once. It doesn't work when the local NTP daemon is running.	ntpdate faketimeserver.com
passwd	Changes a password	passwd username (changes the password for a user named username)
ps	Show names, process IDs (PID), and other information for running processes - Similar to Windows TaskManager.	ps -ef (shows full information about every running process)
reboot	Performs a reboot of the server - Does "force power off" for the VMs	
scp	Securely copy a file from one ESX server to another	scp cdromimage.iso root@mymachine.domain.tld:/isoimages/
shutdown	Generic command for shutting down or rebooting the server	shutdown -h 10 (halts the server in 10 minutes) shutdown -r now (shut down and restart the server immediately)
su -	Switch to the root user	
tail	Like head but displays the last 10 lines of a file unless otherwise stated	tail -15 myfile.txt (would list the last 15 lines of myfile.txt)
useradd	Adds a new user to the system	useradd newuser (adds a new user named newuser)
usermod	Modifies the system account files to reflect the changes that are specified on the command line	usermod -d /home/newuser newuser (modifies the home directory for the newuser to /home/newuser)
vdf	vdf is an ESX Server customized version of the df command. Displays free space for all mounted file systems, including VMFS.	vdf -h
who	shows the user names of all users logged into the system	
whoami	shows the user name you are currently logged in with	

Figure III.2 (continued)   Other Useful VMware ESX Server Commands.

Index

A

Accessing console operating system, 125–128
Add Port Groups, 22, 195–197
Advanced features, 151–164
    consolidated backup, VMware, 158–161
    distributed resource scheduler, 152–154
    high availability, VMware, 154–155
    processor affinity, VMware DRS, 152
    storage VMotion, 157–158
    virtual desktop infrastructure, 162–163
    virtual machine failure monitoring, 155–157
    VMotion, 151–152
Anti-virus configuration, virtual machine
        configuration, 186–187
Architecture, VMware ESX, 31–40
    CPU resources, 33
    memory resources, 33–34
    network resources, 35–36
    physical host server, 32–40
    service console, 36–38
    storage resources, 34–35
    VMkernel, 38–40
Automating, 189–200
    installations, 68–93

B

Backup, 48–49
    virtual machine configuration, 186–187
Benefits of, 11–14
Blue Lane Technologies, 205
Business continuity, 12, 209

C

Cadence and synopsis, 14
Catbird, 205–206
CIM. *See* Common Information Model
Citrix XenServer, 9
Cloning, virtual machines, 20–21
Code samples, 192, 194
Commands, console operating system, 128–132
    consolidated backup commands, 131–132
    networking commands, 130–131
    service console configuration commands,
        128–129
    storage commands, 130–131
    troubleshooting commands, 128–129
Common Information Model, 121
Computer-based licensing, 44
Concurrent user-based licensing, 44
Connectix, 5–6, 14
Console operating system, 17–18, 118–120,
        123–132
    accessing, 125–128
    commands, 128–132
    consolidated backup commands, 131–132
    defined, 123–132
    networking commands, 130–131
    service console configuration commands,
        128–129
    storage commands, 130–131
    troubleshooting commands, 128–129
Console plug-in, 198
Consolidated backup, 158–161
    commands, 131–132
Consolidation plug-in, 22
COS. *See* Console operating system

CPU resources, VMware ESX, 33
Creation of virtual machines, 102–107
Custom plug-ins, creation, 22–23

D

Data backup, 48–49
Data diagrams, 193
Debugging, 12–13, 115, 128
Deployment planning, 42–93
Desktop infrastructure, virtual, 162–163
Dialog box, 106, 156
Direct attached storage, 146
Disk modes, virtual, 100–101
Disks, resource management, 169
Distributed power management, 21
Distributed resource scheduler, 21, 152–154
Documentation outline, 52–53
Documentum, 6
DPM. *See* Distributed power management
DRS. *See* Distributed resource scheduler

E

e1000, virtual network interface card, 135
Editable virtual machine templates, 20
EMC Corporation, 6
ESX service log, ESX support script, 220
ESX support script, 217–221
    ESX service log, 220
    log files, 219–221
    service console messages, 220
    VI client agent log, 220
    VI client installation log, 220
    VI client service log, 221
    VI client system logs, 220
    virtual machine kernel core file, 220
    virtual machine log file, 219
    VMkernel messages, 220
    VMkernel warnings, 219
Extensibility, 189–200
External switch tagging, 140–141

F

Failure monitoring, virtual machine, 155–157

Fault tolerance, 139
Fibre channel SAN, 147–148

G

Gear6, 206
Graphic intensive applications, 12
Greene, Diane, 5–6
Guest operating systems, 98–102
    configuration, virtual machine
        configuration, 182–183
    installation, 105
    performance
        Linux, 185–186
        Microsoft Windows, 184–185
    supported *vs.* unsupported, 45–48
        software vendor support, 46
        unexpected server growth, 46
        virtual machine density, 46–48

H

Hardware, 42–43
    system requirements, 55–57
High availability, VMware, 154–155
History of server virtualization, 3–7
Host machine, 154, 217, 223, 225
Host operating system preparation, 58
Host server configuration, 172–179
    memory performance, 175–176
    network performance, 178–179
    processor performance, 174–175
    storage performance, 176–177
    upgrading VMware ESX version, 172–174
Host server preparation, 57–58
Hyper-V. Microsoft, 7, 10
Hypervisor, 5–7, 9–10, 15–30, 38, 41, 95–96
    centralized licensing model, 20
    cloning, virtual machines, 20–21
    console operating system, 17–18
    core features, 20–21
    deployment wizard, 20
    distributed power management, 21
    distributed resource scheduler, 21
    editable virtual machine templates, 20
    high availability, 21
    live migration, 21

management, large-scale, 20
platform specifics, 17–28
plug-ins, features available from, 22–23
    consolidation plug-in, 22
    custom plug-ins, creation, 22–23
    physical to virtual machine conversion, 22
    update manager plug-in, 22
product background, 15–17
virtual machine file system, 18
VirtualCenter, 23–24
    authentication, 24–25
VirtualCenter, location, 24
VMkernel, 17
VMware ESXi, 25–28
VMware VirtualCenter, 18–20
    components, 19

I

I/O compatibility guide, 56
IBM, 6, 12, 26, 32, 121, 125
Information resources, Web links, 211–216
    InfoWorld Virtualization Report, 213–214
    RTFM Education, 213–214
    TechTarget, 215–216
    Virtual Strategy Magazine, 213
    Virtualization.Info, 214–215
    VMBlog.com, 211–212
InfoWorld Virtualization Report, 212–214
Installation, VMware ESX server, 41–94
    automating installations, 68–93
    data backup, 48–49
    deployment plan, 42–93
    documentation outline, 52–53
    hardware, 42–43
    hardware system requirements, 55–57
    host operating system preparation, 58
    host server preparation, 57–58
    host server usage, 43
    locally, 59–68
    monitoring, 49
    network, 49–50
    performance, 50
    preparation, 58
    requirements, 54–55
    security, 50–51
    software licenses, 43–45
    supported *vs.* unsupported GOSs, 45–48
        software vendor support, 46

    unexpected server growth, 46
    virtual machine density, 46–48
system backup, 48–49
use case, 51–54
Instance-based licensing, 43
Intel, 5–7, 9, 16, 40, 55, 97, 135, 152, 173
Interaction with VMware ESX, 109–122
    Common Information Model, 121
    inventory, 113–116
        additional buttons, 115–116
        administration, 114–115
        events, 114
        maps, 115
        scheduled tasks, 114
        tabs, 113–114
    service console, 118–120
    VI client, 110–121
    Virtual Infrastructure Software
        Development Kit, 120–121
    VMware remote console, 117–118
    Web client, 116–117
Internet small computer system interface,
    148–150
Inventory, VMware ESX interaction, 113–116
    additional buttons, 115–116
    administration, 114–115
    events, 114
    maps, 115
    scheduled tasks, 114
    tabs, 113–114
Invoke, 22–23, 107, 120, 128, 198–199

J

Juxtaposition RDP plug-in, 195, 197–198

L

Legacy application, 5, 11
Legato, 6
Licensing, 20, 41, 43–46, 72, 83
    centralized, 20
    computer-based, 44
    concurrent user-based, 44
    instance-based, 43
    processor-based, 44
    software, 43–45

Link aggregation, 137–139
Linux GOSs performance, 185–186
Live migration, hypervisor platform, VMware, 21
Load balancing, 138–139
Local installation, 59–68
Log files, ESX support script, 219–221
  ESX service log, 220
  service console messages, 220
  VI client agent log, 220
  VI client installation log, 220
  VI client service log, 221
  VI client system logs, 220
  virtual machine kernel core file, 220
  virtual machine log file, 219
  VMkernel messages, 220
  VMkernel warnings, 219

M

MAME. *See* Multiple Arcade Machine
    Emulator
Maps, VMware ESX, 115
Marshall, David, 211–212
Memory
  performance, host server configuration,
    175–176
  resource management, 166–168
    tools, 168
  resources, 33–34
  virtual machine configuration, 181–182
Microsoft Hyper-V, 10
Microsoft Virtual Server, 6, 10
Microsoft Windows GOS performance,
    184–185
Migration, live, hypervisor platform, VMware, 21
Multiple Arcade Machine Emulator, 13
Multiple operating system support, 11

N

Network attached storage, 146–147
Network performance, host server configuration,
    178–179
Network resources, VMware ESX, 35–36
Networking, 133–144
  architecture, 133–142
  external switch tagging, 140–141

  fault tolerance, 139
  link aggregation, 137–139
  load balancing, 138–139
  physical network adapter teaming, 137–139
  virtual guest tagging, 141
  virtual machine configuration, 182–186
    GOS configuration, 182–183
    Linux GOSs performance, 185–186
    Microsoft Windows GOS performance,
      184–185
    VMware tool updating, 183–184
  virtual network interface cards, 133–135
    e1000, 135
    vlance, 134
    vmknic, 134
    vmxnet, 135
    vswif, 134
  virtual switch tagging, 141–142
  virtual switches, 135–137
  VLAN tagging, 139–140
Networking commands, 130–131
Non-volatile RAM, 96
Novell, 6, 98, 206

P

Performance optimization, 171–188
  host server configuration, 172–179
    memory performance, 175–176
    network performance, 178–179
    processor performance, 174–175
    storage performance, 176–177
    upgrading VMware ESX version, 172–174
  virtual machine configuration, 179–187
    anti-virus configuration, 186–187
    backups, 186–187
    memory, 181–182
    networking, 182–186
      GOS configuration, 182–183
      Linux GOS performance, 185–186
      Microsoft Windows GOS
        performance, 184–185
      VMware tool updating, 183–184
    power off idle virtual machines, 179–180
    processors, 180–181
    unneeded virtual hardware, removing,
      179
Performance testing, 13, 50
Peripherals, 12, 43

Physical host server, VMware ESX, 32–40
Physical network adapter teaming, 137–139
PlateSpin, 206
Plug-ins, 22–23
    Add Port Groups, 195–197
    Console, 198
    consolidation, 22
    custom, 22–23
    features available from, 22–23
        consolidation plug-in, 22
        custom plug-ins, creation, 22–23
        physical to virtual machine conversion, 22
        P2V, 22
        update manager plug-in, 22
    hypervisor platform, 22–23
    Invoke, 198–199
    Juxtaposition RDP, 195, 197–198
    P2V, 22
    Storage VMotion, 121, 195–196
    update manager, 22
Portability, 11, 206
Ports, VMware, 223–226
Power off idle virtual machines, virtual machine
        configuration, 179–180
Power state options, 99–100
Processor affinity, VMware DRS, 152
Processor-based licensing, 44
Processor management, 165–166
Processor performance, host server
        configuration, 174–175
Processor virtual machine configuration,
        180–181
Product vendor resources, 201–216
    information resources, Web links, 211–216
        InfoWorld Virtualization Report,
            213–214
        RTFM Education, 213–214
        TechTarget, 215–216
        Virtual Strategy Magazine, 213
        Virtualization.Info, 214–215
        VMBlog.com, 211–212
    third-party vendor resources, 204–211
        Blue Lane Technologies, 205
        Catbird, 205–206
        Gear6, 206
        PlateSpin, 206
        rPath, 207
        Surgient, 208
        Veeam, 208–209
        Vizioncore, 209–210

VKernel, 210
VMLogix, 211
virtualization events, 216
VMTN blogs, 204
VMware Appliance Marketplace, 203
VMware User Group, 203
VMware Web site, 201–202
VMworld Conference, 204

R

RAM Doubler, 5
RedHat, 6, 32, 36, 118
Remote console, VMware, 117–118
Resource management, 165–170
    disks, 169
    memory, 166–168
        tools, 168
    network, 169
    processor, 165–166
        VMware virtual SMP, 166
Resources, 201–216. *See also* Product vendor
        resources
Rosenblum, Dr. Mendel, 5
rPath, 207
RTFM Education, 213–214

S

Scheduled tasks, VMware ESX, 114
Security, 50–51
Security honey pot, 12
Server consolidation, 5, 11, 14, 171
Server virtualization, 1–14
    history of, 3–7
    technology, 7–14
    terminology, 2–3
Service console, 118–120, 123–132
    configuration commands, 128–129
    messages, ESX support script, 220
    VMware ESX, 36–38
Simics, 14
SimOS, 14
Snapshots, 100–101
Software development kits, toolkits, 190–199
Software licenses, 43–45
Software vendor support, 46

SpeedDoubler, 5
Storage, 145–150
  commands, 130–131
  direct attached storage, 146
  fibre channel SAN, 147–148
  internet small computer system interface,
    148–150
  network attached storage, 146–147
  performance, host server configuration,
    176–177
  resources, VMware ESX, 34–35
  virtual machine file system, 145
  VMotion, 121, 157–158, 195–196
Storage/SAN compatibility guide, 56
Supported *vs.* unsupported guest operating
    systems, 45–48
  software vendor support, 46
  unexpected server growth, 46
  virtual machine density, 46–48
Surgient, 208
SvMotion, 22, 121, 158, 196
System backup, 48–49
Systems compatibility guide, 56

T

Tabs, VMware ESX, 113–114
Technology, 10–14
  server virtualization, 7–14
TechTarget, 215–216
Terminology, 2–3
Third-party vendor resources, 204–211
  Blue Lane Technologies, 205
  Catbird, 205–206
  Gear6, 206
  PlateSpin, 206
  rPath, 207
  Surgient, 208
  Veeam, 208–209
  Vizioncore, 209–210
  VKernel, 210
  VMLogix, 211
Toolkits, 190–199
  VI PERL, 191–192
  VMware VI, 192–193
Tools, 101–102
  installation, 105–107
  updating, 183–184
Troubleshooting commands, 128–129

U

UK-EPSRC, 6
Unexpected server growth, 46
University of Cambridge Computer Laboratory,
    6
Unneeded virtual hardware, virtual machine
    configuration, removing, 179
Unsupported *vs.* supported guest operating
    systems, 45–48
  software vendor support, 46
  unexpected server growth, 46
  virtual machine density, 46–48
Update manager plug-in, 22
Upgrading VMware ESX version, host server
    configuration, 172–174

V

Veeam, 208–209
Vendor resources, 201–216
  third-party, 204–211
Vendor support, software, 46
VI client
  agent log, ESX support script, 220
  extensions, 194–195
  installation log, ESX support script, 220
  service log, ESX support script, 221
  system logs, ESX support script, 220
  VMware ESX interaction, 110–121
VI PERL toolkits, 191–192
VI SDK. *See* Virtual Infrastructure Software
    Development Kit
Viridian, 7, 10
Virtual desktop infrastructure, 162–163
Virtual disk, 40, 96–97, 100–102, 129, 131, 145,
    159, 193–196
  modes, 100–101
Virtual guest tagging, 141
Virtual Infrastructure Software Development
    Kit, 120–121, 190–191
Virtual Iron, 9
Virtual machines, 95–108
  configuration, 179–187
    anti-virus configuration, 186–187
    backups, 186–187
    memory, 181–182
    networking, 182–186
      GOS configuration, 182–183

Linux GOSs performance, 185–186
Microsoft Windows GOS
performance, 184–185
VMware tool updating, 183–184
power off idle virtual machines, 179–180
processors, 180–181
unneeded virtual hardware, removing,
179
creation of, 102–107
density, 46–48
failure monitoring, 155–157
file system, 18, 145
direct attached storage, 146
fibre channel SAN, 147–148
internet small computer system interface,
148–150
network attached storage, 146–147
GOSs, 98–102
installation, 105
kernel core file, ESX support script, 220
log file, ESX support script, 219
monitor, 5, 9–10, 181
overview, 95–96
power state options, 99–100
snapshots, 100–101
virtual disk modes, 100–101
VMware tools, 101–102
installation, 105–107
Virtual network interface cards, 133–135
e1000, 135
vlance, 134
vmknic, 134
vmxnet, 135
vswif, 134
Virtual Server 2005 Enterprise Edition, 6
Virtual Server 2005 Standard Edition, 6
Virtual SMP, VMware, processor management,
166
Virtual Strategy Magazine, 213
Virtual switch tagging, 141–142
Virtual switches, 135–137
VirtualCenter, 23–24
authentication, 24–25
VirtualCenter, location, 24
Virtualization, 1–14
events, 216
history of, 3–7
software, 11, 16, 55

technology, 7–14
terminology, 2–3
Virtualization.Info, 214–215
Visual Studio.NET, 5
Vizioncore, 209–210
VKernel, 210
VLAN tagging, 139–140
vlance, virtual network interface card, 134
VMBlog.com, 211–212
VMkernel, 17, 38–40
messages, 220
warnings, 219
vmknic, virtual network interface card, 134
VMLogix, 211
VMotion, 151–152
VMTN blogs, 204
VMUG. *See* VMware User Group
VMware Appliance Marketplace, 203
VMware Community forum, 23, 64, 70
VMware ESXi, 25–28
VMware User Group, 203
VMware VDDK. *See* VMware Virtual Disk
Development Kit
VMware VI Toolkit, 192–193
VMware Virtual Disk Development Kit,
193–194
VMware VirtualCenter, 18–20
components, 19
VMware Web site, 201–202
VMworld Conference, 204
vmxnet, virtual network interface card, 135
vswif, virtual network interface card, 134

W

Web client, VMware ESX interaction, 116–117
Windows virtual machine, 183–185, 225
WINE, 13

X

Xen, 6–7, 9
XenEnterprise, 6
XenSource, 6, 9